Macroeconomics and Gender

Macroeconomics and Gender

Edited by
Ritu Dewan
K. Seeta Prabhu

zubaan

Macroeconomics and Gender
edited by Ritu Dewan and K. Seeta Prabhu
Published (2009) by
Zubaan
an imprint of Kali for Women
128 B Shahpur Jat, 1st floor
New Delhi 110049
Email: zubaanwbooks@vsnl.net and zubaan@gmail.com
Website: www.zubaanbooks.com

10 9 8 7 6 5 4 3 2 1

ISBN 978-81-89884-51-2

DISCLAIMER
The views expressed in this book are those of the authors and do not necessarily reflect those of the Ministry of Women and Child Development and the United Nations Development Programme.

Zubaan is an independent feminist publishing house based in New Delhi, India. It was set up as an imprint of the well known feminist house Kali for Women, and carries forward Kali's tradition of publishing world quality books to high editorial and production standards. "Zubaan" means tongue, voice, speech and language in Hindustani. Zubaan is a non-profit publisher, working in the areas of the humanities, social sciences, as well as in fiction, general non-fiction, and books for young adults that celebrate difference, diversity and equality, especially for and about the children of India and South Asia under its imprint Young Zubaan.

Typset at Tulika Print Communication Services
35A/1, third floor, Shahpur Jat, New Delhi - 110 049
Printed at Print Idea.

Contents

Introduction
RITU DEWAN & K. SEETA PRABHU 1

Gender and Development: Microeconomic Foundations and Macroeconomic Realities
WANDANA SONALKAR 9

Engendering Market Structure: A Normative Analysis
RITU DEWAN & AZANIA THOMAS 26

Engendering Macroeconomic Modelling for Policy Analysis
ANUSHREE SINHA 51

Macroeconomic Complexity and Gender Economics
ROMAR CORREA 93

Indian Taxation Systems and Policies: A Gendered Critique
RITU DEWAN 117

Women's Empowerment through Gender Budgeting: A Review in the Indian Context
ANJALI GOYAL 139

For a Few Pots of Water: Water Rights and Subsidies
ALKA PARIKH 172

Engendering Health Rights in the New Global Economy
RAVI DUGGAL 194

Macroeconomic Methodologies, Approaches, and Policies: Why Gender Matters
PADMINI SWAMINATHAN 208

Notes on Contributors 234

Introduction

RITU DEWAN & K. SEETA PRABHU

The issue of engendering macroeconomic theories and policies has assumed special significance in the context of the increasing importance of macroeconomic constructs and their differential impacts across genders. Gender inequalities at micro and meso levels have macro implications, there being a clear two-way interconnection. However, the polemics as well as the conceptual analysis of inter-linkages in developing countries are still in the formative stage, as are interconnected methodological issues. The fundamental issue is that analysis of engendering macroeconomic theories as well as policies has to be viewed in the context of the market which is not only the primary economic concept but also the main operative reality today. It is being increasingly accepted that markets are imperfect rather than 'perfect' as traditionally assumed. The isolation of the examination of gendered macroeconomic issues from fundamental alterations in market structures therefore needs to be bridged.

One of the main consequences of increasing market imperfections is the acceptance of the reduction of the poor, and amongst them particularly women, into inactive agents in analytical concepts as well as in reality, with little or no role to play in the determination of the nature of their existence either as a class or a group. The urgent task is therefore to re-examine the gendered role of the poor in the political economy of macroeconomics as translated in the actuality of governance, and hence to assess and argue for a more equitable and gender-aware systematic role for State intervention in macro issues.

In recognition of this vacuum in polemics as well as conceptual analysis, a two-day national conference on 'Engendering Macroeconomics and Macroeconomic Policies' was organized in September 2005 by the Centre for Women's Studies, Department of Economics, University of Mumbai, supported by the Department of Women and Child Development (DWCD), Government of India, and the United Nations Development Programme, India Country Office under a joint project *Promoting Gender Equality.* This volume contains selected papers presented at the conference (and subsequently revised and rewritten) which together bring to the fore theoretical possibilities and empirical implications of incorporating a gender dimension into macroeconomics.

Wandana Sonalkar's essay on 'Gender and Development: Microeconomic Foundations and Macroeconomic Realities' focuses on current controversies about measuring the impact of recent global policy changes and economic developments on the conditions of life of the people in developing countries such as India. The author argues that one useful way to adequately address the controversies would be to re-examine the underlying concepts used in the construction of measures of development in terms of the microeconomic foundations of macroeconomics from a gender perspective. Accordingly, the concept of capabilities as put forward by Amartya Sen is examined through a gender lens both as a supplement to incomes in measuring well-being, and as an alternative to utilities as a basis for measuring welfare.

The essay argues that the characterization and quantification of poverty in areas where feudal production relations and traditional forms of activity prevail involves certain assumptions about the framework in which women and men exercise choices about work and consumption. This includes analyses of whether the extension of the scope of the market widens or restricts the set of alternatives available in the context of wide-ranging changes in the macroeconomic environment as well as in economic policy.

In their essay, 'Engendering Market Structure: A Normative

Analysis', Ritu Dewan and Azania Thomas examine how markets reflect the 'behaviours of different groups of people' and thus form part of an intrinsic blueprint that dictates the functioning and outreach of macroeconomic theory as well as policy. They argue that the definition of Pareto-efficiency which determines efficiency in the market is exclusive when defining circumstances of gender discrimination; for example, the Pareto efficient solution of a monopsonist adopting wage discrimination according to gender is clearly in conflict with the principle of egalitarianism. Yet the strategy of profit maximization by a wage discriminating monopsonist on the basis of gender can easily be mistaken for an outcome that is socially inefficient. The process of policy formation therefore needs to carefully take into account the kind of normative measure being used especially when examining the links between gender discrimination and market failure. Gender discrimination may or may not lead to 'inefficient' outcomes within the context of imperfect markets. The authors identify existing situations where gender discrimination does lead to market failure and where there exist possibilities for policy interventions to develop a stronger basis both on egalitarian and social efficiency grounds. Illustrations depicting gender sensitive barriers to market entry include the lack of access to information where women, among some of the many socially disadvantaged groups, are far worse off when it comes to being isolated from, say, credit or labour markets resulting primarily from the dictates of historically defined gender constructs.

Interconnections between gender-sensitive barriers to market access allow policy recommendations to target similar solutions that would reduce discrimination on the grounds of market efficiency. When one examines situations where gender discrimination is socially efficient, then other normative criteria such as distributive justice or access to equal opportunities are more likely to make gender sensitive policies effective.

Although gender-related development issues have prompted serious debate, the absence of appropriate gender-aware macroeconomic analytical tools has penalised quantitative analyses. For economy-wide implications, the impact of macroeconomic policy can be analysed succinctly by using macroeconomic models. Anushree Sinha discusses the constraints of descriptive studies in providing a robust causality in her essay 'Engendering Macroeconomic Modelling for Policy Analysis'.

The essay reviews the literature on engendering macroeconomic models including the issues of measuring and incorporating non-market work into a macro framework. Generally however, macroeconomic analysis and modelling is carried out as if no differences exist between women and men. Yet the evidence from studies that have used gender-aware models confirms that better predictive results are obtained with engendered data. More specifically, trade related modelling methodologies such as the Computable General Equilibrium (CGE) models have the advantage of ascertaining general equilibrium effects on different policy options. The economy wide general equilibrium models need to consider the details of gender composition of the labour market and household work and capture information on non-market work.

In this essay, the proposed CGE model is based on the construction of an engendered Social Accounting Matrix (SAM). The SAM is developed with sectors that have important shares of women workers in different economic activities, the mapping into different types of households being based on NSSO's 55th Round survey data.

Taking the debate further and focusing on institutional dimensions of including gender in macroeconomic frameworks, Romar Correa in his essay 'Macroeconomic Complexity and Gender Economics' explores the role of capital as a principle coordinating both production and exchange. The main objective of the analysis is to examine how the strategies employed by different agents intersect and evolve, leading the system in one direction rather than another. Surveying the literature on norms and institutions, and moving further from micro foundations, the essay appraises the post-Keynesian link between aggregate phenomena and gender, concluding with an approach from the latter end of the divide which focuses on the structural determinants of gender.

It is argued that the relationships between people endure in institutional contexts which both enable and constrain tasks. Long-term contracts describe the non-market activities that take place within households wherein are contingent commitments, liquidity problems, the acquisition and maintenance of capital goods, and borrowing and lending. As households enter into economic transactions with each other, the macroeconomic coordination problem reappears. If one forward contract is violated, a unit will not receive expected income and will be rationed in other markets.

Ritu Dewan's essay, 'Indian Taxation Systems and Policies: A Gendered Critique', that follows analyses the fiscal dimension in the Indian context, an area that has remained relatively unexplored despite own-source revenues being the fulcrum of the ongoing public debate on governmental expenditures, provisioning and pricing. Consequently, the fundamental focus is primarily on examining levels of gender non-neutrality inherent in the theoretical and empirical underpinnings of the Indian taxation system and its policies including identification of biases in major revenue-collection methods separately for direct and indirect taxes.

Analysis is conducted both in economic terms as well as in the context of the prevailing extra-economic gendered reality. The implicit and explicit biases in both direct and indirect taxes examined include those relating to personal income tax, gift tax, property tax, wealth tax, corporation tax and VAT. Aspects focused on include female-headed households, individual and household decisions about consumption, as well as production and investment, and also different personal laws and regulations.

Other illustrations of patriarchal bias presently operative in the Indian revenue system include the issue of standard deductions; lack of tax concessions for child care; lack of sensitivity in pension schemes for female-headed as well as single-person households; non-existence of uniform conditionalities relating especially to medical insurance; gender neutral tax laws for women-only and also women-centric Cooperatives/NGOs/SHGs.

Taking the discussion on fiscal issues further, Anjali Goyal's essay, 'Women's Empowerment Through Gender Budgeting: A Review in the Indian Context', explores the effectiveness of gender budgeting in its present form. The paper emphasizes that most of the activities currently carried out in the name of gender budgeting are *ex post* in nature and oriented more towards gender audits. The initiatives reviewed include resource allocation and expenditure, sectoral audits, macro indicators like maternal mortality rate, access to health, literacy rates, participation in local governance structures including fiscal decentralization, employment statistics, and so on.

The essay suggests that in isolation none of the measures is an effective tool. Also reflected is the concern expressed in Plan documents at the slow progress in achieving empowerment of women despite commitments at the policy level and at the planning stage. An alternative approach is discussed under gender budgeting initiatives to remedy the situation.

Turning to the field level experiences of women, Alka Parikh discusses issues relating to water in her essay, 'For a Few Pots of Water: Water Rights and Subsidies'. It is argued that the two central aspects of concern are availability as well as equitable allocation of water. The National Water Policy has been allocating the highest priority to drinking water, but the priority does not seem to have been operationalized adequately, with water allocation continuing to be urban centric and with a strong elitist bias. Parikh discusses issues of ground water and its privatization, property regimes, costing and subsidies, the difficulty in raising water prices being perceived as a political issue rather than an economic one. The essay ends with a suggestive model for water allocation, which includes the declaration of ground water as community property at least for satisfying domestic needs, exclusion of operation and maintenance costs from subsidies, and the conferring of water rights on women.

Highlighting issues relating to rights of women in the health sector, Ravi Duggal in his essay 'Engendering Health Rights in the New Global Economy' draws attention to health increasingly becoming a tradeable commodity, its delivery being privatized and the role of corporates increasing, thus rendering India highly vulnerable. The GATS mechanism accentuates the problem as India is unable to use the exemption clause in GATS negotiations for the health sector owing to the prevailing political economy. Having signed the WTO treaty on IPR, the country is moving closer to international prices of drugs.

Health status indicators amply testify to the poor state of health and healthcare in India. Gender inequities are quite complex and cross-cutting and hence cannot be viewed only in the context of a specific sector like health. Similarly, discrimination of women in access to healthcare, especially maternal health services such as antenatal care and safe deliveries, contributes to their more adverse health outcomes. Women suffer higher levels of morbidities but these are more likely to remain untreated as compared to men. Further, women are larger users of public health facilities especially for hospital care, and hence when the new macroeconomics impacts public health by reduced investments and expenditures or by the introduction of user fees under so-called reforms, it is women who bear the larger brunt not only in terms of their own health but also by increasingly becoming informal care takers in homes which, because of low purchasing power, may not be able to access private health services or the now user-fee charging public health services.

All these factors have contributed to increased vulnerabilities in access to healthcare and health outcomes, including gender injustice. To change this it is essential to adopt a rights based approach rather than a mere policy based approach to health and healthcare. Health is a public/social good and this needs to be brought to the attention of macroeconomists in order to re-define macroeconomic policies.

Finally, Padmini Swaminathan essay, 'Macroeconomic Methodologies, Approaches and Policies: Why Gender Matters', brings the debate back to macroeconomic constructs through a review of research in order to foreground the critical importance of gender to macroeconomic concerns, followed by an application of gender analysis to the specific situation prevailing in the state of Tamil Nadu.

Despite exhortations to the effect that macroeconomics and social policies need to be integrated, operationally the tendency has been on emphasizing price stabilization and on reducing the role of the State while at the same time adding social policies to address issues such as poverty and women's empowerment. The adding-on-social policy-approach by definition cannot transform macroeconomic policies, but a transformatory approach would, ipso facto, imply that macroeconomic policies and the approach to macroeconomics itself be re-examined.

The signal contribution of feminists and gender studies to macroeconomics is a questioning of the assumptions on which the discipline of economics itself is anchored, a questioning of the methodologies that limit the discipline's understanding and approaches to economic problems, and a questioning of the solutions that it uncritically offers. Nevertheless, the relegation of gender to the social at one level, and the anxiety of feminist researchers including feminist economists to be seen as 'practically relevant' all the time, at another level, is one small example of the continuing tensions that keep surfacing largely also because macroeconomic policies have failed in their basic objectives but have had no qualms in transferring these failures to the 'social sector'—a euphemism for considering all these problems as 'women's issues'. How feminists engage with such reductionism is a challenge waiting to be addressed.

The nine essays outlined here collectively as well as individually highlight the futility of adopting the conventional analytical approach in a world that has fundamentally changed and transformed, and argue for a more gender sensitive approach to macroeconomics. It is our hope that the papers will further the debate on the critical issue of adopting more appropriate frameworks for theoretical as well as empirical analysis and enthuse many more to extend further some of the thoughts put forward in this effort.

Gender and Development

Microeconomic Foundations and Macroeconomic Realities

WANDANA SONALKAR

INTRODUCTION

Assessing the impact of recent policy changes and global economic developments on the conditions of life of the people in developing countries such as India has given rise to several controversies. For example, the claim of the Indian government and international funding agencies that poverty in India declined over the 1990s, has been challenged by critics (see for instance, Jaya Mehta and Shanta Venkataraman's article, "Poverty Statistics: Bermicide's Feast", in the *EPW*, July 1, 2000) who argue that to use the definition of the poverty line initially formulated in 1970, even with periodic upward revisions based on a suitably chosen price index, leads to an underestimation of the extent of poverty. The problem is that the composition of the expenditure of the poor has changed over time, and this is not reflected in the poverty line measurements. Several independent studies on nutrition in fact point to serious deterioration in the nutrition profile of rural and urban populations near the poverty line.

As against this, we have the Human Development Index defined and calculated by the UNDP since 1990 with the purpose of providing a more valid basis than per capita income for evaluating the impact of policies and global economic changes on the populations of different countries, and for making international comparisons of the level of development achieved.

Recently, several states in India have used the conceptual framework of the HDI to examine their performance in comparative terms between states, and also of different districts within the states. An article in the *EPW* by Sangita Kamdar *et al* (2003) questions whether the HDI provides an adequate means of assessing and comparing the level of well-being of persons in various districts. One alternative suggested by them is a Human Poverty Index based on actual attainment, or its absence, of certain basic needs of life, such as drinking water, fuel, and adequate housing.

This essay argues that to address the controversies generated in this debate would require a re-examination of the underlying concepts used in the construction of such indices. We need, in fact, to go back to the microeconomic foundations of the (essentially macroeconomic) analysis of an economy undergoing liberalization and opening up to world markets. A gender perspective is crucial in such a re-examination.

Let us first look at the Human Development Index. The central concept underlying the Human Development Index is Amartya Sen's concept of *capabilities*, on which he has written extensively from about 1984 onwards, a period during which he was also in dialogue with feminist economists; and gender concerns are frequently touched on in his discussion of the concept. Some of the problems in the use of the Human Development Index can be brought out by looking at the evolution of the concept of *capabilities* in Sen's writings. This concept is put forward by Sen on the one hand as a supplement to *incomes* in measuring well-being, and as an alternative to *utilities* as a basis for measuring welfare. So we have to look at how the individual (man or woman) is embedded in the macroeconomic framework implicitly assumed, but not explicitly stated by Sen. This is discussed in the first part of this essay.

As far as poverty line measurements are concerned, the authors of the article mentioned above raise some important issues regarding changes in the composition of people's, especially poor people's, expenditure over a period of about thirty years from 1970. This was a period during which there was an extensive penetration of the market into areas of the economy in which pre-capitalist production relations and traditional forms of activity had earlier prevailed. Our characterization and quantification of poverty in such a time involves certain assumptions about the framework in which people, that is, men and women, make choices about work and consumption. There is also the issue of whether the extension of the scope of the market widens or restricts the set of alternatives available to them. The second part of the essay attempts to bring out and critique some of these assumptions from a gender perspective. The third part will then draw together these two strands of argument and suggest that it is important to be aware of the microeconomic basis of how poor people in a developing country like India are affected by wide-ranging changes in the macroeconomic environment and economic policy.

CAPABILITIES

Let us begin by examining the evolution of the concept of capabilities, which has had a deep-seated influence on how we look at economic development, how we measure it, and the alternatives available to developing countries today. There are several different routes that lead Sen to capabilities, a concept that has borne fruit in the yearly construction of the Human Development Indices for different countries, and has been influential in guiding policy in developing countries since 1990.

One such route is when Sen pursues his critique of utilitarianism, a thread that runs from his 1970 CC&SW through various writings first published before 1980. Sen was in fact attracted to Rawls' theory of justice partly because it had a deontological approach, as opposed to utilitarianism, which is essentially *consequentialist,* judging actions in terms of their results, increasing 'the sum of human happiness' or not. Sen wants to have an ethic that values *liberty* for itself; he explores the idea of liberties as 'negative freedoms', that is, the freedom from being prevented from enjoying certain rights. He then finds the notion of negative freedom inadequate, and wants to include certain 'positive freedoms'. Finally he proceeds to "a characterization of positive freedoms in the form of *capabilities* of persons". More of this later.

The second route also stems from Sen's taking issue with utilitarianism. He finds the notion of *utility* as a measure of human well-being to be inadequate. There are two main reasons for this. Since the term 'utility' refers to the mental state of a person, it does not adequately reflect her physical condition. Secondly, it avoids any criticism of the person's own valuational exercise, which may be influenced by past experience of extreme deprivation, for example, so that a person may be 'happy' even though she is at a very low level of well-being. This, as Sen underlines, is especially typical of women, who tend not to see themselves as deprived.

In Chapter 6 of his 1985 monograph entitled *Commodities and Capabilities*, Sen spells out the implications of his reasoning for the question of collecting empirical data on the living standard, or well-being. If 'utility', 'opulence' and 'functionings' are three aspects of well-being, three type of data corresponding to them are (i) market purchase data, since conclusions about utility and preference maps of a consumer are drawn from her market purchases; (ii) responses to questionnaires (for example, the questions in the Indian census about the type of residential structure a respondent inhabits), and (iii) non-market observations of personal states, such as nutritional status, literacy, etc. He rejects the first two types of empirical data in favour of the third: market purchase data may reflect a person's choice of commodities, but not the choice of functionings. Functionings are posterior to commodities but prior to utilities in the chain: Commodities → Characteristics → Functionings → Utilities.

Capabilities form the link between the commodities and their characteristics, on the one hand, and the functionings a person is able to achieve given a set of feasible commodity purchases. They are linked to personal traits which include, and are influenced by, the gender of the person: her health, mobility, ability to access information etc.

Answers to questionnaires as an empirical source of data on well-being may be coloured by the person's own subjective valuations, to which the above-mentioned remarks apply. In the end, then, Sen favours what he calls non-market observations, such as nutritional status, literacy, and so on, which give direct evidence of the levels of functioning attainable by a person, in short his/her capabilities. This is, of course, the strategy used in formulating the Human Development Index.

Another argument used by Sen in favour of the concept of capabilities is that it is superior to the 'basic needs' approach (BNA) that was adopted by development economists in the early 1980s. In fact the capabilities approach has much in common with the basic needs approach. Sen admits this in a 1983 paper, "Goods and People", which is reproduced in RVD as Chapter 20. He quotes Paul Streeten, one of the economists most closely associated with the basic needs approach: "the basic needs concept is a reminder that the objective of the development effort is to provide all human beings with the opportunity for a full life."

It is in fact interesting to see what Sen says about the distinction between the two approaches; one feels that he is making a straw man of the BNA to some extent. First, he says that the BNA focuses on commodities rather than the capabilities they enable individuals to attain; but this is not quite the case, as "attention is paid to differences in the commodities needed by different persons to satisfy the same human requirements." Also, there is the inclusion of factors such as literacy (which is one of the capabilities used in the HDI approach) in basic needs.

The second point relates to a particular capability that Sen has referred to several times in his writings: the ability "to appear in public without shame", in the words of Adam Smith, or one aspect of "the social bases of self-respect" that figure in Rawls' list of primary goods, or what even Marx acknowledges when he says that what constitutes a 'subsistence' level, changes according to the times. Sen's way of putting it is that "*relative* deprivation in the space of commodities translates into *absolute* deprivation in the space of capabilities." This amounts to saying that basic needs in any specific context have a cultural component; and it is unlikely that development economists drawing up or implementing basic-needs–based programmes were unaware or negligent of this factor.

The third point Sen makes is that the basic needs approach aims at achieving a 'minimum' level, whereas the capabilities approach can be applied to rich countries as well as poor, and can be used as a metric for comparisons of inequality. Here we see that the capabilities approach is being explicitly geared towards the construction of an index for inter-country comparisons. We can perceive an implicit political agenda underlying the counterpoising of the capabilities approach to the BNA: the 'basic needs' approach did at the time imply an *obligation* to provide for people's basic needs, and was in fact used to argue for minimum levels of aid transfers from richer to poorer countries. Sen elsewhere explicitly rejects ethical arguments pressing for such transfers. We can therefore see the implicit rationale of the Human Development Reports: it is to provide a basis for comparisons of well-being among nations, but not to argue for any ethical imperative for reduction of inequalities across borders. Finally, Sen says that 'needs' is a more passive concept than 'capability', and thus the latter is more consonant with the perspective of positive freedom. This is the subject of the next section.

CAPABILITIES AND RIGHTS

We have seen above that libertarian rights are characterized as 'negative freedoms' by Sen, so that he puts forward capabilities as 'positive freedoms'. This is in essence an answer to Robert Nozick, whose list of basic libertarian rights is essentially protective of the status quo: the right to property, the right to earn from one's activity what others are prepared to pay, and not to be taxed on one's income, and so on. However, there are other libertarian systems, such as that of Rawls (who is also discussed at length by Sen), where the list of basic individual rights that are to be given priority includes equality of opportunity, for example. Rawls in *A Theory of Justice* elaborates on his first principle of justice as follows (p. 303): "all social primary goods—liberty and opportunity, income and wealth, and the bases of self-respect—are to be distributed equally unless an unequal distribution of any or all of these goods is to the advantage of the least favoured."

What I wish to point out here is that on the one hand, in talking of 'positive *freedoms*', Sen parts company with the libertarians (both Nozick and Rawls) who set down their respective lists of individual rights that must be upheld by the state, and leave the citizens with the *liberty* to use these rights as they wish; Sen wishes to take moral responsibility for the *outcomes*, i.e. the capabilities individuals achieve. This becomes clear from his extensive discussion of Rawls in this chapter. On the other hand, he has by a kind of sleight of hand done away with the language of *rights* of the individual as citizen. This is because the responsibility of the State in protecting even 'negative freedoms' is glossed over in his distinction between 'positive' and 'negative' freedoms: in fact State action is required to protect 'negative freedoms' even of the Nozick variety. Together with his suggestion that we collect evidence of capability levels attained not from observations of market purchases or by asking persons about various aspects of their well-being, but from 'non-market' observations about their condition, this amounts to an essentially paternalistic approach to development. This would apply, also, to Sen's well-known espousal of gender concerns in development.

We have a striking illustration of this when Sen imparts the concept of women's 'agency' in *Development and Freedom* (p. 189) with his own understanding: "No longer the passive recipients of welfare-enhancing help, women are increasingly seen, by men as well as women, as active agents of change: the dynamic promoters of social transformations that can alter the lives of *both* women and men."

We might think at first sight that Sen's focus on women's agency offers a useful and open-ended alternative to the economic determinism of Ester Boserup, for instance, who argues that the process of economic development and modernization will, albeit with a time-lag, bring about an improvement in women's situation, or what might be called a more 'pessimistic' economic determinism of those who see women's concerns suffering in a global regime of capitalist accumulation. However, when we read further in the chapter in *Development and Freedom* on "Women, Agency and Social Change", the three main examples of women's agency that he gives are: (i) the role of women's literacy in reducing child mortality, (ii) the role of women's literacy in reducing fertility, and (iii) the participation of women in small savings or 'micro-credit' groups. All these examples are in line with the current policies of the international development agencies. The role of agency is almost synonymous with the term 'women's empowerment' which has found its way into the language of development institutions and non-government organizations, also governments of developing countries. The term empowerment refuses to speak of power in the political sense, of resistance to existing power structures: it is a transitive verb, to empower is something one does to someone else. Sen's use of women's 'agency' is thus strictly circumscribed, and we see evidence of this in his choice of examples: he speaks of literacy and not education, perhaps because he is citing easily measurable and comparable indices; he mentions small savings groups whose main achievement is to bring women into the circuit of monetary exchange, rather than to improve their position in the power hierarchy in any significant way.

We may note that Sen's use of the term 'agency' given above is significantly different from the meaning usually given to this term. The *Encyclopedia Britannica* gives the following definition: "the capacity, condition, or state of acting or of exerting power."

If we look more closely, we see that Sen uses the word 'agency' in at least one more sense. In *Ethics and Economics* (1987), for instance, he argues against the view in mainstream economics that an individual acts only in his or her 'self-interest': "While 'well-being' covers the person's achievements and opportunities in the context of his or her personal advantage, ('agency') goes further and examines achievements in terms of other objectives and values as well, possibly going well beyond the pursuit of one's well-being." Elsewhere in this text, he points out that this broadening of the scope of 'well-being' can be fitted into the modern theory of consumer choice. The modern neoclassical theory relies on an ordering of alternatives available to the individual/consumer, without specifying that each alternative basket contain utilities alone: it may include social values, ethical imperatives, and, presumably cultural 'goods'. In fact, Arrow, in his exposition of the theory of social choice, incorporates issues of this type into his social welfare function, saying that it includes values as well as tastes. But Sen proposes to incorporate them into the *individual* valuation function in his system. Sen therefore feels that *capabilities* provide a richer informational content than utilities, but like the latter, they too can be fitted into the neoclassical framework of individual choice.

In *Development and Freedom*, Sen reiterates this position in the context of a typically neoclassical defence of the market mechanism. He says (p. 117): "an important part of the Arrow-Debreu efficiency result readily translates from the 'space' of utilities to that of individual freedoms, both in terms of freedom to choose *commodity baskets* and in terms of *capabilities to function.*"

There is a deliberate play with the word 'freedom' here. In our discussion of Sen's use of 'negative' and 'positive' freedoms above, we noted that the position of the libertarians is much clearer: the role of the State is to guarantee certain basic freedoms, so that persons can then choose their jobs, their lifestyle, their commodity baskets and so on. Sen wants to take ethical responsibility for the achieved states that are implied in a person's *capabilities*, but glosses over the role of the State. In the above sentence too, it is not clear whether he is saying that people choose *capabilities to function*, or that they are the results of their choice, or indeed, that capabilities are the freedom to choose.

Further, it is clear from the above quote that the argument in favour of the market being used here is the general equilibrium framework of simultaneous equilibrium in all markets. One critique of this framework for understanding contemporary economies has been made familiar by Grossman and Stiglitz (1990).

CAPABILITIES AND WORK

Let us turn once more to the chain: Commodities → Characteristics → Capability → (Functioning) → Utility. Gender would appear to be important because an important site where commodities and their characteristics are transformed into capabilities is in the *household.* Women do much of the work involved in this transformation; but Sen is silent about the significance of this work. In fact, the chain refers exclusively to the individual as consumer, not as worker. Again, when Sen looks at the household in response to the work of some feminist scholars, his main concern is with the intra-household distribution of resources rather than the division of labour. This focus in fact goes back to Sen's much earlier work, *On Economic Inequality,* in which he decides that questions about inequality should be considered on the basis of *need* rather than on *merit* or (fair) reward for work. This focus continues in the use of the concept of capabilities as it is reflected in the Human Development Index.

Sen has developed the concept of capabilities to flesh out the 'rational economic man' of microeconomic theory, to include characteristics such as gender, and ethical values going beyond self-interest. And yet, since he retains the abstract framework of neoclassical microeconomic theory, it is hard to see how capabilities fit into the overall macroeconomic picture. I would say that the 'old liberal' framework of price theory is at least clear in its assumptions, in its distinguishing of what the State guarantees and what choices individuals make with the help of the market. Sen, on the other hand, glosses over the role of the State, and also fudges the concept of an individual citizen having certain *rights* vis a vis the State.

I hope this helps us understand why the impressive garnering of facts in the Human Development Report does not really help us to get a clear picture of how economic relations of work, consumer choice, gender division of labour, and poverty and nutritional deprivation within the household are changing, as globalization alters the macroeconomic framework of the economy and influences the rationale of economic policy in developing countries.

I would therefore argue that the problem with Sen's conception of capabilities is twofold. On the one hand, his individual is placed within the theoretical framework of neoclassical consumer theory, while on the other hand the kind of abstraction that that theory makes about the individual as consumer is replaced by a fleshed-out human being with a variety of 'functionings', economic, ethical and social. I have suggested elsewhere that this is a form of *nominalism*, it presumes that only individuals with all their 'attributes' exist, and there is no meaning to any theory that abstracts a particular role of the individual as part of a theoretical exercise. Thus both the 'social being' of Marx and the 'rational economic man' of neoclassical theory are negated; but the conclusions of the neoclassical theory regarding the efficiency of the market mechanism are accepted. The problem with this kind of nominalism is that it creates an illusion of universal applicability: who can argue with a notion of human capabilities that takes account of such a wide range of desirable human functionings of the individual?

However, because it places this individual within the framework of neoclassical *consumer* theory, it ignores the changing macroeconomic framework in which the individual makes choices; and it further totally neglects one aspect of human functioning, that is, *work*. The above applies to Sen's proposal of capabilities as an alternative to *utilities*. However, in the context of the human development paradigm, and particularly in relation to the construction of the human development index, the concept of human capabilities is posed against that of *income* as a basis for judgments about inequality. Here again, it is the *uses* of income to purchase commodities and achieve functionings that is taken into consideration; the work-income connection does not enter the argument at all.

Sen's views have been remarkably influential in recent decades, as globalization extends the reach of the market into all geographical regions and areas of human activity. The emphasis on self-help groups (SHG's) and micro-credit positions poor women as 'good' managers of meagre income resources without offering any improvement in the terms on which their work is rewarded, nor in fact any favourable terms of credit.

Both these aspects are brought out in A.B. Atkinson's contribution to the 1995 Festschrift in Honour of Amartya Sen, entitled "Capabilities, Exclusion and the Supply of Goods". Having quoted Sen as asserting "that, in the chain

Commodities → Characteristics → Capability → Utility,

capability best reflects the standard of living, he modifies the chain to read (p. 20):

Commodities → Activities → Capability → (Utility).

The transformation of income and commodities into capabilities depends not only on the characteristics of the commodity, but on the *activities* of the individual. Feminist economists have brought out the role of housework in the transformation of commodities into capabilities within the household. Here, however, we want to focus on the gender aspects of the embedding of the individual man or woman in the macroeconomic framework of income distribution and employment. As we have seen, the capabilities approach does not help us in this; it in fact diverts us from looking into such questions. There has recently been an attempt to redress this imbalance in the UNDP research agenda by introducing the concept of *livelihoods.*

Atkinson further comments (p. 18): "Where the poverty line is explicitly relative. . ., rising living standards in the community as a whole may lead to a raising of the poverty line in real terms. However, the precise mechanism that relates the necessary income, on the capabilities approach, to the changes in the overall distribution is not spelled out."

In the next section of this essay, we follow Atkinson by asking how the transformation of income into capabilities relates with issues like the availability of work and what the individual, man or woman, requires both to carry out the work that earns that income; and with the overall macroeconomic distribution that determines what work is available. The poverty line approach, as we will see, is also rather negligent of both these aspects.

POVERTY MEASUREMENT: SOME GENDER-RELATED ISSUES

We now go back to the discussions on poverty measurement in India referred to at the beginning of this paper. They bring out the fact that a poverty measure whose structure was worked out in the 1970s and was only periodically adjusted to rising price indices is unable to reflect the implications of changing patterns of consumption among persons whose incomes are near the poverty line. That is why we can have reduced percentages of persons below the poverty line when in fact studies of achieved nutrition levels among the poor—especially among women and children—show an increasing incidence of malnutrition.

At the beginning of their article, Mehta and Venkataraman

(M&V) outline the methodology used in drawing the poverty line: "the 'poverty line' is defined as the aggregate per capita monthly expenditure of that group whose per capita, per diem 'calorie' intake (obtained from the expenditure on food items) conforms to certain specified norms. Defined in this manner, the 'poverty line' incorporates a normative as well as a behavioural component. Hence, expenditure on essential non-food items like rent, fuel, light, clothing, health care, education, transport, etc, are not normative but are empirical. Normatively, the expenditure on non-food items is likely to be seriously inadequate."

M&V's objective is to question government claims that poverty 'declined' in India during the 1990s, not to criticise the poverty line methodology as such. Thus they concentrate on the issue of consumption patterns, especially food consumption patterns. They point to the loss of non-market access to non-cereal food items: "in the past two decades, the rural poor have lost access to common property resources like pastures, forests, ponds and rivers which facilitated a free supply of items like fish, vegetables, fruits, etc. This would rule out any increase in the quantities of non-cereal food items." They also point out that: "Similarly, the shift in favour of particular items in the non-food section does not unambiguously proclaim an improved quality of life."

The poverty line methodology, as we have seen above, is based on an *empirical*, not a normative, measure of non-food consumption. An increased expenditure by those near the poverty line on non-food consumption is directly related to the increase in the cost as well as the consumption of items like fuel, electricity, medical care and education as the government gradually gives up its commitment to providing these at subsidised rates. So this increased expenditure conceals an *increasing* inadequacy in the actual consumption of these items. Similarly, the increasing cost of food items other than basic cereals would rule out any overall improvement in the composition of the food basket, as resources would be diverted away from cereals.

The recent emphasis by State and central governments in India on apparently pro-women policies, for example providing free education to the girl child, or bringing women's self-help groups under government regulation, should be seen against this background. There is now also an attempt to target poor women, especially, as a potential market for the products of large capitalist corporations. Bringing 'gender' into the forefront of development policy programmes often has a blatantly manipulative objective: to draw women into self-help groups and to draw NGOs, government agencies, 'civil society' organizations and even university and college teachers into the activity of building SHGs creates an illusion of bringing everybody into the process of 'empowerment' of women. The emphasis everywhere is on woman as consumer, as the manager of the family's consumption.

M&V have argued that falling proportions of people 'under the poverty line' can coexist with patterns of actual consumption by the poor that lead to a prevalence of severe malnutrition. One response by sections of the government has been to launch campaigns targeting malnutrition in children. For example, the Divisional Commissioner in charge of the districts in the Marathwada region has undertaken to eradicate "all degrees" of malnutrition in children under his jurisdiction, starting from the most severe category. The strategy used involves distribution of nutrient supplements and education of mothers. Again, women are being targeted as 'managers of family consumption' in severely deprived conditions, without looking at the more general causes of the deprivation. The campaign may well have a positive impact in the short term; we are concerned about the limited way in which the 'agency' of women is being portrayed and mobilised.

Shortly after the conference in September 2005 where a draft of this paper was first presented, an article by Ashwani Saith appeared in the October 22 issue of the *Economic and Political Weekly*, which makes a devastating foundational critique of the poverty line approach. Among other things Saith says: "Concepts should clarify and crystallise the nature of a phenomenon; methodologies should provide precision in the identification and quantification of their empirical analogues; do they do so in contemporary poverty studies?" And, further, "It is necessary to register a lament, if not serious dissent, at the disappearance of inequality, not in the world where it seems to be flourishing, but in the discussions on poverty, where it has been pushed into the background and rendered invisible. Absolute poverty cannot really be meaningfully comprehended without acknowledging inequality."

M&V's discussion helps us to see how the poverty line methodology used in India fails on the first count. It really fails to help us see how the poor are making choices about work and consumption in a changing economic environment. Also, the increasing difficulty of finding remunerative work does not come into the picture at all. Our analysis in the previous section should show that increasingly in recent years, an emphasis on measuring poverty in apparently absolute terms has been substituted for any discussion on *inequality*, The influence of Amartya Sen and the capabilities approach has played its role in this diversion of emphasis.

To quote Saith again, " . . . and since inequality and resource availability are closely related, the legitimising of the absolute poverty line as a targeting instrument . . . actually hides, condones, legitimises and perpetuates it (poverty). It is ironical that the more widely used measures of poverty, e g. the Sen Poverty Measure, are lauded for being sensitive to the degree of inequality amongst the poor, while ignoring the issue of inequality between the poor and the rich."

If we are to bring gender into the exercise of assessing the degree of poverty in any meaningful sense, we should be talking about inequality as well as unemployment, or erosion of livelihoods. If this is not done, we are confined to seeing women's agency only in terms of management of consumption within the family, while ignoring their interaction with the macroeconomic environment.

CONCLUSION

I have tried to show above how the capabilities approach to assessment of the impact of development, and the Human Development Index that is based on that approach, omits the question of interaction of the individual with the macroeconomic environment, and concentrates on the role of the individual as consumer. This is contradictory to the connotations of the word 'capabilities', which brings to mind the *capability to work;* this capability in reality is very much related to the availability of employment and the control over assets that might support work for a livelihood.

This has direct relevance to any investigation of the relationship between women and the process of economic development. Feminist economists writing on gender and development have underlined that the present regime of capitalist accumulation tends to divest women in developing countries of their control over productive assets. Where they are offered employment, this is in general on increasingly unfavourable terms. The capabilities approach looks at the evidence on *achievement* in respect of capabilities-related variables like literacy and health without engaging with this kind of analysis. We have tried to bring out how the 'capabilities' framework, with its treatment of capabilities and rights, capabilities and utilities, or capabilities and work, in fact belongs to an analytical framework that excludes any consideration of the individual's rights vis a vis the State. Women are then allotted the role of managing family resources in an increasingly unfavourable economic environment, and women's agency is seen in these restrictive terms. This has a direct bearing on women-related policies adopted by governments in countries like India that have been subjected to IMF-imposed regimes of structural adjustment.

Poverty measures are also formulated in an essentially paternalistic manner that precludes collection of data that might give us an understanding of how poor men and women are coping with adverse terms of employment and access to consumption goods. The question of *inequality*, whether between rich and poor, or between men and women, would also be an essential part of a feminist research agenda.

REFERENCES

Atkinson, A.B. (1995), "Capabilities, Exclusion and the Supply of Goods" in *Choice, Welfare and Development: A Festschrift in Honour of Amartya Sen*, Oxford University Press.

Beneria, Lourdes & Gita Sen (1981), "Accumulation, Reproduction, and Women's Role In Economic Development: Boserup Revisited", *Signs*, 7(2)

Boserup, Ester (1990) "Economic Change and the Role of Women", in (ed.) Irene Tinker, *Persistent Inequalities*, Oxford University Press.

Grossman, S.J. and J.E. Stiglitz (1990) "On the Impossibility of Informationally Efficient Markets" *The American Economic Review.*

Jaquette, Jane S. (1990), "Gender and Justice in Economic Development", in (ed.) Irene *Persistent Inequalities,* Tinker, Oxford University Press.

Kamdar, Sangita and Asoke Basak (2003) 'Beyond the Human Poverty Index: Preliminary Notes on Deprivation and Inequality' *Economic and Political Weekly*, Vol. XXXVIII

Mehta, J. and Shanta Venkataraman (2000), "Poverty Statistics: Bermicide's Feast", in *Economic and Political Weekly,* July 1, 2000.

Rawls, John (1971), *A Theory of Justice* Harvard University Press.

Saith, Ashwani (2005), "Poverty Lines versus the Poor: Method versus Meaning", in *Economic and Political Weekly,* October 22, 2005 .

Sen, A.K. (1984), *Resources, Values and Development,* Oxford.

—— (1981), *Poverty and Famines: An Essay in Entitlement and Deprivation,* Oxford University Press.

—— (1989), *Hunger and Public Action,* Oxford University Press.

—— (1990), "Gender and Cooperative Conflicts", in (ed.) Irene Tinker, *Persistent Inequalities*, Oxford.

—— (1984), "The Living Standard", in (eds) D.A. Collard, N.H. Dimsdale, C.L. Gilbert, D.R. Helm, M. Scott and A.K. Sen, *Economic Theory and Hicksian Themes.*

—— (1985), *Commodities and Capabilities,* North-Holland.

—— (1992), *Inequality Re-examined,* Oxford University Press.

—— (1987), *On Ethics and Economics,* Oxford: Basil Blackwell.

—— (1982), *Choice, Welfare and Measurement,* Oxford.

—— (1976 & 1982), "Rational Fools: A Critique of the Behavioural Foundations of Economic Theory", in *Choice, Welfare and Measurement,* Oxford.

—— (1999), *Development and Freedom,* Oxford University Press, p. 302-3.

Engendering Market Structure

A Normative Analysis

RITU DEWAN & AZANIA THOMAS

'Most economists are trained to think that macroeconomics is about aggregates—for example, the level of employment or exchange rates. What we are trying to demonstrate is that behind those aggregates are the behaviours of different groups of people.'– Nilufer Cagatay, 2005.

INTRODUCTION

Markets reflect the 'behaviours of different groups of people' and form part of an intrinsic blueprint that dictates the functioning and effectiveness of macroeconomic theory and policy. The incorporation of gender discrimination into the mix exposes different constraints about how both function. Some of these constraints are prevalent when light is thrown on the interaction of normative principles and gender discrimination in situations of market failure.

As explained in the second section of this essay, gender discrimination is utilised by markets to achieve Pareto efficiency. For example a monopsonist that wage discriminates on the basis of gender is clearly in conflict with issues of distributional justice (strict egalitarianism). This is even if the strategy of profit maximization adopted by the monopsonist is a socially efficient outcome. In view of possibilities like the one examined, policy formation needs to account for the normative implications that underlie the links between gender discrimination and market failure. In other words, this section shows that gender discrimination though distributively unjust and thereby unequal, may or may not lead to 'inefficient' market outcomes.

Section III examines situations where gender discrimination leads to market failure and can be resolved both on egalitarian and social efficiency grounds. Illustrations of gender sensitive barriers to market entry include the lack of access to information where women (amongst other socially disadvantaged groups) are far worse off when it comes to being isolated from credit or labour markets distorted by historical gender constructs.

Inadequate attention is given to skills in the sphere of non-market work, the purveyors of which are mostly women. Non-market work represents a hidden reservoir which is inadequately recognized as a potential starting point from which development in skills can lead to their marketability across a given trade or enterprise. The outcome of gender discrimination in relation to the issue of non-market work is also socially inefficient.

Finally, isolation from formal credit markets and lack of collateral also poses a serious barrier to credit access for women. This is again mainly on account of the inefficiencies that have resulted from pre-existing historically defined gender constructs. Women were barred from potential sources of productivity as is clearly evident in existing laws relating to private property, for example, The Hindu Succession Act (1956) and Hindu Succession Act (Amendment) (2005). There exists a minute aspect of such legislation that continues to gender discriminate in a socially inefficient manner and also on egalitarian grounds. It is arguably the case that in situations where gender discrimination is socially efficient, normative concerns of distributive justice are more likely to make engendered theory and policy effective. It is with a view to increasing this effectiveness that normative principles need to be examined to reveal the nuances of gender discrimination in a market framework.

ANALYSING TWO NORMATIVE PRINCIPLES: PARETO EFFICIENCY AND DISTRIBUTIVE JUSTICE

This section briefly analyses two normative principles: Pareto efficiency and distributive justice with a view to understanding how they can be used to deal with existing gender inequalities within a market framework.

Pareto Efficiency

Pareto efficiency was a concept first used by Italian economist Vilfredo Pareto in 1906, and was designed to capture the amount of waste or 'friction' within economic mechanisms and thereby indicate how efficiently they operate.

In this context, resource allocation mechanisms such as markets can be Pareto inefficient or Pareto improving, if for a given set of alternative allocations and a set of individuals, there is a facilitated movement from one alternative allocation to another which makes an individual(s) better off while making no other individual(s) worse off. Markets are Pareto efficient where no further Pareto improvements can be made.[1] The case for inefficiency thus implies room for Pareto improvement (where there is the existence of potentially mutual advantageous trade or profitable production decisions. Hence the question of why a particular resource allocation mechanism is inefficient can be rephrased to ask why Pareto improvements do not occur.

This could happen in situations in which (a) Individuals do not have sufficient information to seek out profitable or advantageous opportunities, (b) Individuals do not have sufficient control (or even access) over commodities (including productive assets) to affect profitable or advantageous opportunities, and (c) If individual parties to a trade cannot agree on how to share gains from their mutually advantageous exchange.

Pareto efficient outcomes are not always desirable especially if they are unequal and thereby inconsistent with the principles of distributive justice. Markets function efficiently even in situations where there exists gender discrimination. In other words, gender discrimination can be both Pareto-efficient and unequal, as in the case of the monopsonist who wage discriminates according to gender or in cases where there is a lack of access to productive resources on account of historical gendered constructs.

Distributive Justice

Principles of distributive justice are normative principles designed to allocate goods in limited supply relative to demand. The principles vary along several dimensions depending on the kind of goods sought to be distributed (income, wealth, opportunities etc), the subjects to whom goods are sought to be distributed (individuals, groups, preferences) and the basis on which the goods are sought to be distributed (equality, individual characteristics, according to free market transactions etc).[2] We examine distributive justice in terms of the end-state theory. This theory examines the distribution of goods among members of society at a specific time to assess whether the distribution is just.[3]

The end state theory incorporates strict egalitarianism and on this basis aims to reduce or eliminate differences between individuals or households in a society. It is important to note that advocates of strict egalitarianism most often want to eliminate all forms of gender discrimination on the basis of relative equality. The lack of access to information, credit, productive resources and untapped skill potential which have resulted from fundamental imbalances in gender relations is viewed as unequal amongst the genders from a relative position.

It is however important to mention that certain forms of gender discrimination under the Rawlsian criterion of distributive justice, for instance can be viewed as desirable on the basis of the 'Difference Principle'. John Rawls, in his *A Theory of Justice*, developed the Difference Principle where economic and social inequalities can only be justified, if their most disadvantaged members benefit on account of them.[4] In this context, a monopsonist that wage discriminates according to gender is justified by the fact that more women would be employed, who otherwise would remain unemployed.

GENDER DISCRIMINATION THAT IS PARETO EFFICIENT

We begin here by describing the underlying basis of inefficiency (in previously mentioned point c, p. 28), that is, situations in which individual parties to a trade cannot agree on how to share gains from their mutually advantageous exchange. In the case of a monopsony, there is an inherent deadweight loss, where there is excess involuntary unemployment due to the charging of a singular monopsony wage rate. The mutually advantageous exchange is the potential increase in producer surplus at the cost of hiring more labour. This does not occur, as it is not in the profit maximising interests of the monopsonist to charge a singular competitive wage rate.

The monopsonist can however factor in gender discrimination within profit maximising interests, by hiring total labour at the competitive level and charging for instance, lower reservation wage rates for women as compared to men. In the case of third degree wage discrimination, a monopsonist can further segment labour into markets on the basis of gender, where more women are hired at lower wage rates as compared to men. The result is Pareto efficient, both producers and workers have arrived at how a mutually advantageous exchange or the reduction of deadweight loss can be achieved through gender discrimination.

The analysis then proceeds to find similar ground with neoclassical and segmented labour market approaches to gender discrimination.

A well-documented examination of the economic analysis of discrimination can be found in Stephen. W. Smith's *Labour Economics* (2003), which focuses upon "the possibility that significant wage and employment differences persist between groups in the labour force and how these are not justified by differential productivity and human capital investment. The impact of gender and racial characteristics on earnings and employment outcomes are regarded as labour market consequences of discrimination."[5]

Smith examines two main schools of economic thought regarding discrimination. One is the neoclassical theory stemming from the work of Becker (1957) and Robinson's (1933) 'Theory of Monopsony', where 'prejudice is expressed in discriminatory tastes on the part of employers'. An alternative to the segmented labour market approach is historically traced back to the 'Theory of Non-Competing Groups' in the work of Mill (1885). This approach essentially maintains that the labour market is 'split into sectors including delineations according to sex and racial origin, and that there is very little interaction between the sectors'. Examples of this approach are the 'job crowding hypothesis' and the 'dual labour market' hypothesis.[6]

Perfect wage discrimination by a monopsonist reflects the neoclassical theory of discrimination; in particular, Robinson's 'Theory of Monopsony' (1933). The analysis is augmented by how Pareto–efficiency is achieved within such a market structure by exploiting an existing gender inequality. Third-degree wage discrimination by a monopsonist, however, bears close resemblance to the segmented labour market approach, the only difference being that the latter approach operates within a competitive framework and that the monopsonist is able to wage discriminate between men and women on the same jobs and productivities instead of them being different.

For greater comprehension, the dead weight loss, first and third degree price discrimination of a monopoly is compared throughout with the analogue of a monopsony. We first begin by examining the case of deadweight loss by a monopolist.

The Deadweight Loss of a Monopoly

'A competitive industry operates at a point where price equals marginal cost. A monopolist operates where price is greater then marginal cost. Thus in general, the price will be higher and the output lower if a firm behaves monopolistically rather than competitively.'[7]

This is Pareto-inefficient due to the resultant deadweight loss as denoted in Fig. 1. For the sake of measuring the deadweight loss in either market structure, we costlessly enforce the condition of perfect competition. The monopolist will now sell larger output

Fig. 1: The Deadweight Loss of a Monopoly

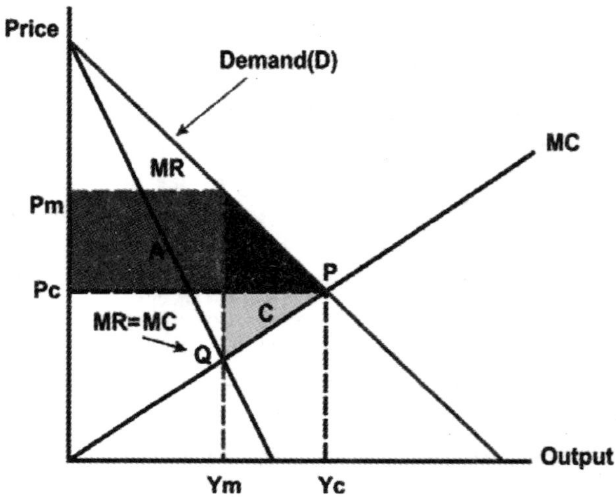

Fig. 2: The Deadweight Loss of a Monopsony

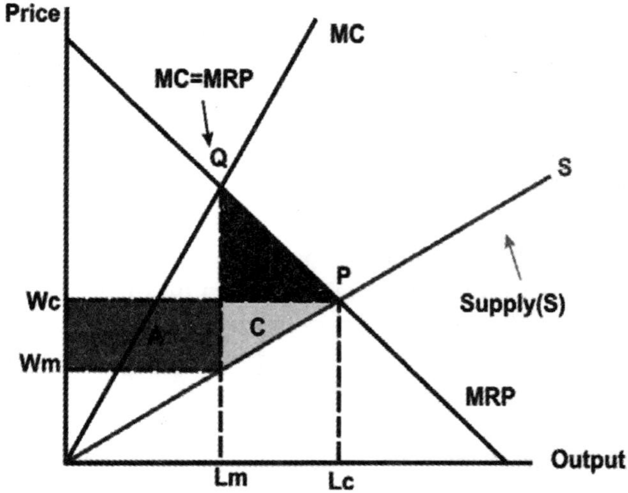

Yc at market price Pc, which is lower then Monopoly price Pm, where output was constricted at Ym. Pareto inefficiency lies in the fact that there is a whole range of output that is not being produced and made available to consumers at lower prices.[8]

The monopolist's surplus goes down by Area A due to the lower price on the units he is already selling. It goes up by Area C due to the profits on the extra units he is now selling. The consumer's surplus goes up by Area A, since the consumers are now getting all the units they were buying before at cheaper price Pc and it goes up by Area B, since they get some surplus on the extra units that are being sold. The area A is just a transfer from the monopolist to the consumer: one side of the market is better and one side is made worse off, but the total surplus does not change.[9]

The Area B+C represents a true increase in surplus—this area measures the value that the consumers and the producers place on the extra output that has been produced. The Area B+C is known as a deadweight loss due to the monopoly condition. It provides a measure of how much worse off people are, paying the monopoly price than paying the competitive price.[10]

The Deadweight Loss of a Monopsony

Similarly, a monopsony will now hire workers at perfectly competitive wage rate Wc and hire labour at Lc, instead of constricting the hiring of labour at Lm thereby exerting control by charging lower wage rate Wm. Pareto inefficiency lies in the fact that there is a whole range of labour that is not being hired (between Lm and Lc).

The monopsonist's surplus goes down by Area A due to higher wages Wc. It goes up by Area B due to the increase in marginal revenue product. The worker surplus goes up by Area A due to higher wages and by Area C due to extra workers hired at Lc.

Area A is a transfer from monopsonist to workers where there is no change in total surplus. Areas B+C, however represent a true increase in surplus value and the deadweight loss at monopsony wage rate Wm.

So how does one factor in such Pareto inefficiency to make it

Fig. 3: Pareto Efficiency and Perfect Price Discrimination Under a Monopoly

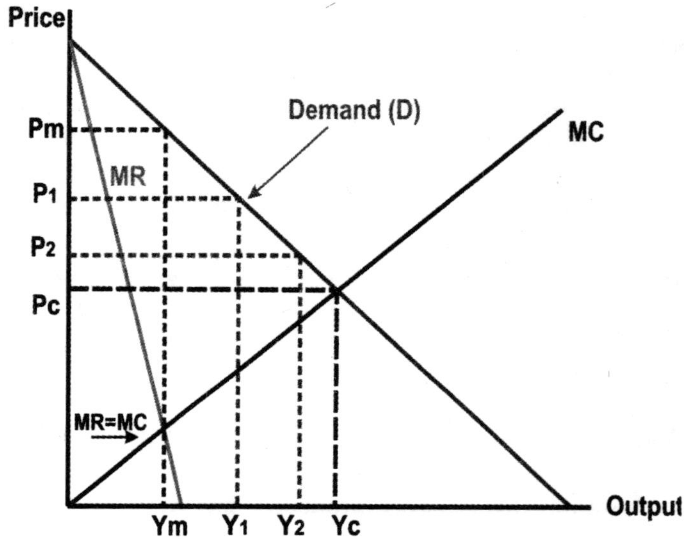

Pareto efficient in the profit maximising interests of both market structures?

The deadweight loss or Pareto inefficiency can be reduced if a monopsonist is able to capture the entire worker surplus and thereby maximise producer surplus by hiring labour at different reservation wages. We proceed to examine the cases of perfect and third degree price/wage discrimination of both market structures respectively.

Pareto Efficiency and Perfect Price Discrimination Under a Monopoly

The monopolist will behave as a perfectly competitive seller as earlier stated. It will produce at an output level where the consumer's marginal willingness to pay equals marginal willingness to produce: at price and output combination (Pc, Yc).

At the same time, the monopolist will engage in the condition of price discrimination, where the aim is to maximise profits (producers surplus) subject to the maximum price (reservation

Fig. 4: Pareto Efficiency and Perfect Wage Discrimination Under a Monopsony

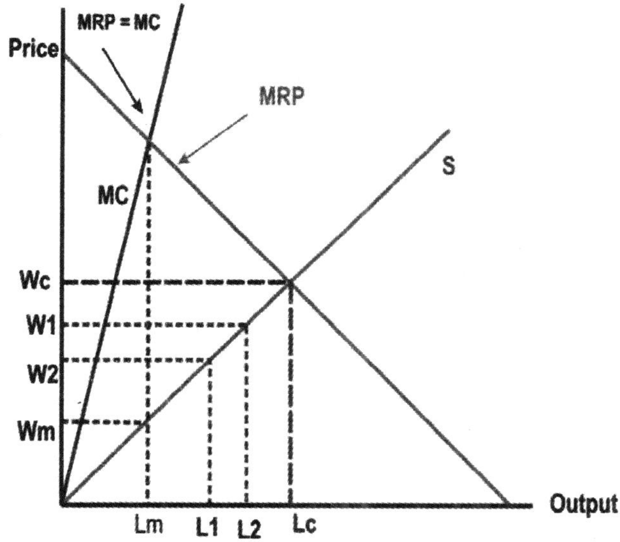

price) that the consumer is willing to pay for the good or service.

(I.e.) The monopolist will charge price P1 (to consumers willing to pay P1 for output level Y1) or charge price P2 (to consumers willing to pay P2 for output P2) and produce a maximum output at marginal cost (At price and output combination (Pc, Yc). In this way the monopolist can maximise producer surplus and appropriate all consumer surplus for itself.[11]

The outcome is Pareto-efficient—there is no way to make both individual consumer and producer better off: the producer's profit cannot be increased: since he/she already has a maximal profit. Consumer surplus cannot be increased without reducing the profit of the producer.[12]

Pareto Efficiency and Perfect Wage Discrimination Under a Monopsony

Similarly, a monopsonist will behave as a perfectly competitive buyer of labour but with a difference. Workers will be hired till a level where the worker's marginal willingness to supply labour equals the monopsonist's marginal willingness to hire labour: At wage rate and worker input combination (Wc, Lc).

The difference is that the monopsonist will still maximize profits (producer's surplus) subject to the maximum wage rate (reservation wage) for that the worker is willing to supply labour. The producer will charge wage rate W1 (to workers willing to supply labour at L1 and accept wage rate W1). In this way the producer is able to charge different reservation wages up to Wc.

The outcome will be Pareto-efficient where there is no way to make both individual worker and producer better off: the producer's profit cannot be increased since he already has a maximal profit. Worker surplus cannot be increased without reducing the profit of the producer.

It is essential to note that the monopolist or monopsonist will need to have perfect knowledge of individual consumers' demand curves or individual workers' supply curves respectively, which may not be possible. But even in the second-best situation, the condition of pareto-efficiency has been established by a monopsonist who is able to exploit situations where fewer women are hired for a lesser wage rate as compared to more men who are willing to be hired for a higher wage rate.

Apart from Pareto-efficiency, perfect wage discrimination by a monopsonist, reflects the neo-classical approach of Joan Robinson's theory of monopsony (1933). Her theory reflects mobility costs incurred by women, due to social convention via the differences in elasticity of supply curves between men and women. The labour supply curve of men is perfectly elastic compared to that of women.[13] In Fig. 4 above, a woman's lack of mobility can also be reflected on lower points of the common supply curve, say at wage rate and labour combinations (Wm, Lm and W1, L1). Apart from mobility costs and ignorance of better job conditions, perfect wage discrimination is also able to exploit a woman's 'amenability' to work for lower paid jobs due to social conditioning on the part of the employer and employee.

We take the analysis further via the description of the more common form of third degree wage discrimination.

Fig. 5: Pareto Efficiency and Third Degree Price Discrimination

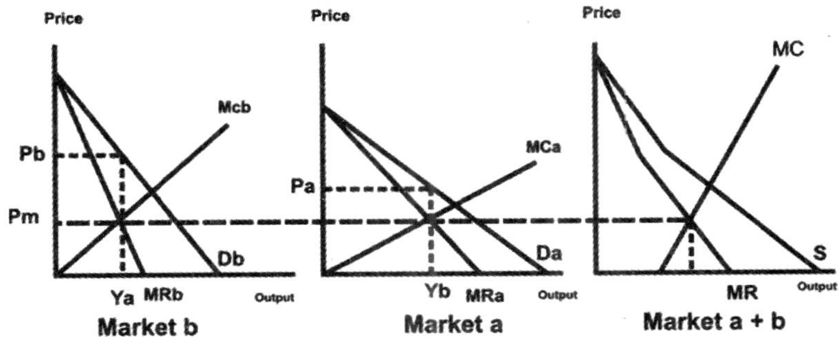

Pareto Efficiency and Third Degree Price Discrimination Under a Monopoly

We begin by examining the analogue of third degree price discrimination by a monopolist.

Consumers are separated into two independent markets (market a and market b) and a separate price is charged for each market. In Market a+b: The MR (Marginal Revenue) curve is found by horizontal additional of two MR curves in market a and market b. The total profit is maximised where MC is equal to MR in each market. MR must be the same in both markets otherwise revenue could be increased by switching output in the market with the higher MR. The profit maximising price in each market will be given by the relevant demand curve.[14]

Thus in market B: Less output (Yb) is sold for a higher price (Pb) as compared to market A: Greater output (Ya) is sold for a lower price (Pa). The lower price is charged to the demand curve that is more elastic.[15] An example of third degree price discrimination is different priced seats on buses for adults and children or different prices for the same product sold in different countries.[16]

Pareto Efficiency and Third Degree Wage Discrimination Under a Monopsony

The monopsonist is able to exploit situations where more women are willing to supply labour at lower reservation wage rates where their supply curves are more elastic.

Workers are now grouped into the two markets a and b, according to the elasticity of their labour supply curves, where a separate wage is charged for each market. Let market b be the market for male workers and market a the market for female workers.

In market, a+b, the MRP curve is found by the horizontal additional of both MRP. curves in market a and market b. Total profit is maximised where MC is equal to MRP in each market; MRP must be the same in both markets otherwise revenue could be increased by hiring labour in the market with the higher MRP.

The profit maximising price in each market will be given by the relevant labour supply curve. Thus in market b: Less male labour (Lb) is hired for a higher wage rate (Wb) as compared to market a: More female labour (La) is hired for a lower wage rate (Wa). The lower wage is charged to the supply curve that is more elastic.

In the case of a monopolist, a necessary condition for efficiency to increase when price discrimination is implemented is that total output should increase. If output remains constant or decreases when price discrimination is allowed, total welfare must necessarily decline. Similarly in the case of a monopsony, a necessary condition for efficiency to increase is that total labour should increase through the condition of wage discrimination.[17]

Without price discrimination, small niche markets may not be well served, if the monopolist is required to charge a uniform price. Similarly, wage discrimination can provide very significant efficiency gains since it allows markets for female labour to be served that would have not occurred earlier if the monopsonist had to charge a singular wage rate.

It is interesting that to prevent the resale of output, a monopolist has to have a definitive manner of segmenting markets, where mechanisms are enforced to clearly differentiate consumers. The 'job crowding hypothesis' of the competitive segmented theory of labour markets depicts how a disproportionate number of women (possessing equal ability as their male counterparts) are excluded from higher paying jobs which depresses wages in the fewer occupations they are crowded into. This is done through the

Fig. 6: Pareto Efficiency and Third Degree Wage Discrimination

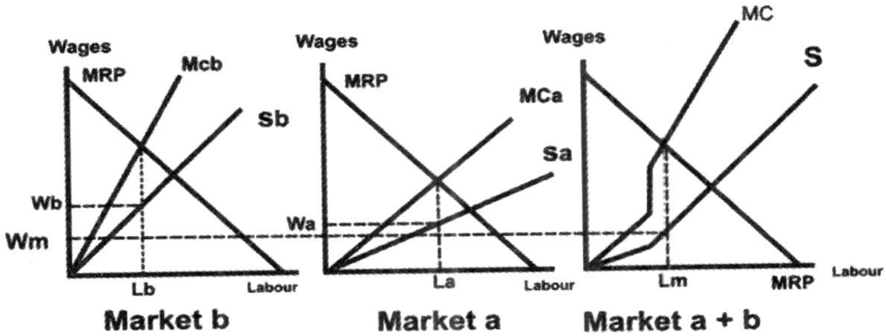

pressure of male trade unions, a crude veto on hiring women, lengthy training or an employment history, which results in the inevitable segmentation of the labour market. The monopsonist is able to effectively segment markets based on the same job and same productivity, by enforcing the latter two conditions i.e. lengthy training or the need for an employment history. (That is, women can be made to perform the same jobs, as trainees or employees that are subcontracted or temporary). This can possibly have an effect on the amenability of more women to work for lower wages thereby depicting a greater elasticity in their supply curves. (See Fig. 6)

HOW CAN GENDER DISCRIMINATION BE RESOLVED EVEN IF PARETO-EFFICIENT?

End-state theories rely on the principle of strict egalitarianism to do away with the forms of gender discrimination incorporated within the market structure of a wage discriminating monopsony. Distributive justice is no longer concerned with reducing the deadweight loss of hiring more workers at different wage rates, but by equalizing wage rates for both sexes.

In this context, we examine the case of equalizing the monopsony wage rate to a minimum wage rate that is equal to all and where more labour is hired. Minimum wage policy is likely to be influential but more so from an egalitarian point of view than from a market efficiency point of view, especially when depicted in the third regime as explained below. There are three classes or regimes, according to the value taken by the minimum wage, as is seen by the following table:

Table 1: Minimum-wage regimes in monopsonistic labour markets

	Minimum wage	*Resulting equilibrium*
First regime	Not higher than monopsony wage	Unchanged from monopsony
Second regime	Higher than monopsony wage but not higher than competitive wage	At kink of supply curve
Third regime	Higher than competitive wage	At intersection where minimum wage equals *MRP*

Source: 'Monopsony', *Wikipedia, The Free Encyclopedia,* 2005.

There is Pareto inefficiency evident in all three regimes denoted by an excess supply of unemployed labour. The first regime being synonymous with the description of the deadweight loss of a monopsony stated above.

We depict the second regime below:

This action would change the supply curve and hence the MC curve (Marginal labour cost). No labour will be hired below the minimum wage Wmin. At this given wage, the monopsonist can now attract a fixed number of workers up to the kink in the supply curve. Here Wmin is higher than the monopsonistic wage rate Wm. At this given wage the firm can now hire all the workers it wants to, up to the supply curve, so that in the relevant employment range its marginal cost of labour becomes effectively constant and equal to Wmin, as shown by the new black horizontal line MCmin. Wmin not only does not serve the profit maximising interests of the monopsonist, but also leads to an excess supply of labour between points A and B, which will remain involuntarily unemployed. This excess supply of labour indicates Pareto-inefficiency, even though all wage rates have been rationalised to Wmin from a strictly egalitarian point of view.

Fig. 7: Second regime: The minimum Wage Distributive Justice

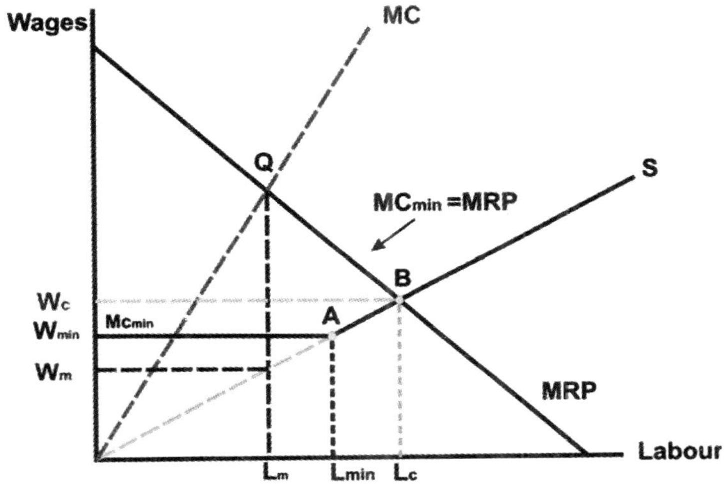

The third regime is depicted below:

At minimum wage rate Wmin, the monopsonist maximises profits at the new intersection point A, choosing the employment level Lmin, which is higher then monopsonistic level L. Beyond point A, however it would be unprofitable to hire additional workers from the monopsonist's viewpoint. There is an excess supply of labour i.e. involuntary employment—equal to segment AB where there is clearly a deadweight loss to society, despite the minimum wage raising the level of employment from Lm to Lmin.

Minimum wage policy is a classic example where policy aimed at distributive justice has resulted in a deadweight loss and where there is a clear trade-off.

FORMS OF GENDER DISCRIMINATION THAT ARE BOTH PARETO INEFFICIENT AND STRICTLY UNEGALITARIAN

This section aims to briefly identify forms of gender discrimination that are both Pareto-inefficient and unequal. Strict egalitarianism as an aspect of distributive justice dictates that all forms of gender discrimination are undesirable, which is a paradox to the Rawlsian 'Difference Principle' that allows for certain forms of gender

Fig. 8: Third regime: The Minimum Wage, Distributive Justice and Efficiency

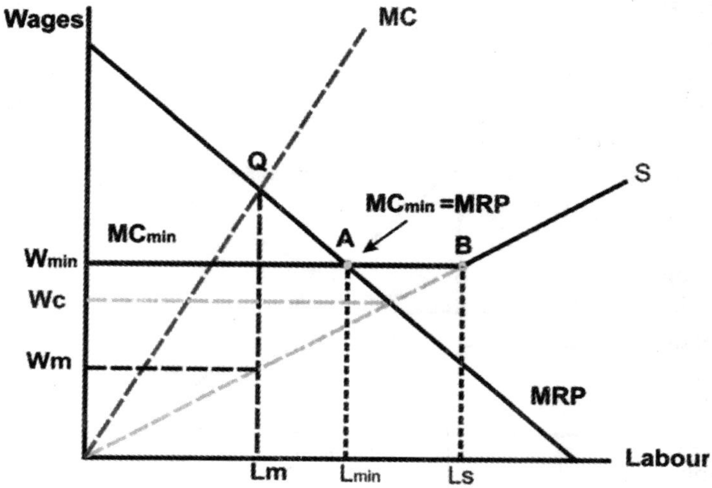

discrimination. In the description of such forms of gender discrimination, we view strict egalitarianism from the point that all individuals in society should have equal power or equal avenues for access to resource allocation mechanisms.

Historically defined gender constructs give rise to inequalities that are exploitable within markets to achieve pareto-efficiency. Such constructs can however lead to inefficient market outcomes, in the following two situations a) when individuals do not have sufficient information to seek out such profitable or advantageous opportunities. b) When they do not have sufficient control (or access) over commodities (including productive assets) to affect profitable or advantageous opportunities.

Lack of Information Access

Access to information is vital to individual and group economic interests and for markets to function effectively. By this we mean, for example, information that would lead to an increase in livelihood options and productivity e.g. labour markets (wage rates, jobs available), credit markets (loan types, interest rate comparisons).

An engendered perspective asserts that clear information access is beneficial for both sexes, except that it is further noticed that women will tend to benefit more considering the historical structuring of their social networks. Women have socially tended to have closely knit familial ties whereas men who are treated as primary breadwinners have tended to extend their networks beyond the family. The spread of information is constrained within a patriarchal structure.

The creation of incentives to resolve this socially inefficient outcome is to create gender-sensitive focal points that will (a) provide information for the individual and (b) encourage the formation of informal social networks that may later evolve into social networks such as self-help groups, women's cooperatives and production associations.

Gender sensitive focal points of information (GSFPIs) can flexibly act both as motivational providers as well as intermediaries of market information to the individual and individuals choosing to group into social networks. These could be incorporated in the workings of existing mechanisms, which would lead to greater levels of efficiency such as labour exchanges, Panchayats and community centres or new GSFPIs through special booths in post offices, railway stations, slums, public wards and points where information is more likely to be received and spread. The underlying principle of GSFPIs is the provision and spread of valuable information to the individual or group in a motivational and simple way.

Lack of Access to Credit

The above point bears a strong interlinkage to gender discrimination and the lack of access to credit. There exist inherent inefficiencies of state-led formal credit systems due to improper targeting, where the poor are still excluded from the benefits of the programme at the cost of the non-poor, improper screening mechanisms of credit worthy borrowers and usage of loans that result in high transaction costs for the poor. The system of directed lending also leads to the creation of non-profit making assets due to poor repayment of loans. Skewed ownership in land patterns and a general lack of collateral does not make things any easier.[18] Women stand on the lower rung of the credit ladder due to added inefficiencies that have resulted from pre-defined social roles.

The importance of social networks cannot be underestimated as societal motivators, and more importantly information providers pose as collateral via the presence of a group. Loan repayments, for example, are easier to monitor via the surveillance mechanisms of a group, which acts as powerful social collateral for access to credit markets. Network effects arise when taking into the account the surveillance mechanism. The total value of the social collateral of the group is roughly proportional to the square of the number of individuals already using that social collateral to seek greater access into credit markets. Hence an individual that adds to a group is able to make use of the social collateral of the entire group. A critical mass point would be reached when the surveillance mechanism fails due to there being too many members within a group.[19]

The issue of network effects and surveillance mechanisms operating within a social network or group is inherent in existing micro-credit schemes. Chavan and Ramakumar (2002) state that these schemes attempt to bridge the gap between the public banking network and women (amongst other socially disadvantaged groups) via the Self-Help Group (SHG). This policy consists of three variants. 1) Public banks either acted as a 'self-help group promoting institutions' (SHPI), 2) Facilitating agencies such as NGOs or government agencies acted as mediators between SHGs and public banks or 3) those who managed the SHGs themselves and behaved as credit providers with public banks providing credit to the facilitating agency. Innovative methods of lending, the exploitation of a vast rural banking network, developed social networks via micro-credit scheme brings the socially disadvantaged, including women in touch with credit markets, which is seen as an efficient outcome.[20]

Of course the question of efficiency depends on how well oiled the mechanisms of micro-credit are. The utilisation of the public banking network for the supply of micro-credit implies accountability in operations, that the interest on SHG loans does not exceed the ceiling fixed by the RBI for small loans (interest rates are fixed to provide a margin to banks and NGOs), if there has been any noticeable contribution to the improvement of skills and technology adopted by SHGs and if there has been a pervasive spread of information towards this end. Also there is the question of whether the micro-credit scheme is gender-sensitive at all.[21]

Untapped Skill Potential

Women tend to largely engage in the trade-off between market work and non-market work. This trade-off exists in degrees depending on the level of importance that social pressures give to the role of non-market work. There exists the accompanying factor of untapped skill potential where attributes and skills acquired in non-market work are not recognised or partially recognised as skill that is both exploitable and marketable, which is therefore not developed to its fullest potential.

A large part of the female workforce is present in industries requiring basic to intermediate skill, because they are seen as having natural given attributes such as dexterity, better concentration for longer hours, good visual responses to detail, comprehension of intricate patterns and the ability to comprehend and assemble the sub-parts of a whole. These qualities reflect training that has been acquired from non-market work like cooking, sewing etc. (Elson & Pearson, 1981).[22]

Skill development is hindered when many of the skills required in women's occupations are not reflected in job designations 'because they mirror domestic tasks which women perform outside the workplace for free' (Lim, L. 1996).[23] The question of skill development needs to be addressed, utilising the recognition of existing skills as a starting point for training, instead of the latter issue being exclusive (Chhachhi, 1999).[24] From an efficiency point of view, this could allow skills to develop at full potential and make them marketable across a given enterprise or trade.

Lack of Access to Productive Resources, Due to Discrimination in Private Property Ownership

Barriers to potential sources of productivity such as private property were clearly identified in previous versions of existent laws such as the Hindu Succession Act (1956) and the Hindu Succession Act (Amendment) (2005). The gamut of religious laws on private property not only discriminate with respect to gender in a socially inefficient manner but are also discriminatory on egalitarian grounds.

Discrimination in access to private property denies women the right to seek better access to credit markets (requiring as they do private property as collateral, the running of small home businesses and where there are adverse generational effects on the productivity of offspring in situations where productivity is positively correlated to access to private property).

Many women's rights activists and legal experts have argued that The Hindu Succession (Amendment) Bill 2005 has not been drafted comprehensively. The Bill is analysed here from the perspective of its inherent gender discrimination that was once socially inefficient.

The amended version of the Bill reduced the following inefficiencies, which existed in the Hindu Succession Act (1956):

- The Mitakshara System of joint family property where women are guaranteed an equal share in the deceased Hindu male's notional portion along with sons and other Class 1 heirs, but are not treated as independent coparceners like sons who by birthright are entitled to an independent share in the joint family property, in addition to their shares in their father's portion.[25]
- Women are not allowed to demand partition of their notional shares if male heirs reside.[26]
- Sons can demand partition of the Mitakshara coparcenary while women cannot.[27]
- A man can convert any part of his separate property into coparcenary property, which can further reduce women's inheritance.[28]

But the Hindu Succession Act (Amendment) (2005) still

contained an aspect that is Pareto inefficient and that was rectified in August of 2006.

> Notably Section 4(2) exempted significant interests in agricultural land such as the devolution of tenancy rights, where states either follow the Hindu Succession Act (1956) or do not specify the order of devolution of tenancy rights and in other states the order of devolution of tenancy rights is gender discriminatory
>
> Here primacy was given (as under the ancient Mitakshara system) to male lineal descendants and women came very low in the order of heirs. Also, a woman got a limited estate and lost the land if she remarried (as widow) or failed to cultivate it for a year or two.[29]
>
> There are inequalities that still do exist and still await rectification: Section 30 of the Act gave a person unrestricted testamentary rights over his/her property. In practice, the provision can be used to disinherit female heirs. This section can and has been used to disinherit women.[30] On the positive side, the amendments might increase the shares of daughters who were unmarried when the amendments came into effect and in the long run increase the shares of all daughters. It will also give daughters direct rights in some property, which the father cannot will away.
>
> But the amendments will decrease the shares of other Class I female heirs, such as the man's widow and mother, since the coparcenary share of the deceased male from whom they inherit will decline.[31]

CONCLUSION

The above is a brief description underlining the importance of the interaction of three aspects: normative measures, gender discrimination and markets. We have seen in Section II, how gender discrimination though distributively unjust and thereby unequal, may still lead to 'efficient' market outcomes, through the example of a wage discriminating monopsonist. We looked at minimum wage policy in direct contrast as an application of distributive justice, to resolve gender discrimination that is Pareto efficient. What will be seen is a trade-off of efficiency versus strict equity. Such a trade off throws light on how gender discrimination can best be resolved depending on the kind of normative measure used.

In Section III, such a trade-off does not always occur. Situations have been examined where gender discrimination leads to market failure and can be resolved both on egalitarian and social efficiency grounds. Illustrations of gender sensitive barriers to market entry include 1) The lack of access to information where women (amongst other socially disadvantaged groups) are far worse off when it comes to being isolated from credit or labour markets distorted by historical gender constructs. 2). Non-market work represents a hidden reservoir which is inadequately recognized as a potential starting point from which development in skills can lead to their marketability across a given trade or enterprise. 3) Finally, isolation from formal credit markets and lack of collateral also poses a serious barrier to credit access for women. This is again mainly on account of the inefficiencies that have resulted from pre-existing historically defined gender constructs. 4) The Hindu Succession Act (1956) and Hindu Succession Act (Amendment) (2005) are prime examples of legislation that barred women from potential sources of productivity such as private property. There still exists an aspect of such legislation that continues to gender discriminate in a socially inefficient manner and also on egalitarian grounds. Daughters might still be included as coparceners at the cost of the widow's property share declining. This anomaly would disappear if the Mitakshara coparcenary is abolished altogether. All property would then go equally to class I heirs, of which the widow is one. Also, given a male bias, an implicit inequality arises from the unrestricted right to will. A man can disinherit her by willing away private property to a person(s) of choice.

It is arguably the case that in situations where gender discrimination is socially efficient, normative concerns of distributive justice are more likely to make engendered theory and policy effective. It is with a view to increasing this effectiveness that normative principles need to be examined to reveal the nuances of gender discrimination in a market framework.

Azania Thomas would like to thank Dr. Sayantan Ghosal, Dr. Dania Thomas, Mr. Chris Way and her mother for guidance, inspiration and support in writing this paper.

NOTES

[1] See 'Pareto efficiency', *Wikipedia, The Free Encyclopedia*. 2005.

[2] See Julian Lamont and Edward N. Zalta, *The Stanford Encyclopedia of Philosophy (Fall Edition)*, 2003.

[3] See 'Distributive Justice', *Wikipedia, The Free Encyclopedia*, 2005.

[4] Ibid, p. 2

[5] See Stephen Smith, *Labour Economics*, UK, 2003

[6] Ibid, p. 96

[7] See Hal Varian, *Intermediate Microeconomics—A Modern Approach*, USA, 1996

[8] Ibid, p. 414

[9] Ibid, p. 414

[10] Ibid, pp. 414-415

[11] Ibid, p. 426

[12] Ibid, p. 426

[13] Smith, op. cit., p. 100

[14] See John Sloman, *Economics*, UK, 1996.

[15] Ibid, p. 265

[16] Ibid, p. 264

[17] See Hal Varian (1996), 'Differential Pricing & Efficiency', *First Monday, Peer Review Journal on the Internet*.

[18] See Pallavi Chavan and R. Ramakumar, 'Micro Credit & Rural Poverty—An Analysis of Empirical Evidence', *Economic & Political Weekly*, 2002.

[19] See 'Network Effect', *Wikipedia, The Free Encyclopedia*, 2005.

[20] See Pallavi Chavan and R. Ramakumar, op. cit.: p. 963

[21] Ibid, p. 963

[22] See Diane Elson and Ruth Pearson, 'Nimble Fingers make cheap workers: an analysis of women's employment in Third World export manufacturing', *Feminist Review*, 1981.

[23] See Lim Lin Lean, *More and Better Jobs For Women: an action guide*, Geneva, 1996.

[24] See Amrita Chachhi, *Gender, Skill and Industrial Restructuring: The Electronics Industry in India*, Hague, 1999.

[25] See Bina Agarwal 'A Bill of Her Own', *Indian Express, Columns*, 2004.

[26] Ibid.

[27] Ibid.

[28] Ibid.

[29] See Kirti Singh, 'Amendments to the Hindu Succession Act—Are they

Enough to Bring About Gender Equality?', *Combat Law, Vol. 4, Issue 1*, 2005.

[30] See Bina Agarwal, 'Women didn't receive rights without struggle', *Indian Express, Columns*, 2005.

[31] Ibid.

REFERENCES

Agarwal, Bina (2004), 'A Bill of Her Own?', *Indian Express, Columns.*

—— (2005), 'Women didn't receive rights without struggle', *Indian Express, Columns.*

Chachhi, A, (1999), *Gender, Skill and Industrial Restructuring: The Electronics Industry in India*, Institute of Social Studies, The Hague.

Chavan. Pallavi and R. Ramakumar, (2002), 'Micro Credit & Rural Poverty—An Analysis of Empirical Evidence', *Economic & Political Weekly.*

Elson, D. and Pearson, R. (1981), 'Nimble Fingers make cheap workers: an analysis of women's employment in Third World export manufacturing', *Feminist Review* 7.

Lamont, Julian and Edward N. Zalta (2003) 'Distributive Justice', *The Stanford Encyclopedia of Philosophy (Fall Edition).*

Lim Lin Lean, (1996), *More and Better Jobs For Women: an action guide*, Geneva: International Labour Organisation.

Singh, Kirti, (2005), 'Amendments to the Hindu Succession Act—Are they Enough to Bring About Gender Equality?', *Combat Law, Vol. 4, Issue 1.*

Sloman, John, (1996), *Economics*, Prentice Hall, Harvester Wheatsheaf, USA.

Smith, Stephen, (2003), *'Labour Economics'*, London, Routledge.

Varian, Hal, (1996), 'Differential Pricing & Efficiency', *First Monday, Peer Review Journal on the Internet.*

'Distributive Justice', *Wikipedia, the Free Encyclopedia*, (2005) *URL*= http://en.wikipedia.org/wiki/Distributive_justice.

'Network effect', *Wikipedia, The Free Encyclopedia* (2005), URL= http://en.wikipedia.org/wiki/Network_effect

'Monopsony', *Wikipedia, The Free Encyclopedia* (2005), URL=http://en.wikipedia.org/wiki/Monopsony#column-one

'Pareto efficiency', *Wikipedia, The Free Encyclopedia,* (2005), URL= http://en.wikipedia.org/wiki/Pareto_efficiency

Engendering Macroeconomic Modelling for Policy Analysis

ANUSHREE SINHA

INTRODUCTION

Since the middle 1980s, a substantial body of work has been produced that analyses and evaluates macroeconomic theory, macroeconomic policy and their gendered impact (Evers, 2003). There is a concern at present that a macro perspective on gender, that includes work that is not marketed (referred as non-market work henceforth) is essential to equitable growth. These and other gender concerns have been incorporated in the Beijing Platform for Action (PFA 1995), which mandated that governments "review and modify, with the full participation of women macro economic objectives and social policies with a view to achieving the objectives of the Platform for Action." The PFA emphasized the need to develop statistical methodologies to capture women's participation in the economy. This would imply that methods of both surveys and other quantitative tools are necessary to fully take into account all types of work, including non-market work undertaken by women.

As expressed in the Beijing PFA there has been a growing recognition of the importance of macroeconomic policy in influencing women's welfare and their prospects for economic empowerment for more than a decade. Policy changes and the integration of developing countries within the global economy could worsen or improve the living standards of women and contribute to narrowing or widening gender gaps in incomes, health, education, nutrition etc. There has also been increasing concern about how gender inequality can constrain the outcomes of macroeconomic policy. For example, recent work (Haddad et al, 1995, Cagatay, Elson and Grown, 1995; World Bank. 1995; Palmer, 1995) shows that economic reforms with decreased incentives can reduce women's output, and restricted access to education can hinder women's ability to develop their human resources. Although gender-related development issues have prompted serious debate, the absence of appropriate gender-aware macroeconomic analytical tools has penalised quantitative analyses. More generally, it must be recognized that there are few instruments which can relate macroeconomic policy and micro economic behaviour.

With this backdrop we examine what kind of techniques can be used to help us evaluate women's contribution to the economy and also to measure the impact of Structural Policy Changes undertaken by most of the developing world to integrate with the global economy. During the last twenty years developing countries have faced major macroeconomic shocks, involving trade policy changes and Structural Adjustment Programmes (SAP). To understand the impact of such changes on women, it is essential to have a comprehensive macro framework such as a general equilibrium model. Even when overall growth in macro variables is recorded it is important to scrutinise further to see which sectors or groups have been impacted differently.

The broader macro framework designed to strengthen competitiveness is the removal of the anti-export bias that arises in most developing countries as a result of continued protection against imports. Continuing protection overvalues the exchange rate and leads to a bias against both exports and import-competing industries in favour of non-tradables such as services. In addition, there is a bias within the tradable sector (that is, importable and exportable products) in favour of import-competing products. This bias results from the incentives that import protection gives for resources to move into import-competing industries and non-tradables, and away from exports. A number of developing countries have adopted a variety of export promotion measures to neutralise these biases. These include export processing zones (EPZs), duty drawbacks and exemptions on imported intermediate products, and in-bond manufacturing. All three in theory allow exporters access to imported inputs at world prices, and EPZs offer, in addition, good infrastructural facilities. Access to imported inputs is especially important in Africa since domestic manufacturing often relies heavily on imports for equipment, spare parts and many raw materials. Export processing arrangements are far more relevant for some subsectors than others. Access to free-trade inputs release exporters from domestic supply constraints, and from quality defects in domestic inputs. It puts pressure on domestic input suppliers to be competitive while mapping out a market for them if they eventually become so. China, in addition to its famous Special Economic Zones, successfully developed labour-intensive manufacturing exports using processing and assembly arrangements, which are now available to exporting firms in general. Where foreign investment is attracted by such arrangements, as in the labour-intensive export industries of China and Indonesia, initially the foreign investors may be entirely export oriented, with little connection to the domestic economy. This raises the question of whether particular developing countries have the institutional capability to operate export-processing arrangements, and highlights the need to introduce policies in line with capabilities. It is likely that duty exemption schemes for imported intermediate goods will work better than duty drawbacks, since drawback schemes require more administration. Similarly, it may be not be possible to extend drawback schemes to indirect exporters (domestic suppliers of intermediate products to final exporters). EPZs, if administered efficiently, are useful ways of kick-starting foreign investment in export manufacturing and have proved so, for example in Mauritius.

It is widely recognized that policy changes such as trade policy reforms through reduction of tariffs, introduction of export incentives and creation of export promotion zones, etc., or programmes such as SAPs would differentially affect women and men. One reason for this is the nature of participation in work.

Moreover, women and men respond differently to economic and trade policies because they have different sets of private resources and levels of access to public ones. Meanwhile, the social and human development impact of trade policy must look at how choice sets have been altered and how alterations have affected women and men. Both kinds of impact analysis, in turn, help determine the changes in the welfare of both genders. What determines status and control over resources? And what determines women and men's choice sets? Households operate in an environment structured by economic incentives and institutional constructs. Greater competition and a need to reduce production costs generally lead to informalization (Portes et al., 1989). It is observed that most of the female workforce is involved in informal activities, and there are indications of an increase in the labour force participation of women in the informal sector (Cagatay, Elson and Grown, 1995). The concern expressed by these studies is that the burden of non-market work undertaken by women has increased with such policies. The studies generally indicate that the quality of life has deteriorated for women with the process of structural adjustment mainly because gender relations and outcomes are not considered while implementing such policies.

In this essay we examine the relevance of formulating a macro framework to study the impact of the various reform measures and structural changes that have been taking place in India since the early 1990s. In the next section of the essay we describe various types of policy changes that are adopted in a developing country while embracing reforms. In the sub-sections of Section II, we describe the qualitative and quantitative methodologies for examining the impact of policy changes on different groups of people. In Section III, we define the strength of Computable General Equilibrium models in carrying out policy analysis, especially with distributional aspects. In this section we introduce the case for engendering CGE models. Section IV describes an engendered model developed by the author at National Council for Applied Economic Research (NCAER) and describes the various data distinguished by gender. This section also illustrates the utility of examining data by gender distinction to understand the status of women in various spheres of her economic and care activities. The model results are also described briefly and then Section V puts forward the scheme of introducing non-market work in a CGE framework and suggests methods of carrying this out. The last section concludes.

ISSUES IN POLICY ANALYSIS

International trade policy influences both macro-economic and meso-economic variables. Gender issues in international trade, however, require an investigation of the transmission mechanisms from policy formulation to implementation and from macro-economic and meso-economic indicators to micro-economic and social development indicators. Macro economic stability and competitive real exchange rates are prerequisites for improved industrial performance but they are not enough in themselves. In a developing country when some institutions grow faster than others there could be unfair practices that would impact the vulnerable sections of society more adversely than others. Regulatory bodies need to be put in place when goods, commodities and services fulfilling critical needs like health, education, transportation, credit needs are supplied by the public/ private sector without any accountability. For example when competition prompts private firms to be more cost-efficient, they are likely to cut down cost through the process of outsourcing work and employment without fulfilling any labour norms. The firms do not find themselves bound to any commitment towards providing any form of security to their casualized labour force, the most vulnerable amongst them being women.

A very critical policy instrument in the process of reforms is also the fiscal policy mechanism. Through use of such policies the government changes the structure of an economy and generates revenues and undertakes expenditure. The impact of fiscal policy changes on women and poverty needs to be examined to make suggestions about how such policies should be designed, modified (if necessary) and implemented so that any adverse impact on women is minimized. The expenditure the government makes needs to be examined in terms of the taxation and benefits these provide to women and men. This aspect has now been recognized by many countries, with India too having shown its intention of formulating gender budgets. Though gender budgeting is a necessary exercise, this can be fully effective only if a framework exists that links women to various activities and socio-economic situations. Without such a framework, a gender budget can be rather unstructured and not in a position to fully direct scarce resources to the benefit of most women in a developing country.

The basic gender framework should be able to spell out how, for example, improved food securities create effective demand and markets for consumer goods and how these affect women workers both in the market and elsewhere. The framework should be able to answer questions such as: do reforms create a coherent new set of signals that could be identified with gender distinction? Was the net effect to stimulate the production of tradable goods that are produced differentially by women and men? Was dispersion in tax burdens lessened for women in the economy? The broader macro framework designed to strengthen competitiveness is the removal of the anti-export bias that arises in most developing countries as a result of continued protection against imports. The composition of government expenditure is as important as its level. This applies particularly to infrastructural investment which encourages rather than crowds out investment by the private sector, and which increases the likelihood that the price incentives provided by liberalization will lead to faster growth. Development expenditure on rural infrastructure may be particularly beneficial to women by increasing supply response and reducing transport and storage costs. Raising living standards of rural households in the immediate future will reduce the damage to the future human and physical capital that results from pressure on livelihoods when people, and in particular women, live in poor conditions.

Good quality data is especially important for this process to have integrity. Currently many countries including India have carried out, or are in the process of carrying out, time use surveys. Data from time use survey is especially significant for gender analysis as well as better quality policy advice across all sectors of government. Such data enable strategic priorities to be addressed better and help to improve the accuracy of forecasting and the scope of potential policy outcomes. The main policy issues which time use data would inform and where gender distinctions can be made are unpaid work, paid employment, health, income support, education and training. On the issue of the importance of mainstreaming gender, Judy Lawrence states the following in an OECD lecture:

> . . . success in gender mainstreaming is largely about strategic positioning, some serendipity and opportunism, and above all good analysis that links the significance of gender analysis to the wider economic debate. Mainstreaming gender analysis has been extremely difficult to implement where there has been no requirement for it to be undertaken as part of the policy analysis process. Small steps have been taken, but hardly mainstreaming in a complete sense. The presence of a department whose main task is gender analysis is not mainstreaming. That will only occur when everyone does gender analysis as an essential part of policy analysis and the capacity to do it exists across government.

Approaches in Analysing Policy Impact

The relationship between policy changes and impact analysis can be carried out through many approaches and most of these can be classified as follows:

The Qualitative Approach

Case studies and surveys can be undertaken to collect and analyse information about the nature of reforms, the exact way such reforms are implemented and the resultant impact on different groups of people within the area surveyed. The studies attempt to build reasonable linkage between the reform and the changes in the welfare of different groups such as women labourers and non-market workers. With such an approach a very detailed understanding of the focus of the reforms, the exact implementation procedures and the changes experienced by the group in which the researchers are interested can be obtained.

There are a large number of studies that analyse the impact of policy changes in developing countries on poverty and inequality.

Squire (1991) and Van der Hoeven (1996) have conducted reviews of the linkage between adjustment and poverty during the 80s. The findings of qualitative analysis about the relationship between reforms and poverty is presented in a short review by Killick (1995). White (1997) provides a more recent review on this. Such work describes, methodically, the reforms undertaken in a country and the changes in a variety of welfare indicators among different household and socio-economic groups. Such studies have been also reported in a series of background papers on "Globalisation with a Human Face" prepared for the Human Development Report 1999 (UNDP, 1999). Similarly Cornia (1999), Handa and King (1997), McCulloch, Baulch and Charel-Robson (2000) provide similar analyses for different African countries.

This approach however cannot identify the exact linkage between trade reforms and welfare changes, as these cannot be tested. The result seen after a policy change could be due to other reasons or mixed outcomes and no direct linkage can be traced without any quantitative connection. Moreover, in case no impact is evident after a policy change this could be due to some countering factors, even though policy changes have had a direct impact on the stated objective. Conclusions through analyses using qualitative studies cannot be taken as general and should be limited only to the specific group interviewed. Such studies are no doubt valuable for in-depth understanding but have strong limitations. The inability of descriptive studies to provide a robust causality between impact and result has made research in modelling approaches more demanding.

The Modelling Approach

The modelling approach has been used for economic analysis for a long time. A model is a simplified representation of the real economy. Econometric models are generally algebraic models that are stochastic in including random variables (as adopted to deterministic models which do not include random variables). The random variables are generally included as additive stochastic terms to account for human measurement errors of data and omissions of variables, etc. Such models can be either linear or non-linear. One of the earlier applications of the econometric models is to the estimation of the demand relationships (Intriligator, 1978). Pioneering work on demand relationships started in the nineteenth century with Engels and continued with Scultz and Moore. The functional forms have varied for such models but the most convenient ones are the constant elasticity log linear specifications. The other form is the semilogarithmic specification and the last important specification, but not of the least importance, is the linear expenditure system. Apart from econometric modelling of demand there has been progress on modelling of production functions. These functions are used to estimate the production of goods with different types of inputs. As in the case of demand equations there are a number of econometric forms of production functions. The most commonly used one is again the constant elasticity log linear specification or the Cobb-Douglas production function (Marsheck and Andrews, 1944, Douglas). In this form the disturbances are treated as exponential. The second widely used form is the constant elasticity of substitution (CES) production function (Arrow, Chenary, Minhas and Solow, 1961). A third specification is the transcendental logarithmic production function (Christensen, Jorgenson and Lau, 1973). Macroeconometric models starting with pioneering work by Timbergen in the 1930s represent very useful applications of econometric analysis to determine the Gross National Product and Gross Domestic Product. These models are used for three major purposes: structural analysis, forecasting and policy evaluation. An extremely useful model of the 1950s was the Klien-Goldberger model of the US economy over the periods 1929-1941 and 1946-1952 (Klien, 1950, Chris, 1960), which also looked at the issue of forecasting GDP and GNP. Two of the models that were influenced by this one were the (i) Brookings model for structural analysis of cycles and for growth and policy evaluation, and (ii) the Wharton model developed explicitly for developing forecasts of the future of the economy such as national income components and employment. They are used regularly to forecast eight or more quarters under alternative assumptions regarding exogenous variables, such as government monetary and fiscal policies.

The social welfare function approach to policy evaluation allows trade offs among the endogenous variables by assuming the existence of a social welfare function that is maximized subject to constraints of the model (Pyndick, 1973, Chow, 1975, 1981). The simulation approach in econometric modelling does not require a welfare function. The policy makers provide the modeller with the alternative policies and the modeller determines the impact of changes on the endogamous variables of the model (Lucas and Sargent, 1980 and Sargent 1981).

General Equilibrium Models

Policy makers are interested in studying the impact of particular policy measures, such as changes in income tax, or the welfare of people below the poverty line and other socio-economic categories of households. It is possible to study the impact of policies that are targeted and are not likely to have a major indirect impact on other variables of an economy. However, economy wide analysis is essential when the indirect impact of policy changes is wide and other groups and other markets are affected as a result of a trade or financial policy.

The general equilibrium models are economy wide models and are multi-agent, multi-commodity models. Such models have the advantage of responding to shocks while fulfilling the conditions of optimality of agents' behaviour, technological feasibility and resource constraints. General equilibrium analysis has a strong theoretical grounding. In the 1970s there were major advances in solution techniques that permitted the application of general equilibrium models to actual data sets. With improvement in data collection and advances in computer technology and software, this has been increasingly used as an advanced methodology of applied policy work. The applied models are treated as representations of reality. Economic theories form the basis to such models, namely, optimisation behaviour, budget balance and market clearing.

CGE MODELS

The Computable General Equilibrium Model (CGEM) can relate macroeconomic policies and microeconomic behaviour. Such models have been applied to a range of policy questions in a number of economic fields over the last ten or so years. They include public finance and taxation issues, international trade policy questions, evaluations of alternative development strategies and implications of macroeconomic policies.

The nature of the links between economic growth, poverty and income distribution is a question that is central to the study of economic development. This has led to the development of tools for counterfactual analysis to study the impact of structural adjustment policies. (Adelman and Robinson, 1988; Dervis et al., 1982; Taylor, 1990; Bourguignon et al., 1991; De Janvry et al., 1991). On the one hand, the construction of macroeconomic models with heterogeneous agents presupposes the availability of representative microeconomic data at the national level, a construction that is often problematic given the difficulty of reconciling household survey data and national accounts data. Among the tools used for the counterfactual analysis of the impact of policies and macroeconomic shocks on poverty and income distribution, computable general equilibrium models appeal because of their ability to produce disaggregated results at the microeconomic level within a consistent macroeconomic framework.

CGE Models have been widely used to simulate the impact of macroeconomic policies on income distribution and poverty. Good examples of such exercises are those that were built in connection with the OECD research programme on Structural Adjustment and Poverty in the early 1990s by Thorbecke (1991), de Janvry, Sedoulet and Fargeix (1991), Bourgionon, de Melo and Suwa (1991). Later Decaluwe, Party, Savard and Thorbecke (1999), Decaluwe, Dumont and Savard (1999), Cogneau and Robilliard (2000), Cockburn (2001) and Agenor, Izquierdo and Fofack (2001) among others attempted to link policy simulations or external shocks to changes in poverty within a group or sub-group of the population.

Gender Focussed CGE Models

Trade policies have different consequences on women and men because women and men differ in their economic and social status. Women and men respond differently to economic and trade policies because they have different sets of private resources and levels of access to public ones. Meanwhile, the social and human development impact of trade policy must look at how choice sets have been altered and how alterations have affected women and men. Both kinds of impact analysis, in turn, help determine the changes in the welfare of both genders. What determines status and control over resources? And what determines women's and men's choice sets? Households operate in an environment structured by economic incentives and institutional constructs. Institutions, both formal and informal, that determine each person's available set of behavioural choices with some choice sets larger than others, govern the behaviour of household members. Clearly international trade policy influences both macro-economic and meso-economic variables. Gender issues in international trade, however, require an investigation of the transmission mechanisms from policy formulation to implementation and from macro-economic and meso-economic indicators to micro-economic and social development indicators.

There are not many current CGE models that have a gender dimension. However, given the importance of understanding the contribution of non-market work a few good gender aware CGE models are being developed (for example check on www.crefa.ecn.ulaval.ca/develop/cge-train.html). A gender aware CGE model would naturally distinguish between men and women in its variables and behavioural relationships. The Fontana and Wood model (2000) allows for capturing the interactions between productive and 'reproductive' sectors of the economy. Female wage rates rise when the leisure and 'reproduction' sectors are omitted. This model considers the details of gender composition of the labour market and household work. The paper studies the impact of world price change on male workers and female workers in terms of both market and non-market work. However, the model does not have detailed production sectors that are essential to understanding the impact of reforms on women workers. There is a concentration of women workers in some sectors and an understanding of how these sectors react to reforms would also provide an understanding of whether the demand for women workers rises or falls due to reforms. The engendered CGE models developed by Sinha for India address this aspect. Apart from introducing sectoral distinctions, Sinha and Sangeeta (2000) distinguish six factors of production by gender and further divide these into rural, urban, formal and informal. Further Sinha et al (2003) augment the CGE model by differentiating factors of production by twelve categories while identifying home-based workers within informal workers as a separate category.

AN ILLUSTRATION: ENGENDERED CGE

The first step in building an engendered CGE model is to construct an engendered Social Accounting Matrix (SAM). In the engendered CGE model developed by Sinha, et al (2003), the SAM is developed with sectors that have important shares of women workers in different sectors of the economy. Moreover workers are distinguished in this study as casual, regular, own account workers, employers and home-based workers. The SAM developed with such distinctions are used as the base for building a Computable General Equilibrium (CGE) Model. In the study, the major concern is to understand the impact of policy changes on the informal sector and on workers distinguished by gender. For this purpose we traced the interrelationship of the informal sector with other sectors of the economy. Once Sinha distinguished the production sectors she mapped the workers differentiated by gender who participated in these sectors. These workers were then mapped into different types of households. Such mappings are done using the data from the NSSO's 55th Round Survey data.

On production, Sinha has used the information from the Central Statistical Organisation (CSO) to break up each sector into formal and informal parts. The formal sector or the registered sector is defined by the CSO as establishments that employ ten or more workers and use power or employ 20 or more workers without using power and are registered in accordance with the Factories

Act, 1951. The remaining manufacturing establishments are treated as unregistered or informal sector. The information of the organized and unorganized sectors is used from the ASI and the Enterprise Follow up Surveys to break up the 115 sectors of the CSO's input/output table for the year 1993-94. These sectors are aggregated to 11 sectors on the basis of their usefulness in providing information about the informal part of the economy and gender shares. As information regarding household members is available, it is possible to compute workers composition in a household.

Input-Output Sectoral Reclassification

The 115-sector input/output table provided by the CSO for the year 1993-94, has been aggregated to 11 sectors (see Appendices C and D) with their formal informal dimensions. As the CGE model had been developed to examine the linkage of workers to the formal and informal sub-sectors of a particular industry sector (including agriculture and services), scrutinising the different process of work (available through NIC classification of processes) within a sector had generated the formal or informal identification of the sectors. While deciding on the sectors, separate sections were formed when these were quite heterogeneous with respect to each other. The sectors are as follows:

1. Agriculture (Informal)
2. Agro-processing (Formal)
3. Agro-processing (Informal)
4. Readymade Garments (Formal)
5. Readymade Garments (Informal)
6. Other Manufacturing Goods (Formal)
7. Other Manufacturing Goods (Informal)
8. Construction (Informal)
9. Other Services (Formal)
10. Other Services (Informal)
11. Government Services (Formal)

Women Workers

The table below (Table 1) shows that a very large share of women are in agricultural sector, which is more than the men's share in

Table 1: Percentage Share of Workers by Sectors

		Female Workers across sectors	*Male Workers across sectors*
Agriculture	I	72.51	52.38
Agro processing	F	1.16	0.72
Agro processing	I	3.24	1.34
Readymade garments	F	0.29	0.35
Readymade garments	I	0.19	0.24
Other manufacturing goods	F	3.15	6.91
Other manufacturing goods	I	3.69	4.76
Construction	I	1.16	4.30
Other services	F	8.62	14.51
Other services	I	4.98	11.30
Government services	F	1.02	3.17
Total		100.00	100.00

this sector by 20 percentage points. Women in the service sector follow this. Men have substantially higher shares of workers in other manufacturing goods and service sectors.

The distribution of workers by each of the 11 sectors into different types of factors of production is computed by using the data from the Employment-Unemployment Survey (Round 55) of the NSSO. In this survey, each household member is asked about his/her status of work. Sinha processed the information and distinguish the following 12 factors of production: Labour Casual—Female; Labour Casual—Male; Labour HB—Female; Labour HB—Male; Labour Regular—Female; Labour Regular—Male; OAW—Female OAW—Male; OAW HB—Female; OAW HB—Male; Employer—Female; Employer—Male

Casual labour, male or female, are informal workers who work as casual wagers both in formal and informal sectors. Regular labour are called formal workers as they are regular wage or salary earners. It is assumed that there are no formal workers in informal sectors. However, the formal part of a sector can employ both formal and informal workers. Own Account workers are informal capital owners. The employers employ either ten or more workers with the electricity or employ 20 or more workers without the electricity. The other employers are informal capitalists. Among the informal workers and capitalists, few are involved in home-based enterprises too. The author maps factors of production obtained from NSSO data analysis by different sectors and distributes the NAS value added for each sector according to the factor ownership. The NAS provide sectoral information with respect to a broad division of registered and unregistered parts of value added. Labour and capital earnings from NAS are then distributed according to NSSO share of each type of labour and capital ownership and wage and capital earning rates both for male and female. NSSO shares have been used to get an estimate of value added distribution by casual labour, regular labour, home-based labour, own account workers, own account home-based workers and employers by gender. The following table (Table 2) shows that of all the women workers, 74 per cent are casual workers, about 4.3 per cent are home-based workers, and 14 per cent are own account workers. Regular workers account only for about 7 per cent of the total female workforce. In the case of men workers, 48 per cent are casual workers, about 4.5 per cent are home-based workers, 34 per cent are own account workers and about 14 per cent are regular workers. Generally women have higher shares of casual workers in all sectors. The exceptions are the readymade garment sector, where men have higher share as casual workers than women. As this sector is a traditionally accepted sector for women to work in, there could be more women entering into formal employment. This is an important point as the earlier study conducted by Sinha and Sangeeta (2001) did not show such findings. The garment sector has also been growing due to the competitive advantage of this sector in the global market. It is therefore important to examine whether the growth of such a sector which employs a large female workforce would have a favourable impact on the women workers.

The factor ownership (Table 2) depicted in the following table reflect the fact that women workers generally are found more in lowly paid jobs compared to their male counterparts in all sectors.

Household Classification

The activity of each member within a household is obtained from the NSSO's 55th round survey (NSSO, 1999-00). Sinha et al (2003) used only labour force activities for building the SAM as a base data set for the CGE model. However, it is important to understand the structure of a household and also the contribution household members make towards the well being of a household through domestic and other unpaid duties.

In this study Sinha distinguishes households first as rural or urban. Next, they are classified as formal and informal by using the NIC, NCO and the "Type" codes of households as formal-informal. The "Type" code formulated on the basis of composite household information, and the household NIC and NCO codes are provided by NSSO. Households in the urban region are classified as formal with "Type" codes as employers and regular wage earners. In rural regions, exceptions are households with NIC agriculture; even with formal "Type" code, such households are classified as informal. Finally, households are classified into different income levels, i.e., poor and non-poor within each broad category. The households are then scrutinised to identify the different types of workers and factor owners distinguished by gender that make up the household as in Table 3.

Table 2: Percentage Distribution of Factor Owners by Industry Sectors

Sector	*Agri.*	*Agro Processing*	*Agro Processing*	*Ready made Garments*	*Ready made Garments*	*Other manufacturing goods*	*Other manufacturing goods*	*Construction*	*Other Services*	*Other Services*	*Government Services*	*Total*
Factors of Production	I	F	I	F	I	F	I	I	F	I	F	
Lab Cas – Female	28.85	14.55	17.36	4.91	6.40	7.87	12.19	8.76	2.63	9.91	0.46	19.76
Lab Cas – Male	39.80	16.07	23.89	20.76	25.73	29.02	35.24	70.35	8.46	45.24	2.54	34.93
Lab HB – Female	0.00	0.00	8.65	0.00	1.53	0.00	5.17	0.00	0.00	1.76	0.00	0.56
Lab HB – Male	0.00	0.00	6.74	0.00	4.43	0.00	9.86	0.00	0.00	8.94	0.00	1.44
Lab Reg – Female	0.00	7.90	0.00	10.25	0.00	3.11	0.00	0.00	11.14	0.00	10.00	1.99
Lab Reg – Male	0.00	29.59	0.00	28.68	0.00	40.60	0.00	0.00	40.21	0.00	87.00	10.20
OAW – Female	4.65	14.41	4.64	7.64	2.41	3.23	0.78	0.15	4.01	1.16	0.00	3.79
OAW – Male	26.69	17.19	12.36	26.54	26.75	15.86	16.35	20.74	33.46	23.51	0.00	24.92
OAW – HB – Female	0.00	0.00	16.12	0.00	12.27	0.00	3.83	0.00	0.00	0.99	0.00	0.59
OAW - HB – Male	0.00	0.00	10.24	0.00	20.49	0.00	16.58	0.00	0.00	8.49	0.00	1.79
Employer – Female	0.00	0.00	0.00	0.00	0.00	0.01	0.00	0.00	0.00	0.00	0.00	0.00
Employer – Male	0.00	0.30	0.00	1.22	0.00	0.29	0.00	0.00	0.09	0.00	0.00	0.04
Total	100.00	100.00	100.00	100.00	100.00	100.00	100.00	100.00	100.00	100.00	100.00	100.00

Table 3: NSSO Household Type Code Description

For Rural Areas	*For Urban Areas*
1. Self employed in non-agriculture	6. Self employed
2. Agricultural labour	7. Regular wage/salary earner
3. Other labour	8. Casual labour
4. Self Employed in agriculture	9. Others
5. Others	

Using these type codes and the status codes, Sinha assigns a separate Household Type codes to each household. This classification of households for rural and urban areas is as follows.

Table 4: New Household Type Code Description

For Rural Areas	*For Urban Areas*
1. Non-agriculturist - Poor - Formal	7. Poor - Formal
2. Non-agriculturist - Non Poor - Formal	8. Non Poor - Formal
3. Agriculturist - Poor - Informal	9. Poor - Informal
4. Agriculturist - Non Poor - Informal	10. Non Poor - Informal
5. Non-agriculturist - Poor - Informal	
6. Non-agriculturist - Non Poor - Informal	

For Rural Areas, NSSO Household Type codes 1, 2 and 3 are all called Informal Agriculturists in our type of classification. These household types are then split into poor and non-poor using the Planning Commission Poverty lines. According to the Planning Commission criteria for the rural sector, those earning less than Rs 327.56 are poor and for the urban sector, those earning less than an average of Rs 454.11 per month fall below poverty line. The Type code 'Self employed in Non agriculture' is further studied and broken into formal and informal parts. The author adopts the CSO definition and assumes that the self-employed are actually formal employers who employ either ten or more workers with the aid of power or twenty or more without the aid of power. Rest of the self-employed are informal employers. These household types are further split into poor and non-poor categories using poverty lines as mentioned earlier. The household incomes are determined by using the different wage rates of workers by industry.

For urban areas, household type 'regular wage earners', as in NSSO classification, is classified as formal households and type 'casual labour' as informal households. Moreover, 'self employed' are both formal and informal, and are again broken into these as in the rural sector. These households are then differentiated into poor and non-poor using the Planning Commission criteria as mentioned above.

The table given below (Table 5) shows that in all types of poor households women have higher shares of members than their male counterparts. The last table of this trio shows that market workers are only 27 per cent in the case of women members compared to 54 per cent male members. The situation of women thus is vulnerable compared to men. This also highlights the fact that reforms even if geared to positively impact all types of market workers within the market economy, would leave the majority of women unpaid workers outside its benefit. In the study, under consideration home-based workers are assumed to be proxy to all types of unpaid work based at home. So any policy that would impact home-based work would be the policies that would impact unpaid work that are somewhat related to specific sectors. The above tables further show that female market work force is mostly informal and even in formal rural households females are engaged more as informal workers.

As noted the data base for a CGE model is a Social Accounting Matrix (SAM). The SAM combines information from different sources in a consistent framework to reflect the economic and social structure of an economy at a particular point in time. The SAM constructed in this work distinguishes factors of production by formal and informal parts as well as by gender. The author mapped the flow of value added from sectors to the different types of factors of production and also mapped the flow of factor earnings 'to different types of factor owners within households, thus determining the factor incomes of these households. The major steps in building the base SAM for the CGE model are explained

TABLE 5: Female/Male Member Activity within formal Informal Households (per cent)

	Rural Formal Non Agriculturist		*Urban Formal*		*Rural Informal – Agriculturist*		*Rural Informal – Non Agriculturist*		*Urban Informal*	
	Female									
	Poor	*Non Poor*	*Poor*	*Non Poor*	*Poor*	*Non Poor*	*Poor*	*Non Poor*	*Poor*	*Non Poor*
Casual labour	12.19	12.30	3.68	1.03	28.52	28.05	16.29	15.16	12.22	7.36
Home-based labour	0.14	0.14	0.04	0.01	0.33	0.32	0.19	0.17	0.14	0.37
Regular Labour	9.79	9.58	5.80	9.14	0.39	0.57	0.31	0.72	1.48	2.40
Own account worker	1.96	6.18	2.32	1.86	2.53	4.23	4.91	6.24	3.87	1.83
Own account worker – Home-based	0.33	1.03	0.39	0.31	0.42	0.70	0.82	1.04	0.64	2.66
Employer	0.00	0.00	0.00	0.01	0.00	0.00	0.00	0.00	0.00	0.01
Worker	24.41	29.23	12.23	12.35	32.18	33.87	22.51	23.34	18.36	14.62
Non-worker	75.59	70.77	87.77	87.65	67.82	66.13	77.49	76.66	81.64	85.38
Total	100	100	100	100	100	100	100	100	100	100
Total percentage by HH category	0.26%	0.81%	2.04%	9.24%	23.75%	37.75%	3.44%	7.87%	6.00%	8.83%

Contd.

TABLE 5: *Contd.*

Rural Formal	*Urban Non Agriculturist*		*Rural Informal – Formal*		*Rural Informal – Agriculturist*		*Urban Non Agriculturist*		*Informal*	
			Male							
	Poor	*Non Poor*	*Poor*	*Non Poor*	*Poor*	*Non Poor*	*Poor*	*Non Poor*	*Poor*	*Non Poor*
Casual labour	8.87	5.23	6.23	2.20	35.50	32.19	11.39	11.31	25.14	18.14
Home-bBased labour	0.11	0.06	0.08	0.03	0.44	0.40	0.14	0.14	0.31	0.99
Regular labour	36.31	47.87	36.01	48.51	1.24	2.22	0.86	1.79	3.34	4.15
Own account worker	0.28	1.32	2.85	2.89	11.83	21.58	32.23	38.99	19.35	28.58
Own account worker: home- based	0.02	0.09	0.19	0.19	0.79	1.44	2.15	2.60	1.29	6.58
Employer	0.00	0.65	0.02	0.18	0.00	0.00	0.01	0.06	0.00	0.10
Worker	45.59	55.23	45.37	54.00	49.79	57.82	46.77	54.89	49.42	58.53
Non-worker	54.41	44.77	54.63	46.00	50.21	42.18	53.23	45.11	50.58	41.47
Total	100	100	100	100	100	100	100	100	100	100
Total percentage by HH category	0.23%	0.83%	1.86%	9.88%	22.16%	38.58%	3.26%	8.06%	5.77%	9.36%

in the following sub-sections. To complete the SAM used information from different authentic sources apart from official statistics like the National Accounts, NSSO, RBI Reports, such as savings rates which are from MIMAP[1] data analysed at NCAER.

Some CGE Findings

The CGE model developed in Sinha, et al (2003) (see Appendix A) is of the type discussed in Devarajan, et al (1996), which details widely used trade focussed models for developing countries. In this model the intention is to characterize the consequences of changes in trade policy for the distribution of income between the formal and informal factors (Sinha and Sangeeta, 2000) distinguished by gender across a variety of household types. The distribution of factor income flows, both formal and informal by gender, between household types is treated as parametric, obtained from the baseline data. Further Sinha (2002) augmented the CGE model by differentiating factors of production by twelve categories. The other important feature in this study is the distinction of 13 types of households in the model with each household type distinguished with information of gender ratios. The model in this study has used the more recent household survey data (NSSO's 55th Round) that also had information on home-based workers. Moreover capitalists are distinguished by gender. Though this did not acknowledge any gender differences in rates of returns due to lack of data.

The findings of the 2003 study show that "working" women benefit in the case of globalization. The findings further show that as a result of removing the market distortion, there is overall welfare gain. As the authors examine the wage differentials between genders they see that in most cases the gap reduces with import liberalization. We must note here that labour market segmentation has not been addressed in this study. However another study (Sinha and Adam, 2006) has shown that in the case of labour market segmentation informal workers face depressed wages compared to formal workers. As women are involved more as informal workers, this has adverse implications for women workers as well.

CGE WITH NON-MARKET-WORK

A CGE model that addresses the concern of impact analysis having gender differentials would have to contain variables distinguished by gender to the extent possible. Apart from data on market work distinguished by gender, it is essential to capture information on non-market work while we build the base data set for a gender CGE model as such work undertaken by women consumes a substantial part of their daily schedule.

Leisure in developing countries can still be considered as a residual activity. So if there is an increase in either market work or care related work for women, their leisure time will get reduced. It is essential to separate all types of activities, i.e., broadly, market work, non-market work and leisure.

SAM with Non-Market-Work

Innovation is necessary in evolving models that recognize behavioural differences by gender. It is important to identify all kinds of work so that most of the work carried out by women is captured. Such work would comprise of:

1. Market work and
2. Non-market work (NMW)

Work needs to be linked to value added and to overall GDP. Market work is linked to value added and GDP through wages. Non-market work has no visible wages and so it is difficult if not impossible to link such work to GDP. A shadow value added measure could be built up on imputation of value for NMW. Studies have shown that a large percentage of women are involved in NMW.

Production Sectors: Gender Focus

I can allow for multiple productive sectors in the proposed model. The differences in participation of women workers in various sectors needs to be recognized while re-aggregating sectors from the 114 input-output matrix of the CSO. This aggregation method follows the one that is described above. When I consider non-market work as well, apart from the input-output production sectors, I introduce a separate sector, the *care sector* and a separate activity which is *leisure* (see Schematic SAM below). This sector uses only labour as its input and provides goods and services to all household members. This conceptualization attempts quantification[2] of the diverse activities carried out by each member of a household and thus allows activities to be differentiated across non-market work by gender. While imputing value for the services provided as non market work, basic market rates of such work would be used which will be recorded as shadow wages as these are not actually distributed to the household members.[3] The output of this sector is also valued as the service itself, rather than the value added provided by the services. For example, if the production of the care sector is roti, then the value addition that the member enjoys from NMW is not the wheat (which is accounted for in national accounting already as part of the households consumption basket), but the services that make the rotis. As the value of the service is imputed both from the production and consumption side of the accounting system I propose, there is overall consistency even after addition of the extra care sector into the standard SAM format.

Factor Markets

While differentiating factor market by gender, it is essential that for each skill-type of labour such as regular workers, (blue collared, white collared, etc.) I introduce the gender dimension. The same needs to be carried out for capital owners as well.

Hence the information of the number of workers by skill and gender employed by the different sectors is classified from the original input-output system of 114 sectors for the base year or the SAM year. Thereafter, it is possible to formulate the CGE model structure whereby a sector employs a type of labour upto a point that the marginal revenue of this sector's production equals the marginal cost of this type of labour. This implies that the base level of nominal wage rate by sector and skill is necessary data information to build the engendered SAM.

In case of a lack of data on gender or skill by each sector, one could use differentials from the sectors where such data are available. I intend to allow for sectoral wage differentials within a skill type

Table 6: A Schematic SAM including NMW

	1	2	3	4	5	6	7	8	9	10	11	12	13	14	15
1 Lab Casual Female										X					Z1
2 Lab Casual Male										X					Z2
3 Lab Regular Female										X					Z3
4 Lab Regular Male										X					Z4
5 Formal Capital Owner										X					Z5
6 Informal Capital Owner										X					Z6
7 NMW-FEMALE											X				Z7
8 NMW-MALE											X				Z8
9 HOUSEHOLDS	X	X	X	X	X	X	X	X							Z9
10 I-O Sectors									X	X				X	Z10
11 CARE SECTOR									X						Z11
12 Leisure									X						Z12
13 CAPTAL A/C									X					X	Z13
14 ROW										X					Z14
15 TOTAL															Z15

Note: ROW is Rest of the World
X implies the cells have values and therefore interlinkages
Z's are totals
Column Total and Row Totals are equal in a SAM

from available data on sector level wages published by the NSSO. To introduce the factor to reflect the gender difference as well we could assume that there is an added fixed differential on the average economy-wide wage for each skill type.

The data for market workers would be used as in the illustrated model given above. However, there is an urgent need to obtain data on time use by household surveys. The data needs to have critical information that would enable these to be linked with other macro level data sets and National Accounting. For example, activities need to be classified so that they could be linked with the 5 digit National Industrial Classification. This would allow us to capture the entire set of activities carried out by women and used in mainstream accounting.

Household Income

While formulating the activities of households, I have already discussed how the types of activities carried out by household members are to be differentiated as market work and non-market work. Work participation needs to be differentiated by time (most likely measure is number of hours of work). So the members of a household could provide both market work and non-market work. In case the member provides market work, we have the remuneration for this work in a straightforward manner. However in case the membera are also/only non-market workers carrying out various types of non-market activities, I need to examine the time spent for each activity type and impute a basic market value for the work or equivalent work performed so that one can measure the shadow wage of such work. The real wage and the shadow wage are what add up to the total wage of a household member.

I assume that households receive (a) wage income from supplying labour plus transfers from government profits from their ownership of capital plus remittance and transfers (if any) and NMW benefits. The CGE specification would have different households with different consumption vectors. The consumption function specified could be extremely simple (derived from a Cobb-Douglas structure) or the more intricate Linear Expenditure Systems.

It is possible in a CGE model to incorporate market work, (also leisure could be incorporated but mostly as a residual above a minimum number of subsistence leisure hours in case of a developing country), and non-market work. Such an exercise would capture the major changes in male and female activities and income if the work-NMW choice would be included. Such a model can be used to study the impact of trade liberalization on female market work, income inequality between males and females and the amount of time they devote to non-market activities.

The structure of the proposed CGE model discussed above, suggests that the Social Accounting Matrix on which the CGE is to be built needs to incorporate details of gender distinguished labour market and non-market work that would also include leisure. The supply of labour for women would be determined through a household utility function. I proceed on the assumption that men would not substitute non-market work with market work. It is only in the case of unemployment in the labour market that men would be involved in non-market work. Leisure in developing countries can still be considered as a residual activity. So in the case of an increase in either market work or care related work for women, their leisure time would get reduced. This again re-emphasizes the data need that essentially separates all types of activities, i.e., broadly, market work, non-market work and leisure. This information would be used differently in formulating functions for men and women. In the case of men one could proceed to having imperfect substitution between non-market work and leisure. In the case of women, there is imperfect substitution between market work and non-market work, but leisure would be determined as a residual of all types of work carried out by women. This is based on the assumption that women would first fulfil all the household chores and responsibilities that come under the "Care Sector" and leisure in hours would be equivalent to (24 Hours—(Market Work Hours+NMW Hours)+Substance Leisure Time (fixed)). The Subsistence Leisure time would be minimum time required for sleep and for personal care. I propose to develop the model in these areas to study the impact of policy changes on welfare of women.

A CGE model would be able to answer questions such as what happens when there is an increase in exports of those goods which employ larger numbers of women workers. If the demand for women workers increases and supply is non-elastic, wages might rise reducing the wage gap. Women would spend more time outside their homes (creating new demands in workplaces) and their leisure and health would be affected. Therefore as the households with such women workers may see some monetary gain, this would have a trade-off in terms of health and other related care activities as well as leisure. Expenditure on childcare and health care might increase and mental stress also might be accentuated in such conditions. Studying the pattern of expenditure on the social sector is possible through the CGE analysis and would be very useful in such an exercise.

One of the direct steps that a government needs to take to help women workers would be to provide hygienic and safe crèches for working mothers. Moreover, increasing the budget for women's health (who would be under greater stress in a competitive global economy) would have a beneficial effect on children's health and save health budgets in the future. Such linkage of policies and economic gains can be simulated through a CGE model incorporating consumption on welfare goods.

To build such a CGE model the information on female and male members of a household will help in obtaining differential earning by gender. The information on activities will determine the resources that women and men can generate. How household income is allocated by gender is a matter of research. It is important to establish any difference in behavioural specifications by gender. The supply of labour for men and women could differ as men generally would not have constraints for shifting from market work to NMW. Women on the other hand might have constraints so that women workers would not respond to market wages in the same way as men.

CONCLUSION

In this essay I have argued that it is beneficial to use of a multisectoral-modelling framework to study the impact of policy changes on women. It is also essential that any future work should include non-market work in such analysis. The importance of gender aware macro-economic analysis has been recognized since more than a decade with many developing countries embarking upon Structural Adjustment Programmes (SAP) and integrating with the global economy. It is now realized that more accurate and conceptually sophisticated gender-sensitive statistics will be useful not only to generate quantitative measurement of women's work, but will also allow more accurate analysis of social and economic conditions, specially in countries undergoing structural adjustment process. Such data and analysis should provide systematic and detailed information for family and welfare policies. There should be an agenda in the budget, and fiscal concerns where the relative poverty of women is considered in order to design macro policies that do not affect women adversely. It is necessary to understand where women are and which kind of policies can affect them, negatively or positively. As a result of the current concerns, gender related issues are now considered not only at the micro level, but also integrated with macro aspects (Beneria, 1995). It is accepted that the first important area is the statistical collection of gender related employment data with greater accuracy than in the past. Another important area is a method based on imputations of the value of non market work to be used in various national accounting frameworks.

Macro policies play an important role in women's welfare and a gender-neutral policy is blind to critical outcomes. There is an urgent need to integrate the gender differences into policy advice, design and implementation with the objective of gender equality and poverty alleviation. Understanding where women are would make it possible to make gender sensitive policies. General equilibrium models are now widely used to assess the impact of economic shocks that reverberate across sectors and, in some cases, regions of a country or even the world. They are capable of producing disaggregated results at the microeconomic level while providing a consistency check on macroeconomic accounts. A general equilibrium model is generally calibrated to a Social Accounting Matrix, which is a complete, consistent, and disaggregated data system. The salient feature of Social Accounting Matrixes is that they quantify—at a single point in time—the interdependence of sectors and regions in an economy. General equilibrium models are typically based on neo-classical theories of firm and household behaviour, and have a time frame long enough to achieve equilibrium in markets. While most are comparative static in nature, dynamic versions have also been developed to address certain types of issues.

An important aspect of engendered modelling techniques is to incorporate Non Market Work in the framework. This is necessary, as women are mostly involved in non market work, which makes their contribution to the overall economy quite invisible. The two main reasons of why such contributions cannot be quantified are: (1) there is a lack of data on how much work the woman is performing in non market activities and (2) the outcomes of such activities are not marketed and there is no systematic recording of such work. In this essay I have argued that it is possible to collect and quantify NMW for carrying out policy analysis.

Without gender analysis policy decisions would be based on untested assumptions: high risk on welfare. Understanding "where women are" implies linkages about women's contributions to the economy are spelled out. This indicates a major need to have macro data disaggregated by sex. Further, apart from information on market related data, it is essential to have information on women's contribution through Non-Market-Work (NMW). Studies have shown that a large percentage of women are involved in NMW. Such work has not been included in national accounting and the value-added generation cycles and thus remains invisible. When governments design policies there is no information on how a policy can impact women who are mainly involved with such work. Hence, scarce resources cannot be allocated for improvement of welfare of non-market workers.

A macro analysis that recognizes such work and translates it into statistical terms is therefore very important. A macro analysis which adopts the CGE methodology allows formulations to distinguish gender aspects. The base of a CGE model is a data set that "already" spells out major linkages in the economy in a Social Accounting Matrix Framework. A SAM for gender analysis has to include gender disaggregated data and preferably also the concept of NMW. Many factors can be addressed simultaneously through such models and the models can be used to analyse trade policies affecting inputs, fiscal policy impacts and impact of technological change that happen through the globalization process. Moreover, such models can be used to decompose the effects of policy changes and they can evaluate feasible policies or "policy packages" in a systematic fashion. The models can assist in policy formulation by permitting comparisons across the set of compatible policy combinations and can be used to track the distributional consequences of policy choices. Further, the benefit of using such models lies in their use for gender analysis by formulating differential gender endowments and behaviours into the framework.

REFERENCES

Adelman, I. and S. Robinson (1978), 'Income Distribution Policy in Developing Countries, Oxford: Oxford University Press.

Adelman, I. and S. Robinson (1988), Macroeconomic Adjustment and Income Distribution: Alternative Models in Two Economies', Journal of Development Economics, 29: 1-22.

Agenor, P., A. Izquierdo and H. Fofack, 2001, IMMPA: A Quantitative Macroeconomic Framework for the Analysis of Poverty reduction Strategies', Washington, D.C.: The World Bank.

Addison, T. and L. Demery (1985), Macro-economic Stabilization, Income Distribution and Poverty: A Preliminary Survey', London: Overseas Development Institute.

Beneria, L., (1995), 'Toward a Greater Integration of Gender in Economics', World Development, Vol. 23, No. II.

Bourguignon, F. J. de Melo and A. Suwa (1991), 'Distributional Effects of Adjustment Policies: Simulations for Archetype Economies in Africa and Latin America', The World Bank Economic Review 5, pp. 339-66.

Bourguignon, F. W. Branson and J. de Melo (1992), 'Adjustment and Incoem Distribution: A Micro-Macro Model for Counterfactual Analysis', Journal of Development Economics 38, pp. 17-39.

Cagatay, N. D. Elson and C. Grown, (1995), 'Introduction" in Gender, Adjustment and Macroeconomics', World Development, Vol. 23, No. 11.

Cockburn, J. (2001), 'Trade Liberalization and Poverty in Nepal: A Computable General Equilibrium Micro Simulation Analysis', Discussion Paper 01-18, CREFA, Universite Laval, October 2001.

Cogneau, D. (1999), 'Labour Market, Income Distribution and Poverty in Antananarivo: A General Equilibrium Simulation', mimeo, DIAL Paris.

Cogneau, D. and A.S. Robillard (2001), 'Growth Distribution and Poverty in Madagascar: Learning from a Microsimulation Model in a General Equilibrium Framework', TMD Discussion Paper 61, IFPRI, Washington, DC.

Decaluwe, B., J.-C. Dumont And L. Savard (1999), 'Measuring Poverty and Inequality in a Computable General Equilibrium Model', Working paper 99-20, CREFA, Universite Laval, Quebec.

De Janvry, A., M. Fafchamps and E. Sadoulet (1991), 'Peasant Household Behaviour with Missing Markets: Some Paradoxes Explained " Economic Journal 101, pp. 1400-17.

Decaluwe, B., A. Party, L. Savard et E. Thorbecke (1999), 'Poverty Analysis within a General Equilibrium Framework', Working paper 9909, Department of Economics, Universite Laval, Quebec.

Defourny, J. and E. Thorbecke (1984), 'Structural Path Analysis and Multiplier Decomposition within a Social Accounting Matrix Framework', Economic Journal 94.

Dervis, K, J. De Melo and S. Robinson (1982), General Equilibrium Models for Development Policy', Cambridge University Press, London.

Fontana, M. and Wood, A., 2000, 'Modelling the Effects of Trade on Women, at Work and at Home', World Development, Vol. 28, No.1173-90.

Fortin, B.,N. Marceau and L. Savard, (1997), 'Taxation, Wage Controls and the Informal Sector', Journal of Public Economics, 66: 293-312.

Kanbur, R. (1987), 'Structural Adjustment, Macroeconomic Adjustment and Poverty: A Methodology for Analysis', World Development 15, pp.: 1515-26.

Karunaratne, N.D. (1998), 'Trade Liberalization in Thailand A Computable General Equilibrium (CGE) Analysis', Journal of Developing Area 32.

Killick T. (1995), Structural Adjustment and Poverty Alleviation: An Interpretative Survey', Development and Change 26, pp. 305-31.

Lawrence, Judy (2000): "*Nordic Council of Ministers/OECD* Gender Mainstreaming Competitiveness and Growth, 23-24 November 2000, OECD Paris.

Levinsohn, James, Steven Berry, and Jed Friedman (1999), "Impacts of the Indonesian Economic Crisis: Price Changes and the Poor." Paper prepared for the Conference on Poverty and the International Economy, October 20-21, 2000. Forthcoming in *Managing Currency Crises in Emerging Markets*, Michael Dooley and Jeffrey Frankel, ed., The University of Chicago Press.

LiD, A., S. Yao and R. Greener (1996), ' A CGE Model of Agricultural Policy Reform in the Philippines'. Journal of Agricultural Economics 47, pp. 18-27.

Löfgren, Hans. 1999, "Trade Reform and the Poor in Morocco: A Rural-Urban General Equilibrium Analysis of Reduced Protection." IFPRI TMD Discussion Paper 38.

McCulloch, N., R.J. Baulch and M. Cherel-Robson (2000), 'Poverty Inequality and Growth in Zambia during the 1990s' , Institute *of* Development Studies Working Paper 114.

Piggot, J. and J. Whalley (1985), 'UK Tax Policy and Applied General Equilibrium Analysis', Cambridge, Cmbridge: Cambridge University Press.

Portes, A., M. CastellI, and L. Benton (eds), (1989): The Informal Economy, Johns Hopkins University Press, Baltimore.

Rauch, J.E., 1991, 'Modelling the Informal Sector Formally", Journal of Development Economics 35: 33-47.

Sahn, D.E. P.A. Dorosh and S.D. Younger (1997), 'Structural Adjustment reconsidered Economic Policy and Poverty in Africa', Cambridge: Cambridge University press.

Sims, C, Stock, J, Watson, (1990), 'Inference in linear time series models with some unit roots', Econometrics 58: 113-114.

Sinha, Anushree and Christophe Adam (2006) 'Reforms and Internationalization: What Lies Behind Jobless Growth in India,' in Guha-Khasnobis, Basudeb and Ravi Kanbur (eds.) *Informal Labour Markets and Development,* London: Palgrave Macmillan.

Sinha, Anushree and N. Sangeeta (2000), 'Gender in a Macro Economic Framework: A CGE Model Analysis' presented in the Second Annual Meeting of the Gender Planning Network, in Kathmandu, Nepal during November 22-24.

Sinha, Anushree (2002), 'Does Welfare of Women Improve by Globalisation: A CGE Model Analysis of India' presented at the 14th International Conference on Input-Output Techniques at the *Universite du Quebec a Montreal,* Canada during October 10-15.

Taylor, Lance (1990), 'Structuralist CGE Models,' in, Lance Taylor (ed.) *Socially Relevant Policy Analysis: Structuralist Computable General Equilibrium Models for the Developing World,* Cambridge, MA: The MIT Press.

Thorbecke E. and H. Jung (1996), 'A Multiplier Decomposition Method to Analyse Poverty Alleviation', Journal of Development Economics 48, pp. 279-300.

Thorbecke E. (1991),' Adjustment and Equity in Indonesia', OECD Development Centre, Paris.

Tongeren, F.W. Van (1994), Microsimulation Versus Applied General Equilibrium Models, mimeo, presented at 5th International conference on CGE Modelling, October 27-29, university of Waterloo, Canada.

Tyler, G.J. and O. Akioboade (1992), Structural Adjustment and Poverty: A Computable General Equilibrium Model of the Kenyan Economy', Oxford: International Development Centre, Oxford.

White H. (1997), 'Poverty and Adjustment in Sub-Saharan Africa: A Review of the Literature', The Hague: Institute of Social Studies.

Winters, L.A. (2000), 'Trade, Trade Policy and Poverty: What are the Links?", Discussion Paper No. 2382, Centre for Economic Policy Research, London.

APPENDIX A: ILLUSTRATED CGE MODEL EQUATIONS

THE MODEL EQUATIONS AS WRITTEN IN GAMS LANGUAGE

The terms of operation are explained below:

*	= Multiplication
**	= To the power of
Sum	= Sum of
Prod	= Products of

The sets are as given below:

IP(I)	PRIVATE SECTORS /AGRIC,AGROPRF,AGROPRIF, RGMF,RGMIF, OTMGF, OTMGIF, CONST, OTSERF, OTSERIF/
IM(IP)	IMPORTABLE SECTORS /AGRIC, AGROPRF, AGROPRIF, RGMF,RGMIF, OTMGF, OTMGIF, OTSERF, OTSERIF /
IX(I)	EXPORTABLE SECTORS /AGRIC,AGROPRF, AGROPRIF, RGMF,RGMIF, OTMGF,OTMGIF, OTSERF,OTSERIF /
INM(IP)	NON-IMPORTABLE SECTORS / CONST /
INX(I)	NON-EXPORTABLE SECTORS / CONST/
IC(IM)	CONSUMPTION SECTORS /AGRIC, AGROPRF, AGROPRIF, RGMF, RGMIF, OTMGF, OTMGIF, OTSERF, OTSERIF/

Where,

A.1. Sectors

AGRIC	Agriculture
AGROPRF	Agro Processing Formal
AGROPRIF	Agro Processing Informal
RGMF	Readymade Garments Formal
RGMIF	Readymade Garments Informal
OTMGF	Other manufacturing goods Formal
OTMGIF	Other manufacturing goods Informal
CONST	Construction

OTSERF	Other Services Formal
OTSERIF	Other Services Informal
PUB	Government Services

A.2. Household Type

RPNAF:	Rural Poor Non Agriculture Forma
RNPNAF:	Rural Non Poor Non Agriculture Formal
UPF:	Urban Poor Formal
UNPF:	Urban Non Poor Formal
RPAI:	Rural Poor Agriculture Informal
RNPAI:	Rural non-Poor Agriculture Informal
RPNAI:	Rural Poor non-Agriculture Informal
RNPNAI:	Rural non-Poor non-Agriculture Informal

A.3. Labour Categories

LCF	Casual Female
LCM	Casual Male
LHBF	Home Based Female
LHBM	Home Based Male
LRGF	Regular Female
LRGM	Regular Male

A.4. Capital Categories

OAWF	Own Account Workers Female
OAWM	Own Account Workers Male
OAWHBF	Own account home based workers Female
OAWHBM	Own Account Home Based Workers Male
EMPF	Employers Female
EMPM	Employers Male

A.5. Price Block

PMDEF(IM)..	PM(IM) =E= PWM(IM)*ER*(1 + TM(IM));
PEDEF(IX)..	PE(IX) =E= PWE(IX)*ER*(1-TE(IX));
CONSUMP(IC)..	PC(IC)*Q(IC)=E=PD(IC)*XD(IC) + PM(IC)*M (IC)$ IM(IC);
SALES(IX)..	PQ(IX)*X(IX) =E= PD(IX)*XD(IX) + PE(IX)* E(IX) ;
SALESN(INX)..	PQ(INX)*X(INX) =E= PD(INX)*XD(INX) ;
ACTP(IP)..	PVA(IP) =E= PQ(IP)*(1-PTAX(IP)) - SUM(JP,IO (JP,IP)* PD(JP));

PVAPUB("PUB").. PVA("PUB") =E= (SUM(LC, WA(LC)*WDIST ("PUB",LC)*L("PUB",LC)))/ X("PUB");

PKDEF(I).. PK(I) =E= SUM(JP, PC(JP)*IMAT(JP,I)); CPIDEF. CPI =E= SUM(IC, WC(IC)*PC(IC));

A.6. Output and Factors of Production Block

ACTEQ(I).. X(I) =E= AD(I)*PROD(LC$WDIST(I,LC), L(I,LC)** ALPHL(LC,I))*KP(I)**ALPHK(I)*KG**ALPHG(I); PROFITMAX(IP,LC)$WDIST(IP,LC).. WA(LC)*WDIST(IP,LC)*L(IP,LC) =E= X(IP)*PVA (IP)* ALPHL(LC,IP);

LMEQUIL(LC).. SUM(I, L(I,LC)) =E= LS(LC);

CET(IX).. X(IX) =E= AT(IX)*(GAMMA(IX)*E(IX)**(1+1/ EPST(IX))+(1-GAMMA(IX))*XD(IX)**(1+1/ EPST(IX)))**(1/(1+1/EPST(IX))) ;

ESUPPLY(IX).. E(IX)/XD(IX) =E= (PE(IX)/PD(IX)*(1-GAMMA (IX))/GAMMA(IX))**(EPST(IX));

ARMINGTON(IM).. Q(IM) =E= AC(IM)*(DELTA(IM)*M(IM)**(1-1/ EPSC(IM))+(1-DELTA(IM))*XD(IM)**(1-1/ EPSC(IM)))**(1/(1-1/EPSC(IM)));

COSTMIN(IM).. M(IM)/XD(IM) =E= (PD(IM) PM(IM)*DELTA (IM)/ (1-DELTA(IM))) **(EPSC (IM));

XDSN(INX).. XD(INX) =E= X(INX);

* XDPUB.. XD("PUB") =E= X("PUB");

QSN(INM).. Q(INM) =E= XD(INM);

CAPRENT(IP).. RK(IP) =E= PVA(IP)*X(IP) - SUM(LC, WA(LC)* WDIST (IP,LC)*L(IP,LC));

A.7. Demand Block

NDEQ(I).. ND(I) =E= SUM(J, IO(I,J)*X(J)) ;

CDEQ(IC,HH).. PC(IC)*(1+ITAX(IC))*CD(IC,HH) =E=CLES(IC,HH)*Y(HH)*(1-MPS(HH))*(1-DTAX(HH));

HHCDEQ(HH).. HHCD(HH) =E= PROD(I$CLES(I,HH),CD (I,HH)**(CLES(I,HH)));

*EINV.. INVEST =E= SAVING;

*EINV.. INVEST =E= SAVING-DK("PUB");

DEPREQ(IP).. DEPRC(IP) =E= DEPR(IP)*KP(IP)*PK(IP) ;

YEQ(HH).. Y(HH) =E= SUM(LC, LFDIST(HH,LC)*SUM (I,WDIST(I,LC)*WA(LC)*L(I,LC)))+ SUM(KC,

```
                      KFDIST(HH,KC)*SUM (IP,RDIST (KC,IP)*
                      RK(IP)))+ ER*RMIT(HH);
KPROF(IP)..           R(IP) =E= (RK(IP)-DEPRC(IP))/KP(IP) ;
KPROFAV..             RBAR =E= SUM(IP, RK(IP)-DEPRC(IP)) / SUM(IP,
                      KP(IP));
HHSAVEQ(HH)..         HHSAV(HH) =E= MPS(HH)*(Y(HH)*(1-DTAX
                      (HH)));
GRUSE..               GOVSAV =E= GR - GDTOT - ER*DEBTSRV ;
* GOVINV..            DKG =E=DSHR*(SUM(HH,DIRTAX(HH))+
                      DUTY-PK("PUB")*DK("PUB")); *DSHR* SUM
                      (HH,DIRTAX(HH))+DUTY-DK("PUB");
TARIFFDEF..           TARIFF =E= SUM(IM, TM(IM)*M(IM)*PWM
                      (IM))* ER;
INDTAXDEF..           INDTAX =E= SUM(IC, ITAX(IC)*PC(IC)*SUM
                      (HH, CD(IC,HH)));
PRDTAXDEF..           PRODTAX =E=SUM(IP, PTAX(IP)*PQ(IP)*X(IP));
DUTYDEF..             DUTY =E= SUM(IX, TE(IX)*E(IX)*ER*PWE(IX));
DIRTAXDEF(HH)..       DIRTAX(HH) =E= DTAX(HH)*Y(HH) ;
TOTSAV..              SAVING =E= SUM(HH,HHSAV(HH)) + GOVSAV
                      + ER*SF ;
* TOTSAV..            SAVING =E= SUM(HH,HHSAV(HH)) + GOVSAV;
KSHARE(IP)..          KI(IP) =E= KP(IP) / SUM(JP, KP(JP)) ;
GREQ..                GR =E= TARIFF + DUTY + INDTAX + SUM(HH,
                      DIRTAX(HH)) + PRODTAX;
GDEQ..                GDTOT =E= (PVA("PUB") + SUM(I, IO(I,"PUB")
                      *PC(I)))*X("PUB") ;
* GDEQ..              GDTOT =E= X("PUB") ;
PRODINV(IP)..         PK(IP)*DK(IP) =E= KI(IP)*(1+ ADJ*(R(IP) -
                      RBAR))*(SAVING-(PK("PUB")*DK("pub")));
IEQ(I)..              ID(I) =E= SUM(J, IMAT(I,J)*DK(J)) ;
TOTINV..              INVEST =E= SUM(IP,PC(IP)*ID(IP)) ;
CAEQ..                SUM(IX,PWE(IX)*E(IX)) + SF + SUM(HH, RMIT
                      (HH)) - SUM(IM, PWM(IM)*M(IM)) - DEBTSRV
                      =E=0;
```

A.8. Market Clearing

```
EQUILP(IP)..          Q(IP) =E= SUM(HH, CD(IP,HH))+ND(IP)+ID(IP);
OBJ..                 OMEGA =E= SUM(HH, HW(HH)*LOG(PROD(I$
                      CLES(I,HH), CD(I,HH)**(CLES(I,HH) (1+GLES))*
                      X("PUB")**(GLES/(1+GLES)))));
```

APPENDIX B: GLOSSARY

B.1. Price Block

ER	EXCHANGE RATE
PD(I)	DOMESTIC PRICES
PM(IM)	DOMESTIC PRICE OF IMPORTS
PE(IX)	DOMESTIC PRICE OF EXPORTS
PK(I)	RATE OF CAPITAL RENT BY SECTOR
PQ(I)	AVERAGE OUTPUT PRICE BY SECTOR
PC(I)	PRICE OF CONSUMER COMPOSITE
PVA(I)	VALUE ADDED PRICE BY SECTOR
PWM(I)	WORLD MARKET PRICE OF IMPORTS
PWE(I)	WORLD MARKET PRICE OF EXPORTS
TM(IM)	TARIFF RATES
TE(IX)	EXPORT DUTIES
CPI	CONSUMER PRICE INDEX

B.2. Production Block

Q(IP)	COMPOSITE SUPPLY
X(I)	TOTAL DOMESTIC OUTPUT BY SECTOR
XD(I)	DOMESTIC SALES
E(I)	EXPORTS BY SECTOR
M(I)	IMPORTS

B.3. Factor Block

AD(I)	PRODUCTION FUNCTION SHIFT PARAMETER
KG	PUBLIC CAPITAL STOCK
KP(I)	CAPITAL STOCK BY SECTOR
KI(IP)	CAPITAL SHARES
WA(LC)	AVERAGE WAGE RATE BY SKILL
LS(LC)	LABOR SUPPLY BY SKILL
L(I,LC)	EMPLOYMENT BY SECTOR AND SKILL
HW(HH)	HOUSEHOLD SIZE WEIGHT
RK(I)	SECTORAL PROFIT
INFSHR(IP)	INFORMAL SHARE OF CAPITAL AND PROFITS
R(IP)	PROFIT RATE BY SECTOR
RBAR	WEIGHTED AVERAGE PROFIT RATE
ADJ	INVESTMENT ADJUSTMENT PARAMETER

B.4. Demand Block

ND(I)	INTERMEDIATE USES
CD(I,HH)	FINAL DEMAND FOR PRIVATE CONSUMPTION
HHCD(HH)	TOTAL HOUSEHOLD CONSUMPTION BY HOUSEHOLD TYPE
ID(I)	FINAL DEMAND FOR PRODUCTIVE INVESTMENT
DEPRC(IP)	DEPRECIATION EXPENDITURE
RMIT(HH)	REMITTANCES (US DOLLARS)
Y(HH)	PRIVATE GROSS INCOME
MPS(HH)	MARGINAL PROPENSITY TO SAVE OUT OF YD
DTAX(HH)	DIRECT TAX RATE
ITAX(I)	INDIRECT TAX RATE
PTAX(I)	PRODUCTION TAX RATE
GR	GOVERNMENT REVENUE
TARIFF	TARIFF REVENUE
INDTAX	INDIRECT TAX REVENUE
PRODTAX	PRODUCTION TAX REVENUE
DUTY	EXPORT DUTY REVENUE
DIRTAX(HH)	DIRECT TAX REVENUE
GDTOT	TOTAL GOVERNMENT CONSUMPTION
HHSAV(HH)	TOTAL HOUSEHOLD SAVINGS
GOVSAV	GOVERNMENT SAVINGS
IMAT(I,J)	INPUT-OUTPUT COEFFICIENTS
SAVING	TOTAL SAVINGS
SF	FOREIGN SAVINGS
DEBTSRV	FOREIGN DEBT SERVICE
INVEST	TOTAL INVESTMENT
SF	FOREIGN SAVINGS (CURRENT ACCOUNT BALANCE)
DK(I)	VOLUME OF INVESTMENT BY DESTINATION
OMEGA	OBJECTIVE FUNCTION

B.5. Parameter Block

ALPHL(LC,I)	LABOR SHARE PARAMETER IN PRODUCTION
ALPHG(I)	PUBLIC CAPITAL SHARE PARAMETER
ALPHK(I)	CAPITAL SHARE PARAMETER IN PRODUC
	WEIGHTS FOR CONSUMER PRICE INDEX

WDIST(I,LC)	WAGE PROPORTIONALITY MATRIX
LFDIST(HH,LC)	LABOUR INCOME DISTRIBUTION MATRIX
AT(I)	CET FUNCTION SHIFT PARAMETER
GAMMA(I)	CET FUNCTION SHARE PARAMETER
DELTA(I)	ARMINGTON SHARE PARAMETER CONSUMPTION
AC(I)	ARMINGTON SHIFT PARAMETER CONSUMPTION
EPSC(I)	ARMINGTON ELASTICITY OF SUBSTITUTION
EPST(I)	CET ELASTICITY OF TRANSFORMATION
CLES(I,HH)	CES CONSUMPTION SHARE PARAMETER
GLES	SHARE OF CONS OF GOVERNMENT OUTPUT IN UTILITY
IO(I,J)	INPUT-OUTPUT COEFFICIENTS

APPENDIX C: AGGREGATION SCHEME FOR 11 INDUSTRIAL SECTORS WITH I-O TABLE

S. No.	*Sectors*		*Input Output Transactions Table 1993-94*
1	Agriculture	I	1-22
2	Agro-processing	F	33-40
3	Agro-processing	I	
4	Readymade Garments	F	48
5	Readymade Garments	I	
6	Other Manufacturing Goods	F	23-32, 41-47, 49-75 76-98
7	Other Manufacturing Goods	I	
8	Construction	I	99
9	Other Services	F	100-114
10	Other Services	I	
11	Government Services	F	115

APPENDIX D: AGGREGATION SCHEME FOR 11 INDUSTRIAL SECTORS WITH NIC CODES

S. No.	*Sectors*		*Input Output Transactions Table 1993-94*
1	Agriculture	I	01111-05005
2	Agro-processing	F	15111-16009
3	Agro-processing	I	
4	Redymade Garments	F	17301-17309, 18101
5	Readymade Garments	I	
6	Other Manufacturing Goods	F	10101-14299, 17111-17299, 18102-18209, 19111-37200, 50200, 50404, 52601-52609
7	Other Manufacturing Goods	I	
8	Construction	I	45101-45500
9	Other Services	F	40101-41000, 50101-50103, 50300-50403, 50500, 51101-52599, 55101-74999, 80101-99000
10	Other Services	I	
11	Government Services	F	75111-75302

Source: Prepared and worked by Sinha et al (2003).

NOTES

[1] Micro Impact of Macro Policies: Data Collected at NCAER.

[2] The prerequisite is data for household members on market and non market work by number of hours through a national representative survey.

[3] I acknowledge that there are various concepts of imputing value for non market work, However, as a practical first step, I suggest that the market wage of the work itself (or similar work) is used to derive at the shadow wage.

Macroeconomic Complexity and Gender Economics

ROMAR CORREA

INTRODUCTION

It is only recently that work at the frontiers of economic science has begun to move beyond the fiction of the representative agent to model macro economies. However, it is still fairly routine to assume that managers, workers and rentiers have identical criterion functions, planning horizons and information sets (Correa, 2005B). Two research agendas have emerged within the gestalt of general equilibrium theory that dispense with this expendable device. One response is to work with the form of utility functions. The path here would lead to the analysis of the endogeneity and evolution of preferences and the appreciation that they are determined by institutions. People are likely to obtain utility not only from outcomes but also from the conditions generating those outcomes. Individuals garner procedural utility from institutions as such (Frey & Stutzer, 2005). Procedural utility emerges in the interaction between people. Thus, individuals get satisfaction from fair and honest dealings, independent of outcomes. By the same token, people measure actions towards them not entirely by their consequences but also by the intent propelling the actions. According to theories of procedural fairness, intrinsic value is attached to the process itself, especially when perceptions of fairness are connected to the idea of agency. Procedures are then evaluated according to the relational information they convey which includes data on impartiality, trust, and the degree of belief of individuals that they are being treated with dignity. Such evaluations have behavioural consequences. In a study about recidivism in cases of domestic violence, it was found that recidivism rates are lower when people are treated with respect by arresting officers. Other pleasures of a procedural kind are the utilities earned by facing and meeting challenges, expressing oneself, using one's talents, and reporting experiences over and above the instrumental value they might have. Of relevance to the theme is the positive utility to be earned from participation. Involvement enlarges the perception of self-determination among men and women. Participation is both an activity as well as a characteristic of an institution. Markets influence preferences in that they provide presumptive reasons why people come into possession of certain commodities and services (Tsakalotos, 2004). Individuals have relational preferences. That is, the terms on which they will transact depends on the perceived relationships among the exchanging parties. Institutions might instigate certain demand and supply functions, self-regarding or cooperative, which feed back to be embodied in the behavioural repertoire of individuals. Markets frame choices. According to experimental evidence, an individual's contribution to public goods and cooperation in prisoners' dilemma situations is a function of context. The more the features of the game resemble a textbook competitive market, the more we expect want-regarding norms and less we would see other-regarding conduct. Markets also act as radical simplifiers in scaling down the complexity with which we, typically, assess an assortment of disparate goods.

The other line of research is to confront the distribution of different agents in the population squarely (Hildenbrand & Kneip, 2005). An index of 'behavioural heterogeneity' for every finite population of households is defined. It is shown that the higher the index of behavioural heterogeneity, the less sensitive is the aggregate consumption expenditure ratio to prices. Already the approach suggests two connections with our theme. Heterogeneity can include the economics of gender, and the dependence of aggregate consumption on (possibly) realized income might suggest an introduction to the economics of Keynes. At any rate, the research strategy is to explain macroeconomic phenomena on the basis of microdata. Less emphasis is placed on the classic axioms and in some innovative work it is shown that even individual rationality might be not required!

We continue with the suggestion that economic relations among agglomerations of individuals can be regarded as a system of higher-order aggregation: the individual, the family, the community, the State and supranational aggregates (Casson & Della Giusta, 2004). In the next section we survey the emergence of norms and institutions as the outcome of the behaviour of agents in all their variety. These outcomes then take on a dynamic of their own that is not easily reducible to the strategies of different players in society. Money is one such coordinating device that is simultaneously social and evolves as the outcome of the deliberative actions of various agents in an economic system. One prominent non neoclassical school that is empirically grounded and that deals with the connection between micro macro and gender explicitly is the Post Keynesian and is the subject of Section III. The following section approaches the topic from the macro end of the spectrum with the Marxian orientation to the subject that is not explicit about the micro realm. We devote Section V to the policy milieu implied by our earlier considerations. Naturally, the norm of complexity suggests that there is no facile answer to the market versus state intervention debate. The conclusion summarizes the arguments.

Norms and Institutions

The attraction of a dynamical systems approach to political economy is that the formulation lends itself easily to an institutionalist interpretation of the solution of economic problems (Correa, 2005A). The context of repeated play is a summary statistic of the cooperative equilibrium among the many that are possible. A requirement here is that the solution must have an objective representation outside the behaviour of the agents in order to coordinate their beliefs. An institution is a social construct and thus endogenous to the repeated interaction of the constituent players. The strategies of agents are functions of the summary representation and their behaviour, consistent with their strategies, confirms the summary representation. Institutions are simultaneously endogenous and objective. Thereby, they at once constrain and enable. Through the dynamic of the State variable, they shepherd agents' actions into cooperative play. At the same time, the State variable is compressed data. An institution enables agents to economise on their data-processing abilities by encouraging them to employ feedback strategies.

Not only markets but aggregate decision-making experiments as well have deepened our understanding of the ability of human beings to create institutions that enable them to discover ingenious ways to satisfy their desires. This process of creation is not always the outcome of deliberative action and is not always upfront in the consciousness of social beings. For an economist, the most salient characteristic of human nature is sociability (Smith, 2004). The human capacity for social exchange has supported investment in the creation and utilization of knowledge beyond the requirements of subsistence. An axiom that applies here is reciprocity. People tend to 'return the favour' when others act so as to benefit them. In the realm of social intercourse, good comes from planned acts of sharing, kindness and reciprocity. The theorem that pro-social preferences influence market behaviour has been attested in experiments and surveys. Pro-social preferences can thus facilitate trade and profit maximization, particularly if they assist in overcoming social dilemmas. If developing countries in which transactions are largely founded on personal exchange and local trade are to make the regime change to a higher trajectory of the growth of wealth, the trust that undergirds the productivity among people known to each other must be transmuted to institutions that enable exchange and the division of labour to be extended to impersonal, arms-length relationships.

A concept that might be useful here is social capital as it exists in communities, networks, families and clans (Tsakalotos, 2004). Social capital is accumulated as people debate and shape their common destinies together. Institutional economies might be associated with superior economic performance in comparison with market systems. The reason is that non-market norms are associated with a stronger collective action goods potential. The literature on the varieties of capitalism suggests that such economies exhibit a remarkable degree of flexibility in decision-making as a result of the existence of trust. The necessity for explicit contracts is obviated and the costly trial and error of search for best practices is reduced. Indeed, sometimes institutions that by neoclassical reasoning would be regarded as rigidities, such as trade unions, may, in fact, be playing a salutary role in resolving a set of public goods problems and reducing risk and uncertainly in economic engagements. Social groups play a pivotal role in generating process-based trust as distinct from ascribed trust which is based on the traits of the interacting partners. It is derived from cooperation and the State has a role to play in promoting networks and, as broker, can facilitate the diffusion of trust across the system.

Relatedly, the theory of the Social Structure of Accumulation (SSA) engages with the problematic of Schumpeter and Keynes about how the incessant flux and uncertainty that is the hallmark of capitalism can create an environment conducive to long-term investment. Institutions evolve to ameliorate some conflicts. Thus, the postwar structure of labour relations outlawed strikes in sympathy with other workers. Conflicts between financial sectors were confined to the determination of the structure of interest rates rather than the development of particular financial markets which were proscribed by law. The SSA structures conflict without eliminating it. It is equally concerned with crisis. Contradictions might reach a critical mass and undermine an SSA. It is not clear what potential SSA might emerge. A related methodological stance is provided by Régulation Theory which is driven by the postulate that the capitalist economy is socially embedded. Both approaches are connected with the study of historically contingent ensembles of complementary economic mechanisms which enable the accumulation of capital. The dynamic tension, once more, is between the stable long-term environment and the conflict inherent in the capital relation. The approach is sensitive to both the anarchic nature of exchange relations as well as the adjunct and supportive role of conventions and procedures in facilitating the reproduction of capital. The relation between the two institutionalist approaches might be stated as follows: a capitalist economy is an ensemble of procedures comprising a regime of accumulation embedded in an SSA. The process of accumulation is a complex process consisting of the self-valorization of capital in and through régulation.

Theorising about money is a case in point. All money is constituted by credit-debt relations, a subset of social relations. The holder of money has a claim on the social product. Money is a credit for the user because it is a liability for the issuer. 'Moneyness' is the specific function that is assigned socially to a process by means of which money becomes an institutional fact (Ingham, 2004). Money has a purchasing power that exists independent of the goods it can command. 'Monetary space' is defined by money of account in terms of which debts are contracted and discharged and transactions conducted. It is the site of potential purchases and sales that can be effected under particular monetary conditions. Money is uniquely specified as a measure of abstract value and as a means of storing and transposing this abstract value. The modus operandi is the social organization of the monetary system. Only by transcending not only the specifics of particular commodities but also the particularities of time and place, can money embody the abstraction of value.

The functions of money have to be constantly rejuvenated in a social process of 'collective intentionality'. Money is a promise and the emission of a promise entails trust. Self-fulfilling trust is based on a social legitimacy whereby anyone may participate in complex multilateral relationships. The assignment of the promise also involves a transparent guarantee that the credit will be accepted back by the issuer in settlement of its own debt. Money exists in vast networks of debtor-credit relationships between issuers and users. Money is produced regularly by the maintenance of the integrity of systems of payment. Confidence is required on both sides of the money relation.

MESOECONOMIC COMPLEXITY AND GENDER

Institutions appear at various points in Post Keynesian (PK) economics (Pressman, 2003). They help explain the consumption behaviour of households, the investment decisions of businessmen and the creation of money in capitalist economies. Consumer preferences are believed to be moulded by acquired social behaviour. In a line of enquiry dating back to Thorstein Veblen, consumer spending is determined by the prerequisites of a lifestyle not different from one's peers and, perhaps, a lifestyle marginally superior to them. Consumption is stable because it is a function of habit. For most middle-income households this means spending a large portion of the pay packet. Consequently, the propensity to consume additional income has a relatively high value and is stable over time. Investment decisions might best be modeled as a herd process wherein everyone watches everyone else. Firms will invest if and only if a sizable number of other firms are investing. On the other hand, if animal spirits are muted, few firms will invest. The concept of money in non neoclassical accounts has been sketched in the previous section. For the present, its role in reducing radical uncertainty in PK theory will be mentioned. Holding money reduces this unquantifiable uncertainty for the firm because it is the common coin of wage payments as well as the discharge of debts. Households feel confident that they will be able to purchase necessities in the future with their money stocks.

Both PK and feminist thought are concerned with the evolution of the mode of production over time (Danby, 2004). The common concern is with sequences: plans are made ex ante based on a mix of objective data and animal spirits, capital goods are then produced before their sale, consumer goods stream out of production lines before they are purchased and so on. Results ex post are unlikely to be equal to plans. The result is a revision of plans and so on in a disequilibrium sequence. Every individual is situated in the present with a unique assemblage of discount rates and information sets. However, patterns of interconnection are pivotal. Enduring relationships between people and institutions affect outcomes.

Gender refers to the social construction of sexual identity, a construction that assigns different roles, rights and opportunities to persons based on their sex. It is simultaneously an enabler and a constraint, something we reconstruct in our daily round with some discretion but far from complete freedom. Social relations are gendered.

The kind of inter temporal commitments that characterize firms and financial intermediaries in PK theory also describe the non-market activities that occur in households like time-dated payment commitments, borrowing and lending and liquidity problems. There are well-known difficulties in coordinating the diverse processes of production and provision of services that occur in households but also in exploring the cognitive armoury of the planner. Contingent commitments are an important component of forward commitments. These, like overdraft facilities, play a vital role in smoothening daily material processes even if never called upon. The approach is not different from the literature on care. 'Care' comprises qualities of attentiveness, expectations and reactions that includes contending with the unexpected as it affects the lives of others. In general, households are not self-contained but need to forge links with intermediaries that are institutions above households and below governments (Casson & Della Giusta, 2004). Intermediaries assist households to access markets. In a sense, they pool households' social resources to enlarge their entitlements to productive resources. Thus, successful microfinance schemes are those in which the mechanisms have worked smoothly as impartial trust-brokers or outsiders. The importance of the subsidy of trust provided by meso-level development agencies is underscored. The role of macroeconomic institutions like governments is to support households, protecting or enlarging their entitlements, and to secure intermediaries. Some concern has been expressed about whether money and care can peacefully coexist (Folbre & Nelson, 2003). According to the Chicago economics view, the movement from caring work into markets might be an efficient reaction to income and relative price changes. From another perspective, the world of commodities and care are disjointed and the fear is that the monetisation of care might crowd out caring feelings. The theory of money outlined earlier does not include the general equilibrium attributes of impersonality and anonymity. Even when money changes hands in the exchange of goods and services, intimate relationships between the parties are not excluded. Childcare markets are one illustration of "rich markets in which the movement of money is only one dimension in a complex relationship of child, caregivers, and parents including . . . elements of trust . . ." (Folbre & Nelson, 2003, p. 115). One merit of creating market alternatives to family care is that it permits women greater freedom. Women were not offered alternatives to providing homemaker, mothering and sexual services. The effects on the demanders of care are salutary as well. The fall in the labour market barriers to entry for women and the greater availability of alternative provision for the young and the vulnerable means that care activity is the outcome more of choice and less of necessity. The quality and costs of care should, therefore, improve. There are potential economies of specialization to be reaped as well. The woman-at-home caregiver is a generalist. Her skills are not likely to range equally from childcare at one end to nurse at the other. Shifting some of the facets of caregiving to trained teachers and doctors in this case should be welfare-improving. The movement from private to public is likely to assist in the economic analysis of work and well-being as we appreciate the value of knowledge and skills in the areas where care is given. At the same time, the dependence on markets for the provision of care presents well-known problems. The sick and the elderly do not meet the definition of the utility-maximizing agent. Care also creates significant externalities that cannot easily be internalized. Many people, not excluding future employers, benefit when children are brought up to be trained and truth-telling individuals. The old gain when the high-income-earning young pay more taxes. Like other externalities, the provision of care induces an incentive to freeride.

Households overlap with each other to create an inter-household domain in which they forge tacit contracts with each other and effect substantial transfers of goods, services and money. If one link in the web of commitments is broken, the aggrieved recipient will find herself constrained in interlocked commitments and so forth. Household systems, at one end, might be internally resilient, or they may be stretched to the point where an exogenous shock snaps ties. It is not clear that household activity breaks down into discrete households; it might be more accurate to speak of wider systems of kin and community in which people are embedded in a variety of relations with each other. The time structure of material activities in the household intersects with the time structure of activities outside the household including those of formal sector employers (working hours, overtime) and state institutions (school schedules, transport). The sphere of the household is not disconnected from visible macroeconomic activity.

THE MACROFOUNDATIONS OF GENDER

A basic principle here is that the functioning of the mode of production under capitalism determines the social organization and the economic foundations of reproduction. Production absorbs reproduction because the access of individuals to the necessary conditions of reproduction (employment at a wage sufficient to support children) shapes their reproductive strategies and their outcomes. Production determines reproduction through the shrinking of choices open to propertyless men and women. Recall here the Keynesian theorem that it is chronically impossible to employ the able-bodied workforce under capitalism. Male and female workers, then, are forced to compete for scarce jobs and this competition is blunted by the evolution of sex-segregated labour markets. Segmented labour market theory (SLM) is consistent with the evidence and offers an institutional critique of orthodoxy and an explanation of the secular unevenness in the distribution of men and women across occupations (Mastracci, 2005). Women simply do not gain access to non-traditional occupations in the primary sector. They do not possess the social capital networks necessary to gain entry into primary-term jobs. Even when they enter higher-mobility jobs, they are excluded from the training and resources that would cement their success.

The segregation extends to other markets as well (Boschini, 2004). In corner cases in asset markets, women are not permitted to own property and to inherit from their husband/father. The implication is that women cannot borrow at market rates of interest as they do not possess collateral. To summarize the gender gap in asset markets in most countries: women are less wealthy than men, borrow less and when they do, are lent less money.

The notion is "the recognition of the complex network of macro-level effects" upon male-female relationships of a mode of production driven by the accumulation of capital (Gimenez, 2005, p. 20). Biologically, and by virtue of the mode of production, men and women are placed in complementary sexual and procreative relations. At the same time, they confront each other on the terrain of reproduction. Male workers have one major source of survival, wage labour; female workers have, in addition, unpaid domestic work. Capitalist production entails class conflicts: between the interests of capitalist women and propertyless women; among the latter, antagonisms exist between 'middle-class' and 'working class' women. On the other hand, reproduction implies critical commonalities of experience that cut across classes, establishing a foundation for women's solidarity.

In mainstream literature sex and gender are clearly differentiated. The former refers to the biological differences between men and women, the latter to the social construction of sexual identity already defined above. However, the radical view is that sexuality and gender are not autonomous (Ebert, 2005). Sexuality is a marker of social difference only in a class society. Gender and sexuality are sites of historical agency and loci of struggle only because of the division of labour and property relations. Under capitalism, the only historical agent is spawned by the penetration of capital, the wage-labourer. Gender inequality, thus conceptualised, is irreducible to microfoundations. It cannot be explained by the preferences and biology of men and women. A skein of macro level phenomena defines the opportunity sets of those who have nothing to sell but their labour power and allocates women mainly to the sphere of domestic/reproductive labour and only secondarily to paid work.

The extension of a Ricardian-Marxian framework to a structuralist account of a developing economy would entail the demarcation of the economy into an industrial and an agricultural sector. The division cuts across the division of the economy into Departments following Marx's schemes of reproduction (Correa, 2005A). Sector I includes Marx's Department II producing luxury goods for capitalists, Sector II is Marx's Department III producing basics for workers and Department I producing investment goods is divided into two parts, investment goods produced in Sector I and investment goods produced in Sector II. This classification is resorted to in order to make non basics and basics output correspond with the output of Sector I and Sector II respectively. A two-sector modelling exercise would have the welcome effect of connecting gender inequalities and macroeconomic outcomes (Evers, 2003). Critical linkages have been uncovered between women's excessive time burdens and macroeconomic stylized facts. For example, in the case of sub-Saharan Africa, gender inequalities constrain supply responses in agriculture. The strict division of labour means that flexibility is severely limited and the substitution between male and female labour virtually absent.

POLICY REGIMES

One lesson from the above is that the issue of market versus state allocation cannot be settled on the basis of efficiency. The preference of individuals for a commodity depends, to some extent, on whether it has been allocated to them by government in the first instance (Tsakalotas, 2004). The initial allocation serves to legitimate and reinforce the collective understanding about normative rights of ownership. The norms that structure market relations have to do with self interest and reinforce 'exit' rather than 'voice'. They complement and reinforce one another. For example, the shortage of social goods underscores the impersonality of the market as does the presumption that market signals are expected to deliver their optimal outcomes by activating the want-regarding impulses of agents rather than their social responsibility. A change in the social equilibrium, say a decrease in the weight of the market with reference to state allocation, will also change the norms that determine that society.

The extension of the market trivializes other non-market values and priorities. For example, 'political' goods coexist uneasily with market norms. One illustration is the proposal to substitute direct provision of education with cash equivalents through a system of vouchers. The objective is the promotion of competition and increase in efficiency. The idea is consistent with the market norm of 'exit' but does not fit well with our perception of the provision of education as a "reflection of received ideals" in which society has a stake. As citizens of the State, we are enjoined to act in accordance with different ends than when we shop as consumers. In the case of political goods, to respect a fellow citizen is to take her reasons for advancing a particular position seriously. Her judgment must be studied and responded to in a public forum. In the end, it must be accepted if found not inferior to one's own. The value here is 'voice' and ideal democracy, distributing goods in accordance with public principles as opposed to given wants.

Alliances, as recommended by the Regulation School, might be a coordination device between the market and the State (Boyer, 2003). They are a mode of governance maintained at first through the consensus of parties operating according to an economic calculus not different from the market. Their merit is that they share the risk and rewards associated with, say, the introduction of new technologies. For example, a question here is how much of the allocation of capital and labour takes place internally in the firm and how much externally in the market. Furthermore, which of the resource allocations are negotiated and which are accomplished through the price system? Duncan Watts is quoted in this context: "where economists see incentives, sociologists can see institutions" (Gibbons, 2004, p. 21). Organizations operate according to ongoing conventions even if the results are not always optimal and efficient by neoclassical standards. At the same time, they are sparing of production and transaction costs and they encourage innovation. To reiterate our earlier theme: the market and State dichotomy reflects a simplistic classification based on two criteria; self-interest privileged by economists or the sense of obligation emphasized by sociologists and horizontal and egalitarian aspects versus hierarchical, unequal aspects of coordination processes. Each of these institutional arrangements is predicated on specific conditions and there is no given optimal arrangement. Post-Fordism, as theorised by members of the Régulation School, has profound effects on gender relations along the dimensions of numerical flexibility, functional flexibility and technological change (Wigfield, 2001). The domain of numerical flexibility is the expansion of part-time work, temporary work and homework. Women are predominant members of this set. Part of the explanation is the traditional role of women in domestic care. However, the provision of welfare has some role to play. The lower the level of welfare, the greater the chance that women will be employed in numerically flexible work. Functional flexibility is achieved by job enlargement and job enrichment. The mode of organization of labour is a critical explanatory variable. It has been found that if models of teams based on the Swedish prototype are grafted, job enrichment is the result. At the same time, if the culture of work is not consistent with this model but with another framework like, say, the Japanese model, the outcome is the negative aspects of job enlargement. Both elements are determined by gender. The suggestion is that if the workforce is predominantly female, work is likely to be organized in a way that enlarges rather than enriches the workforce, the explanation running in terms of the social construction of skill. Finally, the new technology embodied in the Post-Fordist economy upskills some jobs and deskills others and the implications for the workforce are determined by the mode of organization of work. Thus, technological change is pivotal to the Japanese model and deployed in a deskilling manner. The Swedish model, on the other hand, is not dependent on a high order of technological innovation but in the presence of supportive institutional changes, is conducive to upskilling the workforce. The conclusion here is that work is organized and technology utilized in the Post-Fordist workplace in a manner that deskills the jobs of women and upskills the jobs of men.

Moving to consistent macroeconomic policy, the programme of functional finance associated with Abba Lerner was based on the postulate that the issue of new money and the withdrawal of money should be appreciated only in terms of the results of these actions on the economy and not on any doctrine about sound/ unsound finance. The primary financial task of the government is to ensure that the total rate of spending on goods and services is neither greater nor less than the rate at which the current price level would be sufficient to purchase all the goods that can be produced. The second law of functional finance is that the government should borrow money only if it is desirable that the public should possess less money and more government bonds. The government should resort to the printing press whenever the precepts of functional finance dictate that bond sales are not required. The authorities issue bonds to permit the public to hold non-interest-bearing government paper. The prescriptions are for 1. the adjustment of total spending in order to eliminate both unemployment and inflation, 2. the adjustment of public holdings of money and of government bonds in order to secure the rate of interest that induces the desirable level of investment and 3. issue and destruction of money in order to carry out the first two parts. This pure macroeconomic thumbnail sketch is innocent of a gender dimension and there is a need to flesh out a "gender policy regime" (Sainsbury, 1999, p. 77). An unquestioned precept here might be that the unit to be protected from the malfunctioning of the market is the family (Bussemaker & van Kersbergen, 1999). The benefits are conferred upon the head of the household. Income is supposed to accrue to the male breadwinner. Employment and wage policies are targeted at men who are assumed to have support obligations. As a result, generous family incomes are often supported by the State with little concern for individual entitlements. A wife is entitled to the attention of the State only in the form of pension when she becomes the head of the household when her husband passes away. Divorced women are not covered. It may be the case, then, that Keynesian macroeconomic policies reinforce the sexual division of labour. A policy regime of the individual earner, on the other hand, would lead to the ideology that the relations between men and women are coordinating and symmetric. When entitlements are founded on citizenship, for instance, unmarried and married and husband and wife would enjoy equal rights. Paid and unpaid work would provide equal benefits. The financial costs of children and the care of the old and the disabled would be shared through the public provision of services. At the same time, the avowedly liberal philosophy underpinning the citizen is not without its tensions (O'Connor, Orloff & Shaver, 1999). There is a contradiction between a society in which men and women are separate and possess equal rights and the social bonds of private life joining men and women in marriage and the upbringing of children. Macroeconomic policy, operating at the conjunction between State and society, mediates this contradiction. Demands for inclusion on equal terms with men seems at odds with the admission of gender-specific needs.

The present world conjuncture is turning out to be appropriate to recapture the essentially Keynesian view of the economic process. Inflation is not perceived to be a problem any more and the deficiency of effective demand has reared its ugly head. Price stability has resulted in the zero bound interest rate problem. The efficacy of open market operations to lower the interest rate is attenuated. Indeed, when the nominal interest rate is close to zero, any further declines in the inflation rate. causes the real interest rate to rise. Demand is reduced further and a downward price spiral is the result. The time might be ripe for discretionary fiscal policy in a milieu of a sustained downturn, low interest rates and falling prices (Correa, 2003). A stimulus can be achieved without increasing budget deficits if fiscal policy provides an incentive for increased public spending. The focus must be on the structural content of fiscal policy in the form of tax efficiency and the quality of public expenditure. Monetary and fiscal policies are supposed to work in tandem. The exclusive focus on the price level, a characteristic of the old macroeconomics, has been relaxed. Both the arms of macroeconomic policy are to be used to keep real GDP close to potential GDP. In the United States, automatic stabilisers embedded in the fiscal system have been constant since the sixties and have contributed to blunting the edge of business cycles. The objective function of the authorities should be explicit and simple and be consistent with the objectives of forward-looking agents in the private sector. The purpose of sensitizing fiscal policy to gender concerns has been accomplished in many countries by entering into dialogue with women's budget statements (Çagatay, 2003). One proposition that applies here is that women are not a homogenous group. The following criteria might be met of any item of public expenditure. What is the money spent on? How will services be delivered? Who are the providers of services: businesses, voluntary organizations, voluntary groups? Who are the beneficiaries in terms of access to services? Who will benefit in terms of public sector employment? Similar questions could be asked of revenue-raising measures such as taxes and user fees. What, for instance, are the effects of specific policies on particular groups in terms of a reduction in income, consumption, access to services? In particular, which groups would experience an increased workload in terms of unpaid labour time as a consequence of revenue-raising measures?

A complete structural account of the financial development process along the lines proposed by Hyman Minsky would run as follows. The fundamental dilemma in economic organisation is how to preserve the vitality and resilience of a system of decentralized decision making without the attendant instability accompanying an economy in transition. Keynes' solution, the socialization of investment, might be one way of eliminating the extremes of financial instability. Accordingly, the financing of the most capital-intensive processes should be removed from private debt markets. In its place, there should be government financing along with limitations on the liability structure of private business. The symbiotic link between government and the private sector must be restored. The implication is greater deficits when downturns occur. This is not to endorse the basic spending programmes of governments where consumption is supported even while the physical and intellectual capital of society deteriorates. Government spending must create capital assets in the public domain that increase the efficiency of privately owned capital.

In a Keynes-Kaleçki view of the capitalist process, the formation and allocation of profits, in the sense of gross capital income, are central to an understanding of a developing economy. Gross capital income is the cash flow due to the production of goods and services that accrue to business and enable them to fulfil financial commitments. The ability of a unit to put out additional debt or garner funds to pay debt depends on the level and expected profile of profits. Profits, in turn, are a function of the types and sources of demand. The money value of investment in a given period is the basic determinant of money profits in the period. In a system with a small government, profits depend on the pace of investment. With the massive intrusion of the State as direct and indirect employer, the link between profits and investment has been weakened. Since profits are equal to the sum of investment and the government deficit, the flow of profits is sustained whenever a fall in investment leads to a rise in the government deficit. A debt deflation process that is fuelled by falling profits is halted when the deficit increases as income falls. A stabilization policy can be said to be successful when it stabilizes profits. Expansion can take place only when expected profits are adequate to motivate increasing expenditures on investments. The old growth models have been supplanted by a class of new growth stories that provide a formal endorsement of the insight that the accumulation of capital must be self-consciously accompanied by investment in education, health and the like. However, these stylized accounts are yet to elaborate upon the process of social reproduction in which women invest time and money in the education and socialization of children as well as in nutrition and health care for both children and adults (Elson, 1998). The savings (consumption) function is sensitive to being tagged to a man or a woman. Pooling of income within households is incomplete and significant differences between expenditure from female-controlled income and expenditure from male-controlled income exist. As already suggested, women attach a greater weight to expenditure on family nutrition, health and education-related objectives and men have a higher propensity to consume on high status consumer durables. A connection can be made here with the earlier theme of behaviour from more than one utility function driving macroeconomic outcomes. Increasing the aggregate demand for labour through a coherent macroeconomic stance is not connected with a desirable distribution between men and women of paid work in production and paid work in social reproduction. Indeed, the composition of aggregate demand for goods and services might generate overwork for women as their involvement in paid work in production increases while their level of unpaid work in social reproduction does not diminish. Men, at the same time, are unemployed in paid work but are ideologically constrained from undertaking 'women's work' in either production or social reproduction.

The function of the central bank (CB) in this milieu is to act as lender of last resort and thereby limit the losses due to the financial crisis which follows from the instability induced by a boom. A collapse of asset values is prevented. Asset holders can refinance rather than sell out their positions. A combination of rapid CB action and rapid fiscal policy to increase overall liquidity will minimize the repercussion of the crisis upon consumption and investment expenditures. While a CB is not able to determine the short-term path of money, income and prices, it is always able to substitute claims on itself for other claims in the money market, in bank portfolios and in the hands of the public. The terms of exchange sets a floor on the price of the items the CB might acquire. In a world where refinancing of positions is critical, the ability of a borrower to meet financial commitments is jeopardized when the price of its instruments falls sharply. If the CB is willing to introduce claims on itself by buying such instruments, thereby refinancing such borrowers, a floor is set on the price of these instruments. The fixing of this lower bound is an essential lender-of-last-resort function. The function of the CB diminishes the risk of default of the assets it guarantees. Assets with low default risk are liquid. The assets protected by the CB are liabilities of some financial institution, which, in turn, are used to finance positions in assets. Any extension of the monetary authority to extend its domain of lender-of-last-resort protection increases the capacity of the system to lend. Thereby asset prices and lending activity increase. Robust finance, in this context, means that bank assets are heavily weighted in favour of government debt and private debts that reflect hedge financing. In this scenario, it is rational for a CB to operate mainly in government debt. In a robust financial structure, open-market operations can determine the finance available without precipitating massive present-value reversals. A robust system leads to a credit expansion ungrounded in the credit base in the expansionary phase of the cycle. As the system shifts to a financially fragile state, the use of government debt as a position-making instrument by banks decreases. In such a state, variations in bank reserves must correspond to owned assets. The discount window is the right instrument to control reserves.

In the discount technique, bank reserves are furnished when the CB buys or lends on specified types of a paper that are a result of financing business. If bank reserves as well as the currency supply were the result of discounting to-the-asset paper that reflects manufacturing inventories, then as loans fall due and are repaid bank reserves fall. Banks would then have to discount paper and there would be an ongoing relationship between banks and the central bank. The CB creates a market for this paper and gives the assurance that it will have a special status in financial markets. Such paper will therefore belong to a preferred risk class. The guidance of the financial system will be a connection between the portfolio of the CB to a favoured interest rate in the market for eligible paper. In this system, a portion of the reserve base will be extinguished every day and the market will have to discount at the CB in order to replenish reserves. Each bank would have a line of credit at the CB and would be able to borrow up to a bound at a preferred rate. Borrowing above the limit would be at a penal rate. The interest rate for rediscounting would be fixed by the CB. Bank and money market rates for financing would be at a premium over the rate on eligible paper. The volume of bank holdings of eligible paper may decrease because of a decline in the borrowing needs of business, dramatically during a depression. A depression, however, cannot occur with the large deficits that come into play during a downturn. The deficit means that financial markets have to absorb government securities. As private debt decreases, banks are fully invested in government debt. Once banks acquire government debt, the government bonds market is an effective position-making market. When banks are purchasing government paper and the CB desires a rapid growth in reserves, it can increase the resource base by buying government bills from the market. When commercial banks rely on the discount window for a large portion of their reserve position, the CB is concerned with everyday banking matters with member banks. As long as banks value this source of funds, they will conform to business and balance-sheet norms laid down by the monetary authority. In euphoric times, the central bank can impel banks to hedge-finance business. The discount technique is a member of the set of general credit controls that presupposes that markets function efficiently to deliver the expected outcomes. Less well known are selective credit controls that would predispose the CB to act in a discriminatory way. One such device is the Asset Required Reserve Proposal (ARRP) (Kempey, 1997). The device works in the following way. At present, required reserves are held as liabilities by banks. The ARRP would shift this entry to the assets side of the balance sheet of a bank. In other words, required reserves would nestle with the loans and investments of a bank. By so doing, the CB would impact on various credit flows in the system while changing the money supply. For instance, a bank would be encouraged to lend for a gender-sensitive project by the CB creating a negative required reserve on such loans. In general, the use of differential required reserves on the assets portfolio of banks could be used to redirect credit from socially undesirable ends to more productive sectors.

A policy regime must lengthen time horizons as well as reduce the pull of speculative finance. It will be successful if it reduces the conflict of interest between industrial and financial capital and counterbalances the elements that weaken the effects of expansionary fiscal and monetary policy. Investments propelled by the accelerator effects of expansionary policies would be channeled more and more towards investments with high social rates of return and away from asset transfers that consume paper but do not increase output and income. The 'speculative leakage' of expansionary policy would fall thereby. Greater accountability within the financial system would weaken the power of financial capitalists. In turn, this would dispel the bias against expansionary policies.

CONCLUSION

Institutional diversity is increasing in economies and we have made the case for incorporating gender in the consideration of the allocation of decision-making and the organization of the labour market. The introduction would have the salutary effect of extending the notion of the economic agent to more than the propensity to truck, barter and exchange. Thus, to the query "who pays for the kids?" might be appended "what happens when the kids get sick? Who stays home from work?" Institutional arrangements are a bridge from the micro to the macro and back since they operate at an intermediate level between actors and the economic system viewed from a general level. In an endemically flawed macroeconomic system, there is considerable scope for coherent, improving State intervention. At the same time, policy variables should be appraised from the point of view of their disaggregated, differential impacts. Gender is an important dimension along which this evaluation must take place.

REFERENCES

Boschini, Anne (2004) "Engendering Macroeconomics", Lecture Notes, Department of Economics, Stockholm University, pp. 1-10

Boyer, Robert (2003) "Is régulation theory an original theory of economic institutions?" in: Boyer, Robert and Yves Saillard (eds) *Régulation Theory: The state of the art*, eds, Robert Boyer and Yves Saillard, London: Routledge, pp. 320-333

Bussemaker, Jet and Kees van Kersbergen (1999) "Contemporary Social-Capitalist Welfare States and Gender Inequality," in Diane Sainsbury, (ed.) *Gender and Welfare State Regimes*, Oxford: Oxford University Press, pp. 15-46

Çagatay, Nilufer (2003) "Engendering Macro-Economics", in Martha Gutiérrez, (ed.) *Macro-Economics: Making Gender Matter*, London: Zed Books, pp. 22-41.

Casson, Mark and Marina Della Giusta (2004) "The Costly Business of Trust", *Development Policy Review*, Vol. 22, no. 3, pp. 321-342.

Correa, Romar (2003) Book Review: "Money Matters (Not Only, But Also)", *Journal of Quantitative Economics*, Vol. 1, no. 1, pp. 165-167.

—— (2005A) Brahmanada, Chakravarty, Sen: A Golden Braid, in: *Founding Fathers of Indian Political Economy*, ed., D.M. Nachane, Mumbai: Himalaya Publishing House, pp. 208-215.

—— (2005B) "Financial Institutions, in: Issues in Financial Economics", B. Bhattacharya and M. Roy, (eds) Kolkata, Allied Publishers, pp. 97-114.

Danby, Colin (2004) "Toward a Gendered Post Keynesianism: Subjectivity and Time in a nonModernist Framework", *Feminist Economics*, Vol. 10, no. 3, pp. 55-75.

Ebert, Terese L. (2005) "Rematerializing Feminism", *Science & Society*, Vol. 20, no. 1, pp. 33-55.

Evers, Barbara (2003) "Broadening the Foundations of Macro-Economic Models through a Gender Approach: New Developments", in Martha Gutiérrez, (ed.) *Macro-Economics: Making Gender Matter*, London: Zed Books, pp. 3-21.

Elson, Diane (1998) "Talking to the boys: gender and economic growth models", in Cecile Jackson and Ruth Pearson, (eds) *Feminist Visions of Development*, London, Routledge, pp. 155-170.

Folbre, Nancy and Julie A. Nelson, "For Love or Money—Or Both?" in Ellen Mutari and Deborah M. Figart, (eds), *Women and the Economy*, New York: M.E. Sharpe, pp. 108-123.

Frey, Bruno S. and Alois Stutzer (2005) "Beyond outcomes: measuring procedural utility", *Oxford Economic Papers*, Vol. 57, no. 1, pp. 90-111.

Gibbons, Robert S. (2004) "Organization", *New England Economic Review*, Federal Bank of Boston, First Quarter, pp. 18-21.

Gimenez, Martha (2005) "Capitalism and the Oppression of Women: Marx Revisited", *Science & Society*, Vol. 69, no. 1, pp. 11-32.

Hildenbrand, Werner and Alois Kneip (2005) "On Behavioural Heterogeneity", *Economic Theory*, Vol. 25, no. 1, pp. 155-169.

Ingham, Geoffrey (2004) *The Nature of Money*, Cambridge: Polity Press.

Kempey, William M. (1997) "General vs. selective credit controls: the Asset Required Reserve Proposal", in Robin Bartlett, (ed.) *Introducing Race and Gender into Economics*, London: Routledge, pp. 121-124.

Mastracci Sharon M. (2005) "Persistent Problems Demand Consistent Solutions: Evaluating Policies to Mitigate Occupational Segregation" by Gender, *Review of Radical Political Economics*, Vol. 37, no. 1, pp. 23-38.

O'Connor, Julia S., Ann Shola Orloff and Sheila Shaver (1999) *States, Markets, Families*, Cambridge: Cambridge University Press.

Pressman, Steven (2003) "Institutionalism", in J.E. King, Cheltenham: Edward Elgar, (eds) *The Elgar Companion to Post Keynesan Economics*, pp. 196-200.

Sainsbury, Diane (1999) "Gender and Social-Democratic Welfare States", in Diane Sainsbury, (ed.) *Gender and Welfare State Regimes*, Oxford: Oxford University Press, pp. 75-114.

Smith, Vernon (2004) "On human nature", *Daedalus*, pp. 67-76.

Tsakalotos, Euclid (2004) "*Homo Economicus*, Political Economy and Socialism", *Science & Society*, Vol. 68, no. 2, pp. 137-160.

Wigfield, Andrea (2001) *Post-Fordism, Gender and Work*, Aldershot: Ashgate.

Indian Taxation Systems and Policies

A Gendered Critique

RITU DEWAN

I. INTRODUCTION

The issue of engendering macroeconomic theories and policies has assumed special significance in recognition of the differential impact of theoretical and policy perspectives. Fairly substantial research has proven that macroeconomic constructs and policies are not gender neutral. Additionally, it is accepted that gender inequalities at micro and meso levels have macro implications, there being a clear two-way interconnection.

However, the polemics as well as the conceptual analysis of gendered inter-linkages particularly in underdeveloped countries are still in the formative stage, as are interconnected methodological issues. The dominant development paradigm today perceives a nation's goal to be growth combined with rise in per capita incomes, while the basic issues of distribution and equality are given relatively less importance. Gender analysis is thus, of necessity, fully and tightly integrated with broader issues of equity and egalitarianism, patriarchy being perceived as part of an inherently unequal society and not as an 'external' or 'social' issue; by denying this integration we would reaffirm and hence reinforce the marginalisation of women.

The 'Keynesian Consensus' which focused on the role of the State, particularly in distribution, has been replaced by the 'Washington Consensus' emphasizing privatization, liberalization, deregulation, and also reduction of the fiscal deficit. While not implying that the situation was much better earlier, it is widely accepted that this shift has led not only to reduction of social sector expenditures but also reorientation of fiscal policies. Simultaneously, economic restructuring has altered the balance of economic power both between and within developed as well as underdeveloped nations, negatively affecting labour and especially the property-less, the majority of whom are women (see Cagatay, 2003, pp. 15-17).

Taxation systems impact disposable incomes, prices of production inputs, and consumer goods, their consequences hence affect major economic and also extra-economic decisions (see Barnett and Grown, 2004, p. 20). This interconnection operates more significantly in underdeveloped countries where poverty levels are higher and where women are less empowered. Equality thus cannot be perceived in 'formal' terms, but rather must imply substantive equality, particularly in relation to the dominance of the fact that women produce tradables as well as non-tradables not only as informal sector workers but also unpaid family workers.

It is quite surprising that while somewhat substantial analysis has been done focusing on expenditure components, examination of taxation structures and resultant fiscal policies have been quite under-studied. In fact, although some gendered evaluation has been attempted in the international sphere, the gendered implications of India's tax structure and policies are yet to be investigated, and this in spite of the fact that own-source revenues are the fulcrum of the on-going public debate on governmental provisioning and pricing of services. Consequently, the fundamental focus in this essay is primarily on an examination of gender biases explicitly and implicitly inherent in both the theoretical underpinnings and empirics of taxation systems and policies, in the hope that the emerging recommendations in the context of Indian reality will be considered with deserved seriousness.

However, it needs to be specified here that as several of these inter-relationships are being investigated for the first time, especially in the Indian context, it would be presumptuous to assert that all components can be investigated in a short essay. Additionally, at several levels it might be sufficient at this point of time, to identify tentative interconnections and possibilities, rather than to provide 'the' final word and hence a 'complete' solution.

The differential impact of taxation structures and policies needs to be necessarily located in the national pattern of changes in the composition of taxes during the last decade since the implementation of the process of globalisation. Section II therefore gives a short background of the trends in composition of tax revenues in India; it must be noted that obviously a detailed trend analysis is not only beyond the scope of this paper but also would divert from the primary focus. Section III examines illustrations of inherent explicit and implicit gender biases in selected Direct Taxes, while Section IV focuses on the single major form of Indirect tax today—Value Added Tax or VAT—which was introduced in most states of India in the fiscal year 2005-06. The concluding section identifies additional gendered aspects related to taxation structures, and, linking up with a theoretical critique of the fundamentals of tax regimes and policies, attempts to put forward selected recommendations in the specific context of an underdeveloped country like India.

II. TRENDS IN COMPOSITION OF TAX REVENUES IN INDIA

The entire debate has to be necessarily located within the context of the process of tax reforms in India particularly since the early nineties after the initiation of the structural adjustment programme and the subsequent increased focus on the fiscal deficit. Herein will be presented an overview of the pattern of changes in the composition of India's tax revenues over the last decade; the focus will of course be on central sources of revenue, inclusion of state-level data being not entirely necessary for the purpose of this essay.

It has been estimated that although Central Government Taxes as share of India's GDP declined by over a percentage point from 10.4 per cent in 1989-90 to 9.2 per cent in 2003-04, the composition has undergone a significant change with the share of Direct Taxes almost doubling from 2 to 3.8 per cent, and Indirect

Taxes declining from 8.4 to 5.4 per cent. Apparently, the former have risen dramatically from 19.3 to 41.4 per cent, the latter obviously showing an opposite trend 80.7 to 58.6 per cent (Acharya, 2005, Table 3, p. 2065).

However, as can be seen from Graph 1 (see Appendix I: Shares of Sources of Total Central Revenue Receipts: India: 1990-91 to 2003-04), our data differ on some grounds, in that Direct Taxes remain at exactly the same share of 22 per cent after more than a decade, with Indirect Taxes which had shown quite a dramatic decline from 65 per cent to 45 per cent over the last decade, now increasing again. It must be noted here that it is a well-known and accepted fact that Indirect Taxes are more regressive, primarily as the poor—the majority of them women—typically spend a higher proportion of their income on food than the rich do.

While the overall trend is not being negated and we do not deny the fact that the pattern of tax composition seen purely in terms of Direct versus Indirect Taxes is somewhat more equitable today than it was a decade ago, what is debatable is whether the level of equity attained is significant and engendered enough. We give two illustrations of increased gendered inequality in the context of perceived improvement in macro equity levels.

One example of a rise in gender inequality can be perceived from the fact that the rupee value of 'Social and Community Services' as Non-Tax Revenue increased from Rs 377.6 crores in 1990-91 to Rs. 9447.4 in 2001-02. The implication is obvious—a rise in user fees directly and negatively impacts the health of the poor, especially women who are already discriminated against in terms of nutrition, mortality and morbidity.

We came across a quite unexpected and intriguing impact of macroeconomic policy on women during a field-based project conducted last year. Fares of Maharashtra's State Transport buses have increased as a result of the toll imposed after completion of several World Bank-funded road projects. We 'discovered' the gendered impact in Gandhinagar village which is located in the district of Yawatmal. As employment opportunities are low even in the peak season, workers are compelled to migrate on a daily basis to the urban headquarters. With the rise in return bus fares to Rs 16.50, and the prevailing low wages of approximately Rs 40 per day for men and merely Rs 18-20 for women, it obviously becomes quite impossible to even travel in search of employment. Rise in user fees as a source of state revenue thus effectively reduced wages to Rs 23.50 for men, and merely Rs 1.50-2.00 for women. Consequently, the entire state and district highway is crowded every morning with small groups of daily migrant workers trying to hitch rides on trucks, paying drivers Rs 5 each. In the context of existing gender-based wage differences, men thus earn Rs 35 and women Rs 15-20 by avoiding the use of the Maharashtra State Road Transport Corporation which is now going into losses, and may possibly be closed down as in the state of Madhya Pradesh.

Additionally, women, having to leave only after household chores, are obviously not accompanied by males. These women-only groups are invariably taken advantage of by the truck drivers, who insist they all sit crowded in the front cabin. Macro infrastructural policies implemented somewhat blindly in a patriarchal society that is characterised by gender-based labour and wage differentials have thus had the 'unforeseen' effect of institutionalising violence against women (see Dewan, 2003, pp. 48; 52-53).

As an offshoot it must be noted that with the current Reserve Bank of India rules that granting additional loans to revenue-deficit states will be decided on a case-to-case basis, some regions are compelled to access high-conditionality debt from multilateral international agencies. Also, as it is the states that are primarily responsible for public outlays which affect basic infrastructure, health, education, etc, "these expenditures have been very adversely affected in most parts of India" (Ghosh, 2005, pp. 3435). The issue is not that of opposing regulation, but of reassessing centre-state fiscal relations. Another criticism relating to the latest spate of tax reforms in India is that the Twelfth Finance Commission has ignored "the saving-generating impact of investment in an economy where rural and informal sectors are characterised by considerable underutilisation of resources even while the formal sector may not have much slack. . ." (Rakshit, 2005, p. 3448).

III. DIRECT TAXES

We begin by examining gender biases in Direct Taxes as they are more easily identifiable, analysis being based primarily on the Indian reality, while also drawing upon international experience. The taxes dealt with include Personal Income Tax and Corporation Tax, the three taxes relating to Wealth, Gift, and Property being examined separately as a group.

Before making a detailed analysis of each identified source of revenue, it is essential to capture their trends and shares in the composition of Direct Taxes (see Appendix II: Graph 2: Shares of Central Direct Taxes, India: 1990-91 to 2003-04). The share of Personal Income Tax to total has more than doubled over the last thirteen years, this increase making up for the decline in Corporation Taxes. The other three we are analysing contribute virtually nothing to the Central Revenue today.

Personal Income Tax

The most explicit form of gender bias exists in the Personal Income Tax (PIT) as it can be applicable on either individual or family basis, and can hence determine not only the taxpayer but also differential allocations of rates, deductions, and exemptions. It must be noted, however, that PIT is obviously relevant only in the formal sector, where a small proportion—8 per cent—of the total workforce in India is employed. Also, the informal sector accounts for 95 per cent of all women workers in the country, their share of organized sector employment thus being even less.

The basis of tax structures becomes crucial in relation to the impact it has on women's labour supply. Under joint taxation, the greater the difference between the spouses' incomes, the higher will the woman's earned income be taxed, and the less beneficial it will be for her to participate in 'gainful' employment in the labour market. This factor is compounded by the prevalence of the backward-bending supply curve after a certain threshold of income is attained, this threshold being determined by the location of the specific household in the system of production and reproduction. Additionally, the foundation of the chosen tax regime at the macro level and also the 'ideal' threshold income level determined at the meso and micro levels are closely intertwined in the specific context of the predominant notion that the woman is 'normally' a secondary earner. Furthermore, it is obvious that such gender-blind structures and policies do not recognize the existence of a fairly substantial number of female-headed households.

An indirect effect of this type of taxation policy is to "create a disincentive for parents and employers, as well as girls and women themselves, to make investments in women's education. As a result, the perception of women as having low 'skills' and thus low 'productivity' is perpetuated" (Floro, 2001, p. 78).

Individual taxation is preferred because the economic benefit of working depends on how much a woman earns and not the fact of her location in the patriarchal marital structure. Tax structures and policies may thus increase her incentive to take up employment and shift her labour supply curve. Additionally, taxes can also stimulate a woman's participation in the labour market if they are linked to the creation of a social infrastructure such as childcare (see Lofstrom, 2001, pp. 12-13). An independent status as a taxpayer can also strengthen her negotiating position and participation in decision making within the household.

It is in this specific context that the declining role of the State, resulting from the initiation of economic reforms, has to be viewed. Public sector activities benefit women in two ways. "Firstly their possibilities of participating in working life (the public sector provides most of the services women depend on to be able to take gainful employment]. And secondly the supply of jobs increases [both in public and private sectors) and thus the demand for female labour increases. In countries where the activity level among women is high, the proportion of people employed in activities such as education, social services, health and medical care and public administration is also high and vice versa" (Lofstrom, 2001, pp. 13-14).

The impact of gender biases in PIT can be most clearly explained in the context of the South African experience. Till 1995 the income of a married woman was included with that of her husband who alone could file the tax; this combined income thus placed them in a higher tax bracket. Also, women were taxed at different rates as, unlike men, they were classified into one of three categories—'married person', 'married woman' or 'unmarried person'. The highest tax rates applied to 'married women' except when they were the main earners; on the other hand married men who were categorized as 'persons' paid the least. Thus, "taking the extra tax off the woman's income . . . implicitly reduce(ed) her power insofar as money gives power" (Smith, 2000, pp. 10-11). This gender discrimination was abolished with the introduction of a single income tax rate structure applicable to all individuals irrespective of gender or marital status.

Some other international illustrations of reduction in gender biases in PIT include the following

- *France: 1983*: both spouses are now required to sign family tax returns instead of only the husband. Earlier, the wife did not have an independent existence as a taxpayer.
- *The Netherlands: 1984:* equal basic tax allowance replaced the erstwhile higher tax allowance granted to a married man than to a married woman.
- *Britain: 1990*: earlier joint tax could be submitted only in the husband's name, with the wife not being recognized as an independent taxpayer.
- *Malaysia: 1991:* husbands and wives are now treated as separate taxable units with an option for joint treatment, instead of the earlier system where the income of a married woman was attributed to her husband unless she elected separate assessment.
- *Ireland: 1993*: individual taxation as well as an option for the wife to be the 'primary taxpayer' was introduced instead of the erstwhile compulsory joint filing in the name of the husband with choice for separate assessment on labour income (see Stotsky, 1997, pp. 30-31).

It is a given that the marginal utility of income is much more at lower than at higher income levels, the added value of an additional rupee to a poorer person thus implying a much greater effect on income than to those who are richer. This effect is almost always reduced by a progressive income tax system in which marginal tax rates are lower for lower income earners (see also Smith, 2000, p. 9). It is in this broader context that tax systems and issues of feminisation lead to deeper impact on women's income and welfare. And this is precisely why one of the major recommendations we make is to raise exemption limits for single women especially those with dependents and also children who are studying.

Divergent tax rates paid by men and women are further compounded by the existence of gender-based differentials which characterize all economies, particularly those that are underdeveloped, through primarily unequal pay, unequal work, unequal opportunities, and unequal access to opportunities including ownership of productive resources.

The difference in taxes paid by men and women is quite large, given the fact that more men than women are 'regular' employees and hence taxpayers. Amongst the 39.82 lakh persons employed in the Central government in India, women account for 7.43 per cent. However, in this connection it must be noted that the rate of growth of women employed as Central government workers has been declining over time; their share to the total which had almost doubled from 3.5 per cent in 1980 to 7.5 per cent a decade later, began declining in 1991 following the introduction of economic reforms (CSO, 2002, p. 59).

Even so, reduction in gender biases currently contained in PIT would affect a not insignificant number of not only the 300,000 women working at the Centre, but also obviously several lakh times over if the other sectors of 'regular' work are included such as State and semi-state levels, financial institutions, private companies, panchayats, etc. where labour and other related laws are implemented.

Women in India have the choice of filing returns either individually or jointly. The joint option is applicable primarily under the Hindu Undivided Family (HUF), a category that covers four communities—Hindus, Jains, Sikhs, and Buddhists. Under the HUF, the eldest male has the power to file returns for the entire extended family which consists of all other men, their wives, and also unmarried women. HUF's are given several exemptions that are not available to other religious communities including Muslims and Christians who constitute a significant proportion of India's population.

Additionally, the perception of the HUF as a social unit not only ignores but also negates issues of social relationships and dependency in a patriarchal society (see Barnet and Grown, pp. 30-31) It is important to point out that the application of the family as a tax paying unit presumes that information on households is readily available, and also that levels of household well-being are clearly defined.

Wealth Tax, Gift Tax, and Property Tax

In this sub-section we deal with three taxes relating to Wealth, Gift, and Property, all of which have strong gender connotations. Considering the concentration of wealth in the hands of a few, it should make greater economic and egalitarian sense that Wealth and Gift taxes in particular be increased, with higher amounts being taxed severely. However, the process seems to be quite the opposite in India.

While Wealth Tax decreased from Rs 231 crores in 1990-91 to Rs 91 crores a decade later, with a small rise in the last two years, Gift Tax fell from Rs 15 crores in 1994-95 to obviously nil today (finmin.nic).

It is generally accepted that Gifts are a source for large-scale tax evasion, and it was to plug this loophole that the Gift Tax as well as the Wealth Tax were introduced way back in 1957. However, the former was abolished in 1997 on the ground that its revenue potential is low. In 2004, a 'major' loophole was plugged, and accordingly, "purported gifts from unrelated persons, above the threshold limit of Rs 25,000, (will) now be taxed as income. Gifts received from blood relations, lineal ascendants and lineal descendants, and gifts received on certain occasions such as marriage will continue to be totally exempt" (Budget Speech, 2004-05, para. 102). The gendered connotation of this alteration in the Gift Tax is clear—that there need not be any tax-related 'problems' where dowry is concerned. In this sense, therefore, the implications are two-fold—one, that dowry is actually encouraged, and two, that dowry can be continued to be treated as 'women's share in property'.

It is in this context that the issue of women as 'property-less' assumes significance. While not going into greater detail, it is important to point out significant drawbacks of existing laws which impact tax policies, now sought to be removed by the Hindu Succession (Amendment) Act 2005 which has been passed recently:

- Under Section 23, the daughter cannot claim any share by partition in a 'dwelling house' until male members chose to divide the share.
- The same Section denies a married daughter the right of residence in the parental home unless she is widowed, divorced, deserted or separated.
- Women do not get fair share of the revenue generated from devolution of tenancies.
- If a Hindu woman dies intestate, her husband's heirs have the first right to her property, and then her father-in-law's heirs. Her mother's heirs are granted rights only when the woman's 'married' home absolves its share.

However, it must be noted that land is a 'state' subject, and a mere five regions have amended some of these gender biases—Maharashtra, Andhra Pradesh, Tamil Nadu and Karnataka. Further, only Kerala has totally abolished the right to property by males and eliminated the Hindu Joint family system and that too way back in 1975; the significance of this abolition lies in the already examined fact that the Hindu Undivided Family (HUF) is the tax unit wherein gender biases can exist fairly explicitly.

The state of Delhi has recently introduced a gender-differentiated Property Tax—6 per cent for women and 8 per cent for men, with women being given an additional benefit of a 30 per cent rebate. While it is too soon to assess the impact of this, it is possible at this stage to assert that the transfer of property to women in order to avail of these tax concessions could create the basis of economically empowering them, especially in case separation is sought wherein the eternal problem of alternate accommodation would not prove to be a major issue.

Corporation Tax

The gendered impact of Corporation Tax depends on several factors, primarily containing an implicit bias. At one level, it is argued that a reduction would boost both growth and job creation, as not only the national corporate sector but also foreign capital would be provided incentives for increased investment. On the other hand, mopping up of increased revenue by raising rates could have positive economic and distributive effects if invested by the Government in appropriate sectors.

Reduction in Corporate Tax does not benefit women in large companies, as few are either owners or even shareholders. Further, women in medium and small companies would gain only to the extent to which they are employers, and few are. In India the majority of small-scale industries have been converted to captive units of large local and multinational companies, and hence will not and do not benefit from Corporate Tax decreases (see Dewan, 2005). Analysis of the gendered impact of Corporate Tax thus is closely connected to the 'propertylessness' of women.

However, if we presume that private capital does invest its now-raised share of profits, it becomes necessary to examine which sectors are impacted. The first aspect to investigate is whether investment takes place in capital-intensive or labour-intensive industries. Also, in which specific sub-sector does investment occur. If in the readymade garment industry in India where the majority of workers are women, then women would benefit; if in quarrying, manufacturing, etc., then men would benefit. Taxation analysis thus also needs to include Preferential sectoral taxes in the context of prevailing gender-based employment and hence consumption patterns. This sector-wise impact emerges as one of the most crucial areas of further research particularly in the Indian situation.

Corporation Tax in India has been steadily declining as a proportion to Direct Taxes, from 77.3 per cent in 1990-91 to 51.5 per cent a decade later, a small 4 per cent rise emerging in the last two years. However, with the lowering of this tax to 30 per cent from this fiscal beginning April 1, 2005, its share is expected to decline even further. As noted earlier, it is generally argued that reductions in Corporation Tax will increase employment opportunities.

This has proven to be quite the opposite in the most industrially advanced state of Maharashtra, with more jobs being lost than created in the last ten years, the major reasons being closures, lockouts, 'rationalisation', etc. In spite of a large number of revenue and other concessions granted to especially foreign private capital and also local industries in Maharashtra, more than 27,000 small-scale units and 1215 medium and large industries were closed down within a short span of four years from 1998-99 to 2002, displacing over 2.8 lakh workers (Dewan, 2005, p.29). The issue thus is whether the revenue lost in Corporate Tax concessions could not have been of greater benefit if it had instead been utilised to benefit the poor and especially women (see Smith, 2000, p. 19).

IV. INDIRECT TAXES

We focus on the single most important tax today—Value Added Tax—which has been implemented in most states of India from April 1, 2005. Before going further into analysis, it should be noted that although VAT is currently operative in 130 countries, it has historically been implemented in economies where three factors prevail—a high GDP per capita, low dependence on international trade, and existence of a unitary system of government.

As the implementation of VAT in India began barely half a fiscal year ago (at the time of writing), it is obviously too soon to be able to conduct a detailed analysis; we thus focus on theoretical issues, additionally incorporating international experience. Also, while it is out of the purview of this paper to explain all components of VAT, we will present the main salient features.

VAT rates are uniform across states so that prices of goods do not differ. While the prices of some commodities will go up and some may fall, the exact impact will differ depending on the level of erstwhile taxes. VAT is a progressive form of sales tax under the indirect tax umbrella, covering all businesses including importers, manufacturers, distributors, wholesalers, retailers, work contractors and lessors. The objective is to avoid 'cascading', which can have a snowballing effect on prices. It is assumed that due to cross-checking in a multi-staged tax, evasion will be checked, resulting in higher revenues to the government. VAT is—

- A general tax applicable to all commercial activities involving production and distribution of goods, and the provision of services.
- A consumption tax as it is borne ultimately by the final consumer. It is not a charge on businesses.
- Charged as a percentage of price, which means that the actual tax burden is visible at each stage in the production and distribution chain.
- Collected fractionally, via a system of partial payments whereby taxable persons (i.e., VAT-registered businesses) deduct from the VAT they have collected the amount of tax they have paid to other taxable persons on purchases for their business activities.
- Paid to the revenue authorities by the seller of the goods, who is the "taxable person", but it is actually paid by the buyer to the seller as part of the price.

Commodity taxes alter the relative prices of taxed and untaxed goods, and hence transform individual and household decisions about consumption, as well as production and investment decisions. VAT in particular is quite regressive as it has a greater anti-women and anti-poor impact, given the fact that these sections typically spend a larger proportion of their income on basic consumption goods that richer households do; low earners therefore pay a higher average tax rate. Also, VAT is almost always inflationary, as increased taxes are passed on to consumers at every level through the entire chain.

Experience from South Africa reveals that VAT places a heavy burden on labour-intensive firms as compared to capital-intensive ones. This is basically because the ratio of value-added to the sale price is lower for the latter. Also, small producers and traders tend to face high compliance costs, as they lack not only capital, but also human resources and skills including such basic ones as literacy. This is true particularly of women who have higher illiteracy levels than men do.

The long-term implications of VAT thus have to be carefully examined in the specific context of a labour surplus economy where employment rates, particularly for women, are highly differentiated, as are wages and conditions of work. This issue becomes especially significant in economies where the informal sector is both predominant and gendered. One aspect that needs to be urgently examined is whether it is more cost-effective to self-produce or to sub-contract.

In the state of Maharashtra, VAT replaces four legislations

i. The Bombay Sales Tax Act
ii. The Maharashtra Sales Tax Act (Transfer of Right to Use any Goods for Any Purpose)
iii. The Maharashtra Sales Tax (Transfer of Property in Goods Involved in Execution of Works Contract) Act
iv. The Bombay Sales of Motor Spirit Taxation Act.

Gender biases in VAT—as in all consumption taxes—manifest themselves in several ways, including through the choice of commodities and services covered, as well as the different consumption patterns of men and women. We examine the gendered impacts of a few selected commodities specifically applicable in Maharashtra.

Foodgrains, as of now, are zero-based, but only up to the end of the current (at the time of writing) fiscal year. Imposition of VAT on processed wheat, however, can directly impact women, the bias thus not being 'implicit'. Women, as 'carers', may now be compelled to purchase grains, and increase their time spent on 'unproductive' activity. Similarly, a rise in taxes on kerosene combined with reduced subsidies, directly affects the time use pattern of women. Thus increases the 'reproductive' tax that the woman has to pay to the economy as a direct result of change in taxation policies.

Imposition of VAT on Soya and Soya flour seems to be not merely unfair but heartless given the fact that the state has witnessed a spate of droughts over the last six years, with several hundreds of farmers committing suicide. On the contrary, not only should agriculture be declared VAT-free, targeted subsidies should be increased at both the regional and national levels on par with those given in the developed countries. The impact would not only be pro-poor, but also pro-women given three specific facts—that the majority of the population in India is employed in agriculture; that most women are employed in this sector, and that the rate of urbanization has been slowing down since the last decade.

Inexplicably, Maharashtra has exempted certain commodities like petroleum products, lottery tickets, and alcohol. In this connection, it is crucial to recall the anti-liquor movement launched by women in the state of Andhra Pradesh. The main issues highlighted by this statewide struggle were that a significant proportion of family income, particularly of the poor, is spent by men on alcohol thus reducing consumption levels, and that intake directly resulted in increases in domestic violence. As a result of the movement, which gained international attention, alcohol was banned. However, within a short span of time the state government withdrew the ban on the ground that the loss of revenue had led to increased fiscal deficit.

V. POLICY RECOMMENDATIONS

It is difficult to present a formal 'conclusion' or a 'complete' list of recommendations at this point of time in analysis, given that no detailed study has yet been conducted. What we do instead is to point out specific and explicit amendments that need to be made somewhat urgently and can be implemented relatively easily in the Indian context. We have additionally linked up with several other gender biases that are also operative in both perception and policy, and explain them in some detail, before critiquing the fundamentals of the dominant tax regime currently prevalent.

Evaluation of tax policies is generally based on simplicity, vertical and horizontal equity, and neutrality. Normative values also come into play by the inclusion of other functions of a tax system such as economic stabilisation, income redistribution, regulation, and reduction of inequalities. Consequently, a gendered as well as an economically ethical evaluation must of necessity be based additionally on normative values including the fundamental concept of 'ability to pay' (versus benefit principle) particularly in relation to the fact that the debate today in India is increasingly centred around the appropriate degree of tax progressivity (vertical equity) and the 'benefit principle' (user fees).

Gender issues come more strongly into play in several other situations that characterise underdeveloped countries—in relation to defining 'secondary' workers; in the calculation of 'marginal' earners; in single parent families, and particularly in relation to the growing numbers of female-headed households.

The efficiency of a tax system is generally based on the social welfare function which states that the desired revenue and social objectives should be achieved through minimal distortions to individual and business decisions. This method which focuses purely on the market economy, however, has been criticised on several grounds both by mainstream and feminist economists (see Barnett and Grown, 2004, pp.23-24; also, Dewan, 1999; Elson, 1999). We add some of our own points of criticism.

1. Utilities cannot be individually calculated, standardised and then socially collated, the more so in a society that is inherently unequal and patriarchal. The 'greater common good' thus does not imply a collection of 'individual' goods.
2. Non-market time is not leisure for a man and especially not for a woman particularly in economies that are underdeveloped.
3. The current fundamentals of most tax structures negate income-saving and income-augmenting activities that men and particularly women perform in their struggle for survival in economies and also sectors based on 'mere' subsistence.
4. Tax regimes do not recognise nor include the economic contribution made by non-market and extra-market activities which again are performed mainly by women.
5. State withdrawal resulting from the implementation of economic 'reforms' transfer costs from the paid to the unpaid economy, which is deeply gender-segregated.
6. Excluded from any kind of theoretical perspective and hence

policy intervention are 'care' and reproductive activities which contain shadow-economic as well as societal value.

7. Both economic and productive values are not included in public services, even though most women who are 'regular' employees not only work in but also benefit from these sectors.
8. And, ultimately and most fundamentally, tax structures and policies omit even the possibility that fiscal policies can enhance societal and gender equity.

Our recommendations therefore are:

1. Increase in Personal Income Tax exemption limits especially for female-headed households.
2. Increase in Personal Income Tax exemption limits also for those with dependents.
3. Introduction of child-care exemptions under Personal Income Tax.
4. Abolition of Hindu Undivided Family as the basis for filing tax returns.
5. Tax Exemptions for Self Help Groups and Women's Cooperatives.
6. Regulation of Medical Insurance policies: The issue of Medical Deductions and their applications are not regulated by a uniform policy, as we discovered on interviewing two of the largest companies. Consequently, different insurance companies and even different branches of the same company within the same city impose their own rules such as not permitting single women to include their parents in family schemes; the fact that single households pay the same rates as those applicable to entire families; etc. The gender component is quite clear in that women are more likely to have higher medical expenses than men because of additional problems related to reproduction.
7. Policies on Pensions and Post-retirement benefits: The present policy on Pensions is currently quite severely biased against single-headed households, whether male or female. Pensions and other recurring post-retirement benefits cannot be willed or transferred upon death to a non-spouse, not even to dependent parents. While this explicit

bias against single persons exists against both men and women, it is clearly more anti-women in the context of the fact that marriage for women over a certain age 'barrier' is generally not possible, and also as re-marriage is still not socially accepted. Compounding this anti-women stance is the fact that few women have opportunities to become full-time workers and that too in the formal sector where retirement benefits and tax subsidisation policies are operative. The issue of pensions is emerging as increasingly significant in the Indian context as it is now sought to be applied to the informal sector.

8. Another fiscal policy measure that would benefit women significantly is that of granting tax exemptions to Self-Help Groups and also women-managed NGOs. SHGs are today one of the most important aspects of the nation's empowerment policy, while NGOs are increasingly taking over welfare responsibility in the context of State withdrawal after the introduction of economic reforms. At the same time, major exemptions and tax holidays given to Export Promotion Zones not only result in heavy revenue loss, but also favour capital against labour. Thus, it makes sense not only for redistributive justice but also for also economic growth and empowerment to grant women, the majority of whom are poor, at least some concessions.

REFERENCES

Acharya, Shankar (2005) 'Thirty Years of Tax Reform in India', in *Economic and Political Weekly*, Vol. XL No. 20, May 14, pp. 2061-2070.

Barnett, Kathleen and Caren Grown (2004) *Gender Impacts of Government Revenue Collection: The Case of Taxation*, London: Commonwealth Secretariat.

Budget Speech of Finance Minister, 2005-06.

Cagatay, Nilufer (2003) 'Gender Budgets and Beyond: Feminist Fiscal Policy in the context of Globalisation', in *Gender and Development*, Vol. 11, No. 1, May, pp. 15-24.

CSO (2002) *Men and Women in India*, Ministry of Statistics and Programme Implementation, Government of India.

Dewan, Ritu (1999) 'Gender Implications of the 'New' Economic Policy: A

Conceptual Overview', in *Women's Studies International Forum*, Vol. 22, No. 4, Elsevier Science, Pergamon.

—— (2003) *Strategies for Survival in Underdeveloped Maharashtra: Livelihoods in Yawatmal, Jalna, Nadurbar,* Maharashtra Human Development Action Research Study—a UNDP publication.

—— (2005) '*Gender Budget Perspectives on Policies in Small Scale Urban Manufacturies in Greater Mumbai,* Discussion Paper Series—12, HDRC-UNDP, UNDP, April.

Floro, Maria (2001) '*Gender Dimensions of the Financing for Development Agenda*', Working Paper, UNIFEM.

Freiler, Christa, Felicite Stairs and Brigitte Kitchen with Judy Cerny (2001) '*Mothers as Earners, Mothers as Carers: Responsibility for Children, Social Policy and the Tax System*'. Status of Women Canada, Ottawa, Ontario.

Ghosh, J (2005) 'Twelfth Finance Commission and Restructuring of State Government Debt: A Note'. In *Economic and Political Weekly*, Vol. XL No. 31, July 30, pp. 3435-3439.

Government of India (2001) '*Report of the Expert Group on Taxation of Services*' *(Govinda Rao Committee)*. New Delhi: Ministry of Finance.

Karnik, A. (2005) 'Impressive Grandstanding but Empty Coffers,' in *Economic and Political Weekly*, Vol. XL No. 14, April 2-8, pp. 1406-1409.

Lofstrom, Asa (2001) 'A Report on Gender Equality and Economic Growth', Department of Economics, UMEA University, Stockholm (downloaded).

Rakshit, Mihir (2005) 'Some Analytics and Empirics of Fiscal Restructuring in India', in *Economic and Political Weekly*, Vol. XL No.31, July 30, pp. 3440-3448.

Ramanujam, M et. Al. (eds) (1998) *Employment Promotion in the Urban Employment Sector*, New Delhi: New Age International Publishers.

Reserve Bank of India (2003-04). *Handbook of Statistics.*

Slemfod, Joel and Jon Bakija (2004) *Taxing Ourselves: A Citizen's Guide to the Debate over Taxes* Massachusetts: MIT Press.

Smith, Terence (2000) 'Women and Tax in South Africa', in Debbie Budlender (ed.) *The Fifth Women's Budget*, South Africa. World Bank website/ Publicfinance.

Stotsky, Janet (1997) '*How Tax Systems Treat Men and Women Differently*', Tax Policy Division, IMF.

Wanyaka, S. H. (2003) '*Report on Gender Budget Analysis of Taxation in Uganda Focusing on Central Government Taxation*', Uganda Revenue Authority.

Young, Claire (2000) '*What's Sex Got to Do with It? Tax and the "Family".*' Law Commission of Canada.

APPENDIX: I

Graph 1: Shares of Sources of Total Central Revenue Receipts, India: 1990-91 to 2003-04

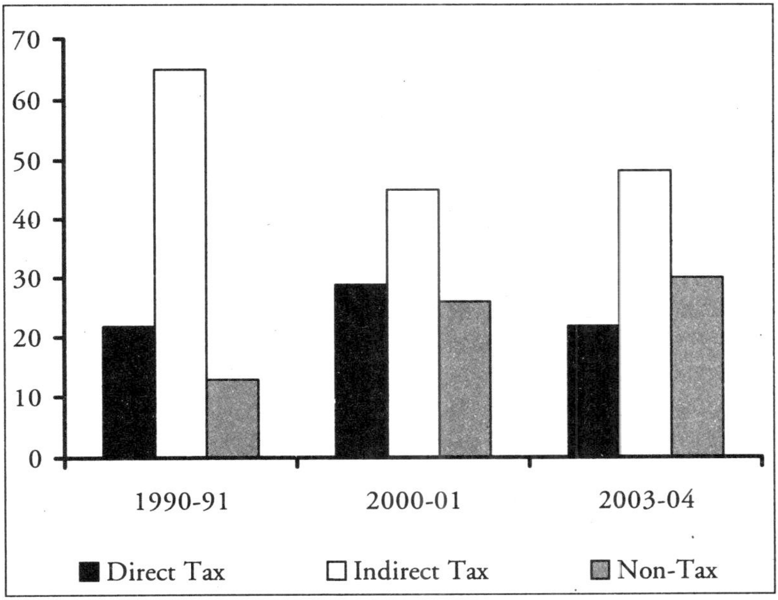

Source: Indian Public Finance Statistics—2003-04, Government of India, Table 2.2, p. 22.

APPENDIX: II

Graph 2: Shares of Central Direct Taxes, India: 1990-91 to 2003-04

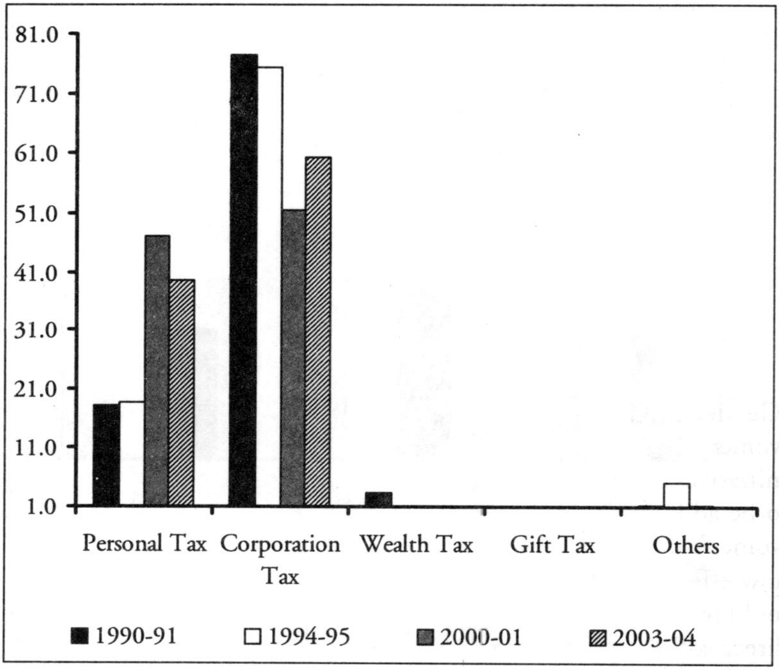

Source: Handbook of Statistics, Reserve Bank of India, 2003-04, Table 102, p. 154.

Women's Empowerment through Gender Budgeting

A Review in the Indian Context

ANJALI GOYAL

INTRODUCTION

'Gender Budgeting' is now recognized as a tool for empowering women. This essay gives a broad overview of the gender budgeting initiatives in India, highlighting certain related issues that need to be addressed for making gender budgeting an effective tool for women's empowerment. The basic question that is posed here is: how effective has gender budgeting, in its present form, been as a tool for women's empowerment in India. While the essay offers no direct solutions, an attempt has been made to bring certain key issues into focus along with suggestions on alternative strategies. The essay lays no claim to providing a list of all the gender budgeting initiatives in the country, and many achievements and activities may not be included because of space constraints.

Section I of the essay briefly introduces the concept of gender budgeting. Section II reflects upon the strategic framework adopted for undertaking gender budgeting in India, highlighting the framework adopted in pioneering countries like Australia and South Africa. Section III mentions a few gender budgeting exercises carried out in India to give a background on the approaches in vogue. Section IV reviews the effectiveness of various approaches under the realm of gender budgeting in the context of empowerment of women. Section V discusses the need to have a second look at the approach to women's empowerment, as reflected in various government initiatives. Section VI describes an alternative strategy to women's empowerment in the context of gender budgeting. Section VII discusses the strategic map of activities based on the alternative approach.

SECTION I

Definition and Concept

The term 'gender budgeting' has become a catch-all phrase to describe various government initiatives that seek to address gender issues in the domain of public expenditure and policy. Two definitions are quoted to introduce the concept.

'Gender-sensitive budgets', 'gender budgets', and 'women's budgets' refer to a variety of processes and tools aimed at facilitating an assessment of the gendered impacts of government budgets. In the evolution of these exercises, the focus has been on auditing government budgets for their impact on women and girls. This has meant that, to date, the term 'women's budget' has gained widest use. Recently, however, these budget exercises have begun using gender as a category of analysis so the terminology 'gender-sensitive budgets' is increasingly being adopted. It is important to recognize that 'women's budgets' or 'gender-sensitive budgets' are not separate budgets for women, or for men. They are attempts to break down, or disaggregate, the government's mainstream budget according to its impact on women and men, and different groups of women and men, with cognizance being given to the society's underpinning of gender relations. (Sharp, Rhonda: 1999)

Gender budget initiatives analyse how governments raise and spend public money, with the aim of securing gender equality in decision-making about public resource allocation; and gender equality in the distribution of the impact of government budgets, both in their benefits and in their burdens. The impact of government budgets on the most disadvantaged groups of women is a focus of special attention. (IDRC, 2001)

The above definitions underline the fact that gender budgeting is now seen as a socio-economic tool for ensuring gender equity in the development process and lays a strong emphasis on engendering public expenditure and policy. Critical activities constituting the gender budgeting exercise include

a) Addressing the gap between policy commitment and allocation for women through adequate resource allocation and gender sensitive programme formulation and implementation.
b) Mainstreaming gender concerns in public expenditure and policy.
c) Gender audit of public expenditure, programme implementation and policies relating to public expenditure, fiscal and monetary matters etc.

SECTION II

Strategic Framework

While several countries across the globe have adopted gender budgeting initiatives, pioneering work was done in Australia and South Africa.

The Australian approach or the "Three-way Categorization" distinguishes between:

1. Gender-specific expenditure;
2. Equal opportunity expenditure for civil servants; and
3. General expenditure (the rest) considered in terms of its gender impact.

In the South African "Five Step Approach" the five steps are:

1. Analysing the situation of women, men, girls and boys;
2. Assessing the gender-responsiveness of policies;
3. Assessing budget allocations;
4. Monitoring spending and service delivery;
5. Assessing outcomes.

In India the strategic framework for gender sensitivity in resource allocation has been earmarking a specified minimum quantum of funds/benefits for women in all women related sectors, supplemented by targeted interventions for women in various sectors like health, education, employment, training, micro-credit etc. A specific focus on gender-based resource allocation is visible from the Eighth Plan onwards.

The Eighth Plan (1992-97) highlighted for the first time a gender perspective and the need to ensure a definite flow of funds from the general developmental sectors to women. The Plan document made an express statement that "... the benefits to development from different sectors should not bypass women and special programmes on women should be complementary to the general development programmes. The latter, in turn, should reflect greater gender sensitivity."

The Ninth Plan (1997-2002) adopted a 'Women's Component Plan' approach as one of the major strategies and directed both the Central and State Governments to ensure "not less than 30 per cent of the funds/benefits are earmarked in all the women's related sectors." Special vigil was advocated on the flow of the earmarked funds/benefits through an effective mechanism to ensure that the proposed strategy brings forth a holistic approach towards empowering women.

The Tenth Plan reinforced commitment to gender budgeting to establish its gender-differential impact and to translate gender commitments into budgetary commitments as the extracts below show

> —the Tenth plan will continue the process of dissecting the Government budget to establish its gender-differential impact and to translate gender commitments into budgetary commitments.
>
> —the Tenth Plan will initiate immediate action in tying up these two effective concepts of Women Component Plan and Gender Budgeting to play a complementary role to each other, and thus ensure both preventive and post facto action in enabling women to receive their rightful share from all the women-related general development sectors.

The Department of Women and Child Development as the nodal Government of India (GOI) Department for gender budgeting took the initiative in 2004 of defining a broader strategic framework for gender budgeting covering a wide range of activities that would collectively contribute to strengthening the gender budgeting initiative. This is given below:

Mission Statement—"Budgeting for Gender Equity"

Framework of activities

- *Quantification of allocation of resources for women in the Union, states and Local Administration budgets and expenditure thereof.*

  - Refining and standardizing methodology and development of tools.
  - Trend Analysis
  - Analysis of change in pattern, shift in priorities in allocation across clusters of services etc
  - Variations in allocation of resources and actual expenditure
  - Adherence to physical targets

- *Gender audit of policies of the government—monetary, fiscal, trade etc. at the Centre and state levels*
  - Research and micro studies to guide macro policies like credit policy, taxes etc
  - Identification of gender impact of policies/interventions viewed as gender neutral
  - Micro studies to identify the need for affirmative action in favour of women towards correcting gender imbalances

- *Impact assessment of various schemes in the Union and State budgets*
  - Micro studies on incidence of benefits
  - Analysis of cost of delivery of services

- *Analysing programmes, strategies, interventions and policy initiatives from the perspective of their impact on the status of women as reflected in important Macro Indicators like literacy, MMR, participation in work force*
  - Analysis of substance and content of various interventions directed at health of women and correlate the same with indicator like MMR to establish need for corrective action in formulation of scheme/approach.

- *Institutionalizing the generation and collection of gender dis-aggregated data*
  - Developing MIS for feedback from implementing agencies
  - Inclusion of new parameters in data collection in Census and surveys by NSO, CSO etc

- *Consultations and capacity building*
  - Collation of research and exchange of best practices
  - Developing methodologies and tools for dissemination
  - Forums and Partnerships among experts and stakeholders.

- *Review of decision making processes to establish gender equity in participation*
  - Review of extant participation of women in decision making processes and to establish processes and models aimed at gender equity in decision making and greater participation of women.
  - Formulation and reflection of *satellite accounts* to capture the contribution of women to the economy by way of their activities in areas that go unreported like the care economy, unpaid work in rearing domestic animals etc.

Formal institutionalization of the gender budgeting exercise in the annual budgeting process of the Government of India has taken place with the inclusion of a gender budgeting statement in the Union Budget 2005-06 (Statement 19, Volume 1, Expenditure Budget 2005-06).

SECTION III

Approaches to Gender Budgeting Initiatives in India

A wide variety of women empowering initiatives have been taken up over the last few decades in the government and civil society. A few milestones in the context of gender budgeting are briefly mentioned below to enable reflection on the different approaches to gender budgeting.

i) As mentioned in Section II, the Government of India adopted the Women's Component Plan approach for ensuring gender sensitive resource allocation. Reviewing the performance of the WCP during the Ninth Plan, the 10th Plan document indicates that 39 per cent of the GBS of 15 women related Ministries/Departments flowed to women under the Women's Component Plan.

ii) The first formal exercise in gender budgeting at the national level was undertaken by the National Institute of Public Finance and Policy (NIPFP) when they analysed the Union Budget. The Report of NIPFP categorized public expenditure under three main types

a) women specific allocations which are specifically targeted to women and girls,
b) pro-women allocations which are the composite expenditure of schemes with women component, and
c) mainstream public expenditure that have gender differential impacts.

The study highlighted the low proportion of women-related allocation in the Union Budget and the tendency for revised allocations being less than budgeted projections. The study concluded that the gender incidence of the benefits of public expenditure is difficult to measure in precise quantitative terms, since the bulk of the expenditures are meant to provide services that are essentially public in nature. The suggestion was that the expenditures meant primarily for women be shown separately so that they can be easily culled out from budget heads of social and economic services in which it is possible to segregate such expenditures. With this objective in view, the report recommended the following priority actions for gender-sensitive budgeting:

- Mechanism to collate gender disaggregated data from relevant Departments so that it can be developed to obtain the gender-wise relevant statistical database, targets and indicators.
- Gender audit of plans, policies and programmes of various Ministries with pro-women allocations.
- Segregation of provisions for women in the composite programmes under education, health and rural development in order to protect the provisions by placing restrictions on their re-appropriation for other purposes.

iii) Studies in select sates were commissioned by the Department of Women and Child Development through the National Institute of Public Cooperation and Child Development using the same model.

iv) The Department of Women and Child Development also commissioned a study on gender analysis of budgets of all states for the period 1993-94 to 2002-03 so as to generate a time series data on budgeted expenditure for women by state governments for the years 1993-94 to 2002-03.

In this report, the programmes for women have been classified under 5 sectors:

a) Education and Training—General education of girls above senior secondary level, training of women in technical education, extension work, etc.
b) Women in Need—pension/financial assistance for destitute/handicapped women and widows and their children for purposes like marriage/education, etc., shelter homes, rehabilitation of prostitutes, etc.
c) Health—maternity and child care, hospitals for women, community health programme for women, etc.
d) Women Empowerment programmes—working women hostels, self-help group schemes, women cooperative banks, etc.
e) Miscellaneous measures

Apart from highlighting the fact that more than 50 per cent of expenditure on women is from the state budgets, the study also brought out significant variations in interstate positions on trends of expenditure on women when seen in correlation with female population.

v) At the state level, the state government of Karnataka was a pioneer in gender budgeting of public expenditure. The state undertook to earmark resources for women in most sectors. States like Kerala and Tamil Nadu have achieved a high degree of progress in gender related indicators on literacy, health, employment etc. through the introduction of several successful gender related programmes (especially through the self help group movement).

vi) The initiatives taken in the last few years by Ministry of Finance have reinforced the commitment of the government to gender budgeting as a tool for women's empowerment.

- The Ministry of Finance had constituted an Expert Group on the classification system of government transactions under the Chairmanship of the Chief Economic Advisor to the Government of India. One of the terms of reference of the Expert Group was "to examine the feasibility of and suggest the general approach to Gender Budgeting and economic classification. The report of the Expert Group has since been accepted by the government and an inter-departmental committee was constituted in November 2004 with representation of the Ministry of Finance, Planning Commission and the Department of Women and Child Development.

- Recognizing the need to spread gender budgeting initiatives in the entire government machinery, the Inter Departmental Committee recommended that all departments establish a Gender Budgeting Cell. To begin with, eighteen departments were asked to reflect scheme-wise physical targets and expenditure benefiting women in their Performance Budgets for 2004-05.
- The Department of Women and Child Development has drawn up detailed guidelines on gender budgeting initiatives for these cells, and workshops have been organized for dissemination of gender budgeting practices and initiatives.

vii) There is abundant action research in academic circles by gender and public finance experts and studies have been conducted at national, state and district/local levels. The approach has been essentially to carry out a gender audit of public expenditure and policy. The studies give an insight into the trends and patterns of public expenditure from a gender perspective, both at the national and state levels. There are several studies on the status of women and public expenditure for women in sectors like agriculture, industry, labour and so on; there are also micro level studies that cover gender analysis of budgeting practices and implementation at panchayat levels. Considerable research also exists on the gender impact of important government programmes like the Employment Guarantee Scheme, Swarajayanti Gram Swarozgar Yojana etc. These studies have highlighted important areas of concern these are as follows:

- The overall inadequacy of allocation for women in budgets at both national and state levels
- The multiplicity of schemes with small budgets which have limited impact and coverage
- Too many layers of administration impeding the smooth flow of funds and delays in implementation
- Shortfalls in implementation on account of gender insensitivity in implementing agencies or failure to address core gender related issues. Scheme formulation not in line with field level requirement. Scheme design does not address barriers to access by women.
- Lack of availability of gender disaggregated data to isolate expenditure on women in pro women schemes
- Lack of transparency in indicating physical targets and achievements
- Lack of women's involvement in decision-making

Summarizing the above,

- Gender budgeting activities in the government generally comprice:
  i) A conscious decision to earmark funds for women related programmes and enhance allocation under women specific programmes and pro women programmes
  ii) Implementation of women specific schemes for training and skill upgradation (STEP, Swawlamban, Training women in agriculture extension activities etc.) and mobilization of the collective power of women through self-help group based schemes (Swayamsidha, Swashakti, Kutumbashree, SGRY), extension of micro credit (Rashtriya Mahila Kosh) and so on
  iii) Addressing improvement in women related macro indicators like literacy, maternal mortality rate (MMR) etc. through focus on coverage of women in education and health services.
- Gender Audits have focused on the depiction of quantum and trend of resources allocated for women in government budgets at the national, state and lower levels of administration, commenting on the adequacy or inadequacy of the allocation

and reality checks on translation of budgetary provision into actual expenditure. They also include an analysis of the impact of expenditure and a review of the effectiveness of public programmes targeted for welfare and development from the point of view of design and implementation and comments on the status of women's access to select public services. A third aspect is the adoption of a few macro indices like MMR, work participation, literacy etc. that dominate the measurement of gender status and highlighting gender differentials to focus attention on the need for enhanced allocation for women in certain sectors like health, education and employment.

SECTION IV

With this background, we now examine Gender Budgeting as a 'tool' for women's empowerment. A logical starting point for this would be to look at the constituents of 'Women's Empowerment'. These are defined in the Tenth Plan document quoted below:

- *Social Empowerment*—to create an enabling environment through various affirmative developmental policies and programmes for development of women besides providing them easy and equal access to all the basic minimum services so as to enable them to realize their full potential.
- *Economic Empowerment*—to ensure provision of training, employment and income-generation activities with both 'forward' and 'backward' linkages with the ultimate objective of making all women economically independent and self-reliant.
- *Gender Justice*—to eliminate all forms of gender discrimination and thus allow women to enjoy not only the de-jure but also the de-facto rights and fundamental freedom on par with men in all spheres, viz. political, economic, social, civil, cultural, etc.

Gender Budgeting Tools

As mentioned earlier, gender budgeting initiatives in India have been undertaken using several different approaches. Some of these are discussed below.

A) Quantum and trend analysis of gender based resource allocation and expenditure

The term gender budgeting by its very definition and nomenclature has underpinnings in financial resource allocations and thus most of the gender budgeting exercises focus on quantitative resource allocation for women, under gender specific and pro women categories of public expenditure.

It is no doubt necessary to get a macro position on trends in allocation for women. However this approach has several limitations as a means of empowering women. Some of these are listed below:

a) How do we judge the adequacy of allocation without the availability of a benchmark based on an assessed gap in availability of public facilities? The general concern expressed is: when women are under 50 per cent of the population why should public expenditure on them be less than 5 per cent of the budget? There is no apparent rationale behind a WCP of 30 per cent and that too only in the social sector's budget. Why not 50 per cent or 75 per cent?

b) The overall size of allocation also obfuscates details like actual utilization of expenditure by women. Core issues like the design of programmes and their effectiveness from the gender perspective, too many small interventions, barriers to access etc, remain opaque in macro level analyses of quantitative allocations for women.

c) A rising trend in allocation of funds for women does not necessarily translate into enhanced benefits or wider coverage. The rise in allocation may just cover enhanced cost of delivery of services with no increase in the quantity of services or even in their quality.

d) The tendency is to analyse expenditure at each level of government in isolation. For example gender analysis of Union budgets is carried out without linking it to state expenditure. In the federal setup this gives an incomplete picture. Any comment on, say, expenditure on health for women is incomplete if we look at the Government of India Budget or State

Budgets in isolation. Both have to be seen to get the complete picture.

e) Without the availability of gender disaggregated data it is difficult to comment upon the true position of incidence of public expenditure from a gender perspective.

B) Gender audit of sectors like education, agriculture, health, industry etc.

Many gender budgeting studies have presented gender profiles of sectors like health, education, agriculture, employment and so on at a national or state level. This is certainly a more effective mechanism than the first approach based on quantification of resources. However in most of these studies, the issues raised are deficiencies in design and/or implementation of programmes, based on field level surveys. Little attempt has been made to benchmark the scale of resources required to empower women meaningfully, or to examine their availability or the reliability of services. Another limitation is that this approach does not recognize the need for holistic empowerment of women. Can we address women's empowerment in isolation on a sectoral basis? If a woman has access to a Primary Health Centre but no income to feed herself and is debt ridden due to lack of adequate sustainable income, would we say she is empowered? Effective improvement in health for women, for example, requires not only access to a medical centre but also transport (road), employment (food), water and sanitation and so on. A sectoral approach is thus uni-dimensional when rated as an empowerment tool.

C) Gender audit based on the position reflected by gender related macro indicators

The status and trends of certain gender related macro indices, for example, MMR, women's access to health, literacy rates, participation in PRI, employment statistics etc., are quoted as proxy indicators for levels of women's empowerment. Adverse gender indices are cited as justification for enhancement in the quantum of allocation. However, this approach again is constrained in that there is no benchmarking of the quantum of allocation required to achieve the targeted improvement in these indices. Thus the effectiveness of this approach is questionable.

Further, these are just averages. They require a reality check in terms of regional imbalances, class based differentials, gross inequalities and so on. These indices also do not address issues of availability and access. For example, if say, coverage of water and sanitation facilities is said to be universal for all habitations. Is this true of all areas in desired quantum and quality? Coverage has to be seen against an acceptable yardstick for availability and reliability of service. These indices are also found wanting on the scale of holistic empowerment. Planning for improvement in MMR cannot be done by merely addressing the provision of health facilities. This has to go in tandem with education, adequate water, sanitation, nutrition and roads for emergency situations. If a health infrastructure is created, manning it effectively may require basic infrastructure like water, sanitation, roads and electricity. A single macro indicator may thus not serve the purpose.

D) Women's participation in gender budgeting through fiscal decentralization and local level institutions

This could prima facie be an ideal solution that would take into account field level requirements of women and with their participation in planning and implementation, an achievable outcome is more likely. However, desirable as it is, we have to recognize the constraints in the current context.

a) The biggest constraint is limited financial devolution. The structure of public finances and expenditure in India is a multi-tiered one and resources flow to the field through several layers of administration and through a variety of modes—centrally sponsored, central sector, state sector, additional central assistance and so on. The net result is that very little devolution of financial powers rests with the local level administrations. Further, schematic designs and conditionalities leave them with virtually no flexibility. Accountability too is diffused. These problems are faced even in some of the states that are upheld as best models. In a study commissioned by the World Bank (India-Fiscal Decentralization to Rural Governments), some key findings based upon studies in Kerala and Karnataka, indicate that (i) Inter-governmental relations are mostly hierarchical. The design and implementation of the decentralization programme are a state government responsibility. However, implementation of key aspects of the programme is lagging. Districts and blocks have no powers to tax and little expenditure autonomy. Both in Karnataka and Kerala, they more or less function as spending agents of higher-level governments; (ii) Both states have weak, outdated and poorly functioning financial management systems that debilitate the policy making and planning process, as well as the management and accountability of the decentralized system. In the absence of reliable information on the revenues and expenditures of local bodies, neither the states nor the centre can lead a reasonable fiscal decentralization programme; (iii) An important lesson learned in these case studies is that one necessary condition for a well-functioning system of fiscal decentralization is a healthy State financial position. Because the Constitutional Amendment defined decentralization to be a state subject, until state governments can improve their deficit position, local governments can expect continued under-funding of their present grant entitlements, resistance to new programme development, and hesitation in assigning more own source revenues to local governments.

b) Another constraint is the limited *effective* participation of women in field level planning and implementation. Women's participation in local administration is constitutionally provided. However the effective impact would require immense capacity building and overcoming of socio-economic barriers. Field level studies conducted in Karnataka indicate a few problems. For example, elected women representatives (EWRs) in PRIs are not well endowed or trained in technicalities of budgeting even though they may be aware of their needs at the local level like water, sanitation, security etc. They are not always given an equal opportunity to express themselves or impose the perceived requirements of women.

c) Identification and promotion of gender audit based Best Practices: There are abundant instances of best practices in the realm of gender empowerment. Projects have been taken up to successfully demonstrate the strength women draw in collectivity, as for example in self-help group schemes and cooperatives etc. There are also projects reflecting the potential for women in skill upgradation, micro credit based entrepreneurship etc. However, most of these efforts are not taken to scale. Whatever best practices there are tend to be project and culture specific. National level applicability often poses problems.
d) Reliance on women specific schemes: We devise women-specific schemes for nutrition, education, vocational training and so on. These are no doubt critical in the empowerment process. However, they tend to be uni-dimensional in focus and do not serve as a tool for holistic empowerment.
e) Reliance on convergence of interventions: Given the multitude of schemes and programmes for women, spread across various departments and ministries of the government, one approach towards empowerment of women is seeking to converge these interventions, mostly through self-help groups (SHGs) or women cooperatives. This could prove an effective empowerment approach and also finds support in the Tenth Plan documents.

Extract from the Tenth Five Year plan 2002-07
2.11.63 As much of the success of empowering women depends upon the holistic impact of various sectoral achievements, efforts will be initiated/intensified during the Tenth Plan to converge the existing services, resources, infrastructure and manpower available both in the women-specific and women-related sectors with an ultimate objective of optimizing the benefits with greater cost effectiveness. To this effect, efforts will be made to converge the services of health care, nutrition supplementation, safe drinking water, adult/functional/legal literacy, gainful employment both wage and self-employment, sanitation, health and nutrition awareness, knowledge and information about management of diseases, counseling towards safe motherhood practices, nutrition, welfare services, etc.

> The integrated approach adopted by the two on-going programmes of women's empowerment viz. Swa Shakti and Swayamsidha will be further strengthened and expanded during the Tenth Plan with an ultimate objective of universalizing the same through the already available grass-root level networking of SHGs.

While the SHG groups and collective power of women is critical in the empowerment process, in the absence of an institutional mechanism for convergence, it would prove difficult to have universal success, given the involvement of a number of departments and schemes, at the functional level. Success stories rest on individual efforts rather than institutionalized mechanisms. Central sector schemes and centrally sponsored schemes have limited flexibility and may require a re-look at the design and implementation of the schemes. Further the SHG movement is not uniform in its success and spread across the country.

Summing up it is submitted that while all the above approaches have merit and benefits, but in isolation, these approaches are not complete in themselves to achieve women's empowerment.

Having looked at the limitations of the above approaches it would also be pertinent to look at a few development related issues which need to be addressed for arriving at an effective alternative strategy for women's empowerment.

SECTION V

Extant Approach to Women's Development—A few comments

1) While planning for women's empowerment, the outlook has been one of looking at *women as a beneficiary segment* rather than as equal participants in the development process. As a consequence, the gender budgeting exercise has mostly focused on the provision of resources and programmes for women in the social sector. Sectors like Education, Health, Nutrition, Employment etc. are no doubt critical in the empowerment paradigm, but it is necessary that we look beyond this. Women must be recognized as *equal* players in the economy whether they participate directly as workers or indirectly as members of the care economy. It has to be accepted that *every*

policy of the government, whether fiscal, monetary or trade, has an impact on the well being of women and that in many cases there would be a gender differential in the impact. Thus it is not adequate to restrict the gender budgeting exercise to a *few* sectors of the economy which are traditionally considered to be women related. The analysis has to cover every rupee of public expenditure. It has to cover the way schemes are conceptualized and how women friendly they are in implementation and targeting of beneficiaries. It has to embrace a gender sensitive analysis of monetary policies, covering the impact of indicators like inflation, interest rates etc., and fiscal policies covering taxation, excise etc. Thus a gender budgeting analysis has to go hand-in-hand with gender mainstreaming for meaningful empowerment of women. A direct spin off of this would be immediate expansion in access of women to public resources and the consequent strengthening of their economic identity.

2) At present, a very limited gender perspective is kept in mind while formulating fiscal and monetary policies and taking decisions on issues like withdrawal or introduction of subsidies etc. This has to be initiated if we are to speak of meaningful women's empowerment and thus has to form an integral part of the gender budgeting exercise. Without this, the gender budgeting exercise may be enhancing resources in the social sector but the impact may be nullified by, say, inflation, costlier credit, withdrawal of subsidy, imposition of taxes, excise/custom duties on essential commodities etc. If a policy of the government unwittingly has a significant gender adverse bias, arresting that may be more critical than enhancing resources for women specific programmes. Thus there is a strong case for gender-based review of fiscal and monetary policies as an integral part of the Gender Budgeting exercise.
3) If certain planning and implementation issues are not addressed, the gender budgeting initiatives may meet the fate of several other development initiatives and remain more of a paper exercise with limited outcomes, the more so given the lim-

ited bargaining power of women. These issues would include

- Synergy in resources for women in various budgets—national, state and local
- Weeding out overlapping interventions that obfuscate the status of actual beneficiaries
- Scheme design and implementation from a gender perspective to consciously address socio-economic barriers faced by women in accessing services

The administrative set up in our country has multiple layers of governance and budgeting. Each of these has a multitude of departments and ministries with their own programmes and schemes. The end result is considerable overlap in interventions for women. This only goes to enhance the overhead costs of delivery of services and may not be to the benefit of women. For example vocational training and skill upgradation programmes are run by several GOI departments and by state governments, each government agency bearing the administrative cost of delivery. Despite so many agencies, the countrywide geographic balance/imbalance cannot be ascertained. This also makes it difficult to ascertain the total allocation flowing to women and conduct a gender audit in a meaningful fashion.

4) Reliance on the voluntary sector for outreach has come to stay. But this has to be institutionalized and optimized so as to ensure more transparency and accountability. Interventions may be well designed but the implementation process entailed in grants-in-aid schemes is such that voluntary sector organizations apply for grants. There is no decisive decision-making to ensure that voluntary sector is co-opted where required to ensure balanced coverage. The modality of most grants-in-aid schemes has been seeking applications from willing voluntary organizations. No pinpointing of areas of requirement so as to progressively achieve universalization of an intervention is being implemented. The time has perhaps come to look upon the NGOs as *"social contractors"*. The order of events needs to be reversed. The spatial context should get

first preference and selection of implementing agencies from voluntary organization more transparent to promote accountability, especially at the field level.

5) Creating gender budgeting tools based on resource allocations and concomitant follow-up activities and gender audit should not become an end in itself. We have to move away from looking at this exercise as an accounting exercise with focus on "higher women related allocations." The expected end outcome is women's empowerment Thus this exercise has to be seen in the perspective of a *process* which entails looking at multi dimensional activities, many of which do not necessarily have a specific allocation in public expenditure. To state a few:
   - Looking at alternative ways of achieving desired outcomes based on effectiveness;
   - Participation of the stakeholders (women) and building their decision making and enforcing capacities;
   - Effective implementation of legislations that seek to establish gender equality, which may not necessarily translate into a specific resource allocation but are just as critical for achieving the goal of gender empowerment;
   - Social re-engineering on gender attitudes through a review of education curricula;
   - Gender sensitization of administrative cadres;
   - Taking corrective measures in interventions based on results of evaluations and reality check reports.

SECTION VI

Gender Budgeting for Women's Empowerment: An Alternative Strategy

Women as Stakeholders

Awareness about gender budgeting and policy level commitment to women's empowerment is at a peak today. Various enabling measures like setting up of gender budgeting cells in ministries of the Government of India, reflection of a gender budget statement in the Union Budget 2005-06 and adoption of the women's component plan by some states have been undertaken. The midterm appraisal of the Tenth Plan has identified adverse child sex ratio, high MMR, wide gender gap in literacy and wage rates, violence against women and female feticide and infanticide as burning issues for women besides the vulnerability of women in low paid hazardous and insecure jobs in the unorganized sector and in export processing/special economic zones. This document also states that there is a need to review the stagnation in implementation of the women's component plan.

> Extracts from MTA Tenth Plan document para 4.35
> The Tenth Plan envisaged tying up WCP and gender budgeting to "ensure both preventive and post-facto action in enabling women to receive their rightful share from all the women-related general development sectors". The reality is that women still remain largely untouched by gender-just and gender-sensitive budgets as well as WCP. This stagnation needs to be shaken up across the board.

It is thus perhaps an opportune time to explore an alternative strategy towards gender budgeting, that builds upon the vast experience gained in the past few decades. The challenge is how to make gender budgeting an effective tool for women's empowerment.

There is no denying that participative budgeting with women being directly involved in the decisions related to planning, financing and programme implementation is the ideal situation. However in the Indian context, given the limited devolution of finances to local administrations and socio-economic and political barriers to women's effective participation, an alternative strategy is proposed.

An alternative strategy: Macro level planning for micro needs

The strategy proposed here is *Macro level planning for micro needs.* The perspective on gender budgeting has to be *turned upside down.* It is not the allocation of resources in the budget at national and/or state levels that has to seen but the resources that flow to and are available to women at the field level (i.e. the women in the villages, cities and towns) that need to be monitored. Planning for empowerment should then be based on a reality check on what is the level of empowerment of women at the field level based on regional geographic spatial maps.

Two inter-related mechanisms are suggested as a part of the proposed strategy

a) *Spatial Mapping of infrastructure and resources:* How do we translate financial commitments into 'monitorable' measures of empowerment? How do we overcome disparities in empowerment across various regions and across classes? Macro level resource allocations and financial and physical indicators do not adequately address these questions. The solution offered is *spatial mapping.* The states have to be asked to do spatial mapping of social infrastructure and access to employment opportunities for women, clearly indicating resources available, overall gaps, resource allocation required based on size of population and yardsticks for availability of facilities etc. so that universalization is achieved progressively, and allocations and interventions are more focused. These spatial maps would then form the basis for concomitant regional plans and projections on funds for gender requirements, with maximum local participation. This would also enable taking into account regional requirements and building in culture specific changes necessary in interventions for women. Such mapping initiatives have been undertaken over the past years but in a piecemeal manner, for relatively uni-dimensional issues but not for gender specific concerns. Thus the technology and methodology is in place.

b) Centralized coordination of macro level planning for micro needs with the Planning Commission: Till financial devolution improves and social change takes place and participative budgeting becomes a reality, the Planning Commission will have to coordinate *Planning at macro level for micro level* needs. Public expenditure flows to the end target group through a plethora of administrations, schemes, and agencies. So planning for and implementing and monitoring at the field level would require centralized coordination of all the interventions. The Planning Commission will have to take over the role of coordinating gender budgeting initiatives in the realm of providing basic infrastructure for women, employment opportunities, economic empowerment etc. that is seen as necessary for the well being and development of women.

This suggestion being given in the gender budgeting context is not administratively impossible. It is to be found in the Tenth Plan MTA document in the context of achieving balanced regional growth. The coordinating role of Planning Commission has been recommended as below

Regional Balance and Planning (extract from MTA of the Tenth Plan).

The Planning Commission should be the bridge between the Centre and the states that its present role enables it to be. This is necessary because the Planning Commission is the only agency that directly supports the development Plans of states and is engaged in a regular development dialogue with them. This means that the Commission must see itself in a more proactive role in championing the cause of the states with Central Ministries in key policy issues that have strong equity and regional balance dimensions.

In line with its original mandate, the Commission's role and influence must be leveraged more effectively with both the states and the Central Ministries for bringing about greater intra-state and inter-state regional balance.

A similar exercise with a wider dimension will have to be carried out in the gender context. Through coordination, the Planning Commission will have to essentially address all gender issues including issues like overlap in initiatives (across departments in Government of India and state governments), need for synergy in provision of funds at centre and state levels etc. This would be facilitated by the information reflected by the spatial mapping exercise and benchmarking of financial resources required based on region specific requirements of women. The process envisaged is an end to end approach, similar to the Backwards Districts

Initiative scheme initiated by the Planning Commission for 100 districts. This is perhaps the only viable approach to address a hard-core problem like women's empowerment.

SECTION VII

Strategic Map for Women's Empowerment

A strategic map is proposed to depict all the inter-related activities necessary for women's empowerment and to enable a better focus in resource allocation under Gender Budgeting. Taking a cue from Robert S. Kaplan and David P. Norton's paper (*Harvard Business Review* Sep-Oct 2000) we may map our strategy under the following four components:

Client (women) perspective	Internal Processes perspective	Financial perspective	Learning perspective

The detailed Strategic Map is at Chart I.

Client/Stakeholders (women)perspective

- *Basic socio-economic infrastructure*: Health, education, water and sanitation
- *Economic Empowerment*: Economic identity, employment, assets, credit, skills, markets, risk coverage
- *Social and political empowerment*: Political participation, gender equality in inheritance, marital laws, security

The three concerns identified for the stakeholder are distinct in that they require a different strategy, funding pattern and implementation approach.

Basic socio-economic infrastructure

At the macro level, provision of some basic infrastructure on a universal access basis is necessary for survival and dignity of living. This includes water, sanitation, electricity/power, roads etc. It may be debatable whether expenditure on these utilities should be included in quantification of resources allocated for women and what percentage of this should be treated as a women's component. But it cannot be denied that these facilities are critical for the well-being of women. In particular, water and sanitation and

Chart 1: Strategic Map for Gender Budgeting as tool for Women's Empowerment

Perspective	Basic Infrastructure	Economic empowerment	Social and political Empowerment
Clients (women's) perspective	**Basic Infrastructure** Water & san, fuel power, roads health facilities, schools etc. 1. Universal & adequate access 2. All components available with reliability	**Economic empowerment** Economic Identity for women 1. Sustained livelihood with minimal displacement 2. Risk alleviation, security net 3. Ownership rights of women over productive assets 4. Access to training in high productivity skills, credit, markets 5. Support services like crèches, working women hostels etc. 6. Equal pay for equal work	**Social and political Empowerment** 1.Effective and equal participation in political process - representation in political bodies, legislatures, local bodies 2. Equal rights in inheritance, marital laws etc. 3. Social security
Internal Processes perspective	1. Spatial maps indicating gaps in infrastructure. 2. Planning Commission to coordinate for synergy in funds and schemes of Centre and States. 3. Devolutions of responsibilities and funds to local self-help groups and women rep.s in PRI s. 4. Yardsticks for universal availability 5. Performance Targets—outlays and outcomes 6. Monitoring systems	1. Preparation of spatial maps to indicate gaps in access to sustained livelihood. 2.Converge schemes/design programmes to universalize access to sustained livelihood for women based on region specific requirements, Coordination by Planning Commission 3. Promoting sustained economic activity in women self-help groups/cooperatives 4. Gender mainstreaming in "gender neutral sectors" through high skill training, facilitating access to credit, tapping new avenues of productive employment etc. 5. Facilitating & promoting asset ownership by women	1.Changes in societal attitudes-engendering school/college curriculum 2.Incorporating gender mainstreaming concepts in education and training 3.Gender sensitization in administrative cadres 4.Institutionalizing political participation of women 5. Promote social awareness in self-help groups 6. Focus on implementation of gender related laws 7. Increase recruitment of women in law enforcing agencies

Chart 1: *contd.*

Perspective			
Financial perspective	1. Assess funds required based on yardsticks to cover infrastructure gaps 2. Prioritize funds allocation to cover spatial gaps 3. Better fiscal management to stretch resources 4. Reduce delivery costs by weeding out overlapping schemes and multiple channels of flow of funds	1. Enhanced Allocation for schemes for training women in higher skills for more productivity 2. Expansion of availability of credit facilities for women 3. Gender based review of fiscal and monetary policies 4. Incentives for gainful employment of women 5. Financing support services like creches and hostels 6. Satellite Accounts for unaccounted work of women	1. Financing gender awareness and sensitivity oriented media campaigns 2. Setting up research forums on gender issues 3. Financing training and capacity building for leadership amongst women 4. Financing programmes for social security of vulnerable women
Learning perspective	1. Harnessing information technology to develop spatial maps 2. Training of administrators in gender budgeting. 3. Bridging gap between research and policy/implementation/administrative action 4. Reality checks through surveys and evaluations 5. Develop MIS for gender disaggregated data on beneficiary incidence 6. Awareness about targets at stakeholder level 7. Promote public private partnership, eg. health insurance cover	1. Redesign programmes/schemes to match field level requirements 2. Build in flexibility for regional differences 3. Universalize best practices 4. Impact analysis to guide improvements in design and implementation 5. Research and innovation in women friendly technology to promote productivity and employment 6. Entrepreneurial capacity building for women 7. Concurrent evaluation of success	1. Capacity building amongst women in political process, awareness on rights etc 2. Review of Policy and Legislations from gender perspective to establish gender equity 3. Gender sensitization of law enforcing agencies 4. Design special programmes to address problems of vulnerable women (widows, disabled, destitute etc) 5. Reality checks on law enforcement

fuel, as the bulk of time for women goes in water and firewood collection. Drudgery apart, this work is purely unpaid labour and leaves them with no time to pursue more remunerative options. Thus the economic identity of women gets downplayed despite the critical labour they put in for survival of the household. Connectivity by rail/roads again is often critical for survival in times of crisis on health grounds or to market produce or seek employment.

Another reason for ensuring universal availability of this critical infrastructure is the impact it has on effective delivery of other services-particularly health and education and employment opportunities. Availability of medical services in crisis, manning of primary health centres and schools often suffers due to lack of availability of basic infrastructure like electricity and water/sanitation in rural areas. In a study carried out by World Bank (Anil B. Deolalikar, 2005) it has been concluded that universal road, electricity and sanitation coverage in the poor states would be associated with reductions of 40 per cent in the child underweight rate and 60 per cent in the infant mortality rate.

Thus provision of these facilities i.e. water and sanitation and electricity/bio gas may be deemed to be gender friendly and we may treat them as critical for women's empowerment. However the focus has to be on universalizing these services with attention on adequacy, access and reliability. One drawback has been benchmarking. For this exercise to be successful it is necessary that we benchmark resource requirement of the physical infrastructure after establishing yardsticks for availability, translate these into financial projections and then plan ahead. This has to go in tandem with spatial maps for progressive universal coverage and to facilitate monitoring.

Economic Empowerment

Despite the tremendous amount of effort devoted by women in the care economy and support in survival of the household, much of this is unaccounted for and unpaid. Creating an economic identity for women is critical for empowerment. This requires a more micro level approach but coordination at Planning Commission level is still important because of the multitude of small budgeted interventions. Further resource allocation has to be seen in conjunction with reality reflected in spatial maps on access to productive livelihood in different areas of the country. Universal access to productive livelihood for women would serve as a stabilizing factor for the entire family. The strategy may entail tapping the economic potential of collective power of women besides training in the higher skills. This has to go hand-in-hand with gender mainstreaming. The induction of women in the workforce of the entire public machinery in greater numbers, opening up more training institutes etc., and universalizing access to support services like accommodation, crèches and micro credit for women is critical for economic empowerment are also important. The approach has to be creative and gender sensitive.

Social and political empowerment

This entails relatively less resource allocation and more focus on effective implementation of laws and legislations and change in societal attitudes on gender. Effective empowerment for women would rest on equity in political processes and participation. A successful strategy would entail more concentrated participation of women in this realm through induction in law enforcing agencies and in legislating and administrative bodies.

Internal Process Perspective

This would include

i) Exercise of preparation of spatial maps by each state up to say village/block/district level on gender friendly infrastructure and livelihoods/employment sources/asset ownership etc, clearly indicating gaps in infrastructure and access to livelihoods
ii) Developing yardsticks for access to socio-economic infrastructure
iii) Coordination by Planning Commission for synergy in resource allocation at centre and state levels and facilitating convergence of multi-departmental interventions
iv) Redesigning interventions from a gender perspective
v) Gender mainstreaming in all public expenditure

vi) Developing monitoring mechanisms to ensure progressive universalization of infrastructure and employment opportunities based on spatial mapping

vii) Involving women self-help groups and women elected representatives in PRIs to take decisions and participate in programme implementation and monitoring with defined roles.

(This no doubt would require greater devolution of powers and training. Some amount of untied funds could be made available at the field level to enable women groups to address their gender priorities.)

viii) Gender based review of fiscal and monetary policies

ix) Gender based review of legislations and effective implementation of gender related legislations

Financial perspective

Action areas would cover

i) Translation of physical projections into financial projections based on spatial maps of resource gaps, yardsticks for resources required to universalize the availability of services for women's empowerment

ii) Enhancing allocations to universalize access to basic socio-economic infrastructure

iii) re-prioritization of resource allocation to cover infrastructure gaps and imbalances

iv) Synergy in state and national level resources

v) Monitoring utilization of resources based on targets achieved

vi) Gender friendly review of revenue, tax and subsidy policies

Learning and Innovation perspective

This would require among other activities

i) Better fiscal management to stretch existing resources

ii) Employment generation for women in new areas

iii) Developing MIS to generate gender disaggregation in data, harnessing technology for resource mapping

iv) Training of administrative cadres in gender mainstreaming

v) Social re-engineering through the gender component in the education process—gender issues compulsory in research, training and so on.

vi) Capacity building for stakeholders (women) in budgeting, higher productivity skills and training, improvement of women's bargaining power-collective strength through setting up self-help groups and cooperatives

vii) Bridging gap between research and administrative action, identifying impediments in effective implementation. Evaluation and micro level reviews

The above strategic map is only suggested as an example of the kind of activities holistic empowerment of women would entail. Enumerating activities more comprehensively would require a process of consultations with all concerned Ministries and Departments in the Centre and states as well as with local administrations. The Planning Commission would play a vital role in the above strategy because they provide a powerful meeting ground for all the players and constituents to converge. No doubt the above approach requires considerable effort in areas like spatial mapping and benchmarking of resources. However, with the slow progress reflected in women's empowerment being a major concern, the effort is perhaps now required. Further the advances in Information Technology could be fruitfully harnessed to this end.

CONCLUSION

Despite all legislation and policy commitments and planning, women remain a vulnerable group. If we are to translate the policy commitment of Women's Empowerment into a reality we would have to go beyond the current outlook on gender budgeting which excludes several dimensions of the problem. We have to go in for a more broad based approach that addresses planning, adequate resource allocation, programme design and formulation, targeted intervention and implementation based upon the requirement of women residing at the field level with their participation. This has to be supplemented by relentless reality checks at the field level. Gender mainstreaming has to be a guiding force in all these activities to maximize outreach of public expenditure and benefits for women. Further universalizing access is very important for meaningful outcomes. Inter-state and intra-state imbalances have persisted for a long time and need to be addressed more forcefully. Some overlap of gender and developmental issues will take place: this is inevitable given the wide gap in availability and requirement of socio-economic infrastructure in the country.

The strategy of macro level planning for micro needs and the strategic map for gender budgeting as a tool for women's empowerment has been proposed keeping in view the need for a holistic approach to empowerment of women. Any successful strategy for women's empowerment will have to account for the fact that

a) Empowerment cannot be successfully achieved till all aspects—social, economic and political are addressed.
b) Empowerment should cover women in all regions of the country
c) Gender concerns have to be mainstreamed in all aspects of public expenditure and policy as women are equal citizens in the country
d) Participation of women in decision making is necessary given their specific needs and to recognize them as equal members of society
e) Societal attitudes have to be re-engineered

Resource allocation and public expenditure are important inputs in the empowerment process and thus Gender Budgeting has a very critical role to play. However, the tool of gender budgeting has to lend itself to this process based upon the requirements of women's empowerment. The allocation and expenditure process has to be focused and appropriately prioritized. The tool should not become an end in itself. The gender budgeting tool thus has to be honed through

a) Spatial mapping of status of women and resources to ensure progressive universal coverage.
b) Coordination of the flow of public resources to facilitate and ensure convergence of resources with synergy across and within various levels of government

No doubt the resource allocation involved would be of a high order. However, this investment itself could contribute to gender empowerment if utilized in an efficient outcome oriented manner with more involvement of the stakeholders (women) in decision-making and implementation. Further this would lay the foundation for other women-specific interventions to be effectively implemented. And last, meaningful empowerment of women in India would have to rest on a shift in societal attitudes. This has been very well documented in the following extract from the Sixth Plan document.

It is more important to create a general awareness and understanding of the problems of women's employment in all the top policy and decision making and executive personnel. There is also the special problem facing women like the preference for male children for social and cultural reasons. This will require awareness, understanding and action. The best way to do so is to educate the children, orient the teachers, examine the text books and teaching-aids and ensure that the next generation grows up with new thinking.

Note: The author is presently working as Director, Finance in the Department of Women and Child Development. The views expressed in this paper are the personal views of the author.

REFERENCES

Sixth Five Year Plan Document (1980-85), Planning Commission, Government of India

Seventh Five Year Plan Document, Planning Commission, Government of India

Eighth Five Year Plan Document, Planning Commission, Government of India

Ninth Five Year Plan Document (1997-2002), Planning Commission, Government of India

Tenth Five Year Plan Document (2002-2007), Planning Commission, Government of India

Mid Term Appraisal of Tenth Five Year Plan (2002-2007), Planning Commission, Government of India

Annual Report 2004-05 of Department of Women & Child Development, Government of India

Nirmala Banerjee, Poulomi Roy: 'What does the State Do for Indian Women?'—*Economic and Political Weekly* October 30, 2004

Gender Budgeting in India, UNIFEM and NIPFP: 'Follow the Money Series—South Asia, Vol. 3; Gender Budgeting in India

Maitreyi Krishnaraj, Divya Pandey, Aruna Kanchi; Research Centre for Women's Studies, SNDT Women's University, Mumbai—'Follow the Money Series—South Asia, Vol. 5: Gender Sensitive Analysis of Employment Guarantee Scheme

Nirmala Banerjee, Joyanti Sen, Sachetana, Kolkata—Swaranjayanti Gram Swarozgar Yojana—A Budgetary Policy in Working; 'Follow the Money Series—South Asia, Vol. 6

Robert S. Kaplan and David P. Norton: Having Trouble with Your Strategy? Then Map It (Harvard Business Review Sep-Oct 2000).

Anil B. Deolalikar (2005) Attaining the Millennium Development Goals in India (World Bank, 2005)

India—Fiscal Decentralization to Rural Governments, (January 2004, World Bank)

Debbie Budlender and Guy Hewitt Engendering Budgets—A practitioner's guide to understanding and implementing Gender-responsive Budgets-(Common wealth Secretariat)

For a Few Pots of Water

Water Rights and Subsidies

ALKA PARIKH

- According to an IFPRI study (2002), more than one billion people in the world already lack access to fresh drinking water. Forty per cent of the world's people live in countries where water is scarce; by 2025, this figure is expected to rise to 66 per cent. In other words, one person in six lives without regular access to safe drinking water. The World Bank estimates that by the year 2025 one person in three, or 3.25 billion people in 52 countries will face water shortages.
- The same IFPRI study reports that dirty water kills 2.2 million people a year in developing countries.
- According to the Annual Report of the Ministry of Water Resources of 2001-02, the per capita availability of potable water in India in 1951 was 3,450 cubic meters. In 1999, it came down to 1,250 cubic meters.
- The Ministry also reports that in 1993, 23 per cent of rural and 15 per cent of urban Indians did not have access to potable water.
- It is feared that major metropolitan centres may go dry as early as 2015 on account of over-exploitation and misuse of water resources (Bansil, 2004).
- The women of drought affected villages in Rajasthan and Haryana travel upto 8 kms a day to fetch water for their families (Bansil, 2004).

It is odd to use the word 'scarce' to describe a resource that covers three fourth of this planet. And yet, as time passes by, not only is the availability of fresh water becoming increasingly problematic but demand for it is increasing in direct proportion to economic development. Water is needed not just for survival, but for cooking, cleaning and bathing in homes; for irrigation in agriculture; for cooling and mixing in industries; for entertainment and various other purposes. The irony of the situation is that even as demand for water has been increasing, pollution from untreated industrial and sewage waste has been killing existing water bodies, reducing the overall supply of fresh water. Thus, a scarcity of water has become a bitter reality in today's world, and rights to water resources come increasingly under threat as fresh water becomes scarce.

Assigning property rights to water is a completely non-acceptable proposition for many people who firmly believe that rights over something that is not just a basic necessity of life, but a *source* of life, cannot be assigned to some individuals or a group of individuals. Water is needed for survival, not just by human beings, but by all living creatures on earth. How then can it belong to just a few (Barlow and Clark, 2002) A key argument is that every human being should have access to water, and everyone should be able to get what they need for survival, because water is a common good. Those who support this argument further believe that water cannot therefore be a property right for anyone, rather it should be a fundamental right for everyone.

However, it is argued by others (Iyer, 2003) that when water is used for commercial purposes (for irrigation, industries, water parks, etc.) rather than for survival, it should not seem unethical that the ones who benefit from its use should pay something in return for it. Such water should be allowed to be traded and markets can be set up for such purposes where water becomes a commodity, rather than a basic right.

It is not easy to see how smoothly the same resource can, based on the use to which it is put, act as a 'fundamental right' at one instance and become a marketable commodity at another. Are there checks and balances in the system that can ensure that water is available to everyone for survival first, before it can be used for other purposes?

As noted above, millions of Indians do not have access to water; and even fewer have access to safe drinking water. At the same time, it is not that because of this, water is not available for commercial purposes in India. Rather, in this, the elite have usually had precedence over the survival needs of the poor. It is not even true that water is not available only in arid regions due to geographical factors. A river full of water might be flowing alongside a village and yet the same village might be facing a severe water shortage, because the river water is used by the urban supply system, and hence not allowed to be used by the villagers. More than the physical atmosphere, it is the political economy of a region that defines who gets water and how much.

Present drought conditions do not happen merely because of weather or monsoon failure, which precipitated it, but also because of human factors which have led to over-exploitation of ground water, misuse of surface water and pollution of both. It is interesting to know that, in the nineteenth century while there were famine related deaths due to the non-availability of food, there was no talk about the lack of drinking water (Bhatia, 1992). As water is being cornered for use by a few and as its demand is increasing, droughts in today's world have changed their meaning: water scarcity precedes food scarcity in a drought-affected region.

As Jairath (2003) strongly argues, "Droughts as the inevitable consequence of water scarcity thus obfuscate its socially manufactured nature. Efforts that focus on the augmentation of water supply per se and ignore the skewed social control over extant water resources by the privileged minority are fraught with failure. Increased water availability subject to the same inequity of access merely reproduces the relative shortage for the majority. It is this relativity of socially generated water scarcity that is hidden by presenting droughts as an absolute shortage of water availability in a region."

Haven't we all witnessed lush green patches of irrigated fields in the middle of severely drought-affected regions? Isn't it known that water is provided through canals for irrigating sugarcane in one area while the neighbouring area may be be suffering from severe drinking water shortage? Worse still, it has been noted that in the villages through which canals pass, the women struggle to get potfuls of water from failing water sources, but are not allowed to touch the gallons of water flowing by in the canals (Shah, 2002). Water is often easily available in thousands of gallons for water parks and swimming pools in luxurious residential colonies, and women in the nearby slums wait for hours to fill up just a few pots. As the Narmada Bachao Andolan leader Medha Patkar says, water scarcity is a result of a wasteful economy where a culture of wastefulness is practised by a few at the expense of the needs of many (Rajesh, 2000).

While emphasizing the realities of water allocation, we cannot deny the seriousness of the problem of a limited quantum of water. The need for water conservation is acute. Water is limited in nature and hence should be used with care, so that the demand for it remains manageable. Although this essay focuses on water rights and subsidies, it fully recognizes and acknowledges the crucial importance of water conservation.

WATER: A CRUCIAL ISSUE FOR GENDER RESEARCHERS

Collecting water for domestic purposes is the responsibility of women. An average woman asks for water for the purposes of drinking, cooking, bathing, house cleaning, washing clothes, and for animals. There is no controversy over the theoretical point that water for such domestic purposes should be available to all, without any discrimination. The National Water Policy 2002, in fact assigns the first priority to drinking water (Iyer, 2001). There is no policy, however, that states that water for such domestic purposes should take precedence over any other use of water. There is no guarantee in the Constitution that this use is a basic right that should supersede all other uses of water. In other words, no action is taken anywhere to ensure that drinking water indeed gets the first priority. The National Water Policy does not try to operationalise the priority given to drinking water.

Bina Agarwal (1994) argues for title over land for women. However, it is equally important, if not more so, to demand priority rights over water for women. Women should have the very first right over water when they demand it for drinking and domestic use.

Why should water rights be included as a topic in gender studies? Consider the suffering and hardship so many women have to undergo just in order to fetch water: rural women in water poor villages, for example, spend hours walking long disances to fetch water. They develop severe backaches and legaches, and some even complain of hair loss from carrying heavy pots of water on their heads. In villages or shanty towns where each area has a tap or a hand pump, the women spend a lot of time filling water (that often comes only as a trickle) from this source. Even middle class women in many cities spend considerable amounts of time filling water, because the pressure of the flow is often very low, and shortages are common for at least half the year. Considering that these three groups would account for at least two thirds of the population of women in India, the problem of water becomes a burning problem for any gender researcher. In this context, it is interesting to note that whenever an all-women panchayat is formed, one problem that the members invariably attend to is that of water (Datta, 1998).

Throughout this essay, we argue that water for domestic purposes should be given precedence over all other uses. It is tragic that this needs to be even said and it is difficult to believe that such an important resource is so frivolously allocated. Researchers and policy makers have simply not paid much attention to water rights; rather they have focused much more on land and forest rights. In the absence of research on the subject, the National Water Policy makers might have indeed found it difficult to operationalise the priority accorded to drinking water.

Right over water is not so much of an issue in urban areas. The main debate about water supply in urban areas revolves around the availability of water and water charges. In the face of a fiscal crisis in many regional governmental bodies, the problem of water subsidies has become acute. At the same time, resorting to raising water charges may lead to lesser accessibility to water for poor families. Thus this question needs to be discussed in the context of accessibility to water for all urban families.

This essay deals with two key issues: property rights over water and subsidies given for water. When water is not provided by the government, as is the case in many villages, it is rights over the resource that will determine the accessibility to water. When, on the other hand, water is provided by the government, the question of how much the user pays for the infrastructure supposedly determines the quality and reliability of services. Thus the price of water becomes an important issue.

It is our contention in this essay that first rights over water should be for drinking purposes (this will impact on women, since they are the ones who shoulder the responsibility of fetching water) before it is made available for any other purpose. To operationalise the concept of granting first rights over water to women, we first need to understand the prevailing property rights regimes. Three property rights regimes are discussed in the literature on water: riparian, public allocation and prior appropriation. We look at these in the second section of this essay. Issues related with equity for each of these property rights are also examined. The third section discusses property rights over ground water specifically, since most of the drinking water for the rural areas comes from this source.

Making water reach the taps of urban and rural households involves costs. The problems of management of man-made water supply systems are discussed later in this essay. The debate mainly deals with two issues (1) the advisability of allowing the private sector into water supply systems and (2) water charges.

This essay also looks at experiments with various property rights regimes in other countries and tries to draw lessons for India. Based on all these studies, we put forward a tentative model for water management. We then summarise the discussion and offers some concluding remarks.

PROPERTY RIGHTS OVER WATER

Ostrom et al (reference missing) maintain that in situations of scarcity, when water users interact without the benefit of effective rules limiting access and defining rights and duties, substantial free riding in two forms is likely: overuse without concern for its negative effects on others and a lack of contributed resources for maintaining and improving the water resource itself. The authors argue that under such circumstances, group or individual property rights regimes can help in more effective management of such a natural resource. In this section, we discuss the prevailing property rights regimes existing in India: in other words, who owns water, who can access it and how much is allowed to be used.

Types of Property Rights Regimes in Water

Property rights can be based on three systems (Jyotishi and Rout, 2005): riparian rights, public allocation and prior appropriation rights. Riparian rights link the right to use the resource to the community/individual geographically closer to the resource. Such rights have always been recognized in India: the people living close to a river/stream always have the right to use the water, although they can not divert it or stop it without the approval of the government. In spite of general acceptance of such rights, it is interesting that once the water is stopped through dams by the State, riparian rights cease to exist. In such cases nearby villages do not have the right to use the water that they have traditionally been using; the dammed water becomes the sole property of the government.

Medha Patkar and her associates from the Narmada Bachao Andolan have been demanding riparian rights for the village communities living beside a river, whether there is a dam on the river or not. The idea is to change the pattern of water allocation from urban centric to rural centric. Also, if the rights are awarded to the community rather than individuals having their lands beside the water body, the activists hope that this will lead to much more equitable distribution of water. It should be noted though that riparian rights are not always equitable. If granted to individuals, the one with the longest straw gets the most water.

Water rights are not connected to land rights in all countries; but in India, they are. The wisdom of granting such rights is justifiably questioned often. Reddy (EPW, July 13, 2002) argues that delinking of water rights from land rights (abolishing the riparian rights) will help in addressing equity issues effectively. However, the transaction costs of enforcing such a system would be enormous. Political factors, for example, will make it extremely difficult to change the ownership rights over ground water. This is discussed in more detail later.

Public Allocation

Public allocation involves distribution of water by government agencies. Water supplied by pipelines comes under this sets of rights. Water tanks in villages which have outlets nearby for filling water also fall in the same category. The water needed for urban/ rural water supply systems belongs to the government. In other words, property rights for water meant for public allocation belong exclusively to the government. The riparian rights of the nearby villages are superseded for such water bodies. As mentioned in the Introduction, an urban-centric and elitist bias exists under such rights regimes.

Within the public distribution system, water for domestic purposes gets priority over other uses. In other words, under public allocation, it is not easy to divert water from residential areas to industrial/entertainment areas. Such a move would surely result in a public uproar. Thus priority needs to be given to water for drinking and domestic purposes. However, even under public allocation, the bias remains elitist.

Prior Appropriation Rights

Prior appropriation rights are limited only to those who first claim the resource. Let us take an example. The right to dig wells theoretically belongs to all. However, in cases of excessive withdrawal, a blanket stay on digging wells can be imposed. Under such circumstances, the rights enjoyed by the well owners who had already dug wells become the prior appropriation rights. It is obvious that even this regime can be very inequitable. In India, except for surface water bodies that are used for public allocation, the water rights are riparian or prior appropriation rights. Most of these rights are neither granted nor enforced by the State, rather the users have simply enforced their rights over a resource.

Given the fact that women are usually not empowered enough to enforce their rights, their rights over water are generally superseded by others; even though the purposes for which these property right holders use water might be of lesser importance than human survival.

PROPERTY RIGHTS OVER GROUND WATER

There is an asymmetry in Indian law about ownership between flowing surface water and groundwater. In respect of the former, the law does not recognize ownership rights; there are only rights of use. However, in terms of the Indian Easements Act, the ownership of land carries with it the ownership of the groundwater under it, subject to regulation and control by the State (Iyer, 2001). Thus water rights for ground water are connected with land rights. When about 85 per cent of the rural drinking water comes from ground water, this Act has very serious implications for women who fetch water for their families. Serious inequities have come into existence because of this law. And many of these concern women.

One factor which leads to serious inequities because of this law is the competing uses of water. About 50 per cent of the irrigated water comes from ground water and 85 per cent of rural drinking water also comes from ground water (Iyer, 2003). Well irrigation has led to heavy exploitation of groundwater, resulting in a reversal of the ratio of withdrawal and recharge of water. It should be emphasized that in spite of population pressure in rural areas, the demand for domestic water is never so much that it could dry up the aquifer. Large scale over-exploitation of ground water in rural areas always comes from its commercial use, not the domestic. And yet, when aquifers go dry, women have no one to turn to; it is perfectly legal for the landowners to withdraw as much ground water as they please.

The groundwater policies of the government have also (perhaps unknowingly) tended towards encouraging over-exploitation. These are in the nature of providing incentives for groundwater development such as subsidized credit, and subsidized power or diesel/kerosene. While these have helped in promoting groundwater development in the regions where such development was below potential, they have also led to over-exploitation of the resource in fragile resource regions. It is interesting that no attempts were made at the policy level to strengthen the natural resource base in terms of replenishing the water table (Reddy, 2002). Over use of irrigation has made even drinking water scarce. Such priority given to irrigation over drinking water has surprisingly not been questioned.

Water rights being connected to land rights affect the poor adversely, since most of them do not own land and hence would not have access to water easily. Small and marginal farmers cannot afford to drill borewells or tubewells (they usually own dug wells which, in many areas, have gone dry). Thus the economically backward people are denied their genuine share in the common pool resource (Reddy, 2002; Iyer, 2001).

Even though it is politically difficult to do so, it is important to enact legislation that makes all water bodies available first for domestic purposes and only after that for others.

Water Subsidies and Privatization

When water is fetched directly from a source and there is no middleman to distribute it, the question of who gets how much is decided according to who has water rights. But people living in urban areas do not fetch their own water from a source, rather water is made available to them through the water supply system built by the government. Thus water is not a 'free gift of nature' for the city dwellers, it reaches them after considerable expenditure is incurred by the system. Therefore there has to be a charge for the end users, in this case, city dwellers.

There is no controversy about whether or not there should be water charges. Indeed, there seems to be general agreement that this is a necessary thing to do. The controversy is really about how much the user should pay. The World Bank thinks that the users should pay the entire cost of building the water supply infrastructure and maintaining it. Barlow and Clarke (2002) feel that users should pay minimum charges, or no charges. The dilemma is: if too much is charged for water, the poor are deprived of the most basic necessity of life. And if too little is charged, it could result in extremely poor maintenance of water supply and the sewage system, leading to very little availability, considerable wastage, poor quality of water, large unserved areas, and so on.

The normal criteria in such cases would be to recover the operation and maintenance costs from the charges levied on the users. Since water is a basic necessity, the cost of building the infrastructure can, therefore, be borne by the government. However, determination of water charges seems to be more of a political issue than an economic one. People living in Hyderabad, Mumbai and Chennai pay more than 100 per cent of the operation and maintenance costs (i.e. a part of capital costs are also recovered from the water charges), while people of Kolkata pay just 14 per cent, and those in Delhi a mere 26 per cent. Mumbai charges a flat rate of Rs. 3.50 per kilolitre of water while Delhi starts at 30 paise per kilolitre for small users.

Do people in Mumbai feel that they are paying too much for water? We decided to ask some people living in the city's slums. Instead of asking whether they feel that water charges are high, we just asked them how much they pay for water and what were the main problems they faced regarding water. They told us some heart-rending stories about their water problems: not only does the supply come at unearthly hours, it sometimes does not come at all, there is just one tap among 40-50 households and every morning there are bitter fights over water. While everyone spoke of this, no one complained that the costs were too high. Thus the ability to pay for water does seem to exist among the poor in Mumbai. If affordability was the criteria, the poor of Delhi should be able to pay at least as much as the Mumbai poor pay. But they end up paying 10 times less. It is difficult to justify such low charges on economic grounds and difficult therefore to justify the huge subsidies given for water by Delhi and Kolkata.

Raising water charges might prove to be politically very difficult for the governments of Delhi and West Bengal (however much they can ill afford it), because water is treated as a 'non-tradable commodity' and a fundamental right. The government of Delhi has found a solution for this problem: it has handed over the management of the water supply system to private companies. These companies can raise water charges and the government can distance itself from them, hence not letting it affect them. Although this is an effective way for the government, there are many issues involved in privatizing water supply systems that need discussion.

The World Bank was one of the main proponents of the idea of privatizing water supply systems. It states that 'public water and sanitation services are often plagued by inefficiency' (Bosch et al, 2000). Most of the problems faced by the developing nations regarding water, are shown in World Bank literature to be mainly a result of poor and corrupt management by government bodies. It is argued that the more efficient management practices of the private sector can help to improve the situation.

The World Bank also advocates that given the scarcity of water and the fact that often water is more wasted than used, full cost pricing of water is advisable. Full cost pricing would not only lead to water conservation, but would also ensure proper operation and maintenance of the water supply infrastructure. It is also possible to treat sewage water appropriately with full cost recovery (Cosgrove and Rijsberman, 2000). Full cost pricing will also ensure that additional investments in water infrastructure be made so that coverage is extended to the unserved poor (Faruqui, 2003).

Barlow and Clarke (2002), in their famous book "Blue Gold: The Fight to Stop the Corporate Theft of the World's Water", counter these arguments. They argue that privatization of water leads to many damaging effects, including rate hikes, cut-offs to customers who can't pay, reduced water quality, huge profits for corporate investors, secret contracts, bribery and corruption. They also point out that for private corporations, the prime targets have been water services in larger tourist areas and urban centres, leaving the smaller, less populated and less lucrative municipalities to governmental stewardship.

Their most forceful argument, and one that has gained much support, is that privatization of water supply might result in exclusion of the poor from the water market altogether. They give the example of Mexico city. In 2001, Vivendi (a private company that had a contract to provide water to Mexico city) increased its rates by 60 per cent, which led to payment defaults and, consequently, service cutoffs mostly affecting poor residents in that quadrant. Another often cited case is that of Cochabamba, Bolivia, where a private company was given a contract to supply water. They increased the water charges beyond the reach of most; public protests and riots forced the government to revert the decision on privatization (Barlow and Clarke, 2004).

Faruqui (2003) replies to these criticisms by arguing that it is not correct to say that the poor will be made to pay more under the privatization scheme. "The unserved poor often pay 10 to 20 times the price that the served non-poor pay per unit for water". However, the fact remains that not all poor pay such high prices for water; and even when they do, it is only for some days in a year, not every day.

Calculations are easily available, but given that the price of water with subsidies could be Rs 4-5 per kilolitre, we feel that not many people in India would be able to afford water at full cost price. Full cost pricing does not seem to be a humane solution for water supply problems. It can expose the poor to untold hardships. That is the reason we advocate a system where operation and maintenance costs and only 10-20 per cent of capital costs are recovered by water charges (as happens in Mumbai).

One more concern exists regarding privatization: much more importance might start being given to 'high valued' use of water over 'low valued' use, thus resulting in allocation of water towards such high valued uses. The low valued uses include water needed for survival. Thus priority might be accorded to commercial uses over survival uses of water. Privatization, thus, could go against the interests of the urban poor.

Above all, in tackling the problem of water scarcity, demand management is more crucial than supply management. There is no guarantee that increasing water charges would reduce water wastage at the household level. Otherwise, by the same logic, an increase in fuel prices should have reduced fuel consumption. Unless the value of water is realized by citizens, and their demand for water starts falling, water shortages will persist. Privatization cannot be expected to solve the fundamental problems plaguing the water situation.

WATER RIGHTS: LESSONS FROM OTHER NATIONS

Continuing from the privatization debate of the previous section, it should be noted that the argument against charging full cost price holds only if water is used for domestic purposes. As far as commercial uses of water (like irrigation for commercial agriculture, industrial processes, or luxury uses like sauna) are concerned there is no controversy about charging for these. It would be informative to learn how this problem is solved elsewhere in the world.

In South Africa (Reddy, 2002), to promote efficient use of water, user charges are imposed. These charges are determined on the basis of full financial costs of providing access to water. All water uses are covered under this new pricing policy, except survival use. The policy makers decided that water for basic human needs will be provided free of cost. This is achieved by providing the first 25 litres of water per capita per day free to all. Nations can decide how much quantity they would like to provide free of charge for cooking, drinking, bathing and cleaning, but giving water for most basic necessities free is a lesson to be learnt from South Africa.

In Mexico (Shah et al, 2004), agriculture's role has been declining in the economy and the non-agricultural demand for water has been rising. Hence in 1989, land ownership was separated from water ownership. The design manual of the CNA provided that no user could impound or divert more than 1080 m^3 of water except by obtaining a 'concession' from the CNA. In sum, all water used for purposes other than domestic personal use needed a licence. Although this system worked well for large users like industrial and commercial establishments, municipal councils or modulos (the associations of farmers managing surface water for irrigation), the real difficulty has been with water rights of numerous agricultural users who account for over 80 per cent of water use. Here, the sheer numbers of users involved and the logistical complexity of processing their requests for concessions is proving to be a great challenge.

Mexico thus offers a warning signal. It is not easy to regulate the uses of water. If Mexico is finding it difficult to regulate its 70,000 tubewell owners; on the last count, India had 20 million private pumpers, and this number has been growing at a rate of 1 million a year in recent years (Shah et al, 2004). Clearly, the system of private water rights through issue of licences that is proving so difficult to work on tubewell owners in Mexico, will prove nearly impossible to implement in India. There do not seem to be easy solutions for the ground water problem; be it for a specific use or regulation over water withdrawn for conservation purposes.

In China (Shen, 2003), all water resources are owned by the state. A water drawing permit system has been implemented to authorize the transfer of water to the users. In other words, private individuals are given operational rights over water, if not direct property rights. The permit gives user rights and disposal rights to the users whereas the owner state regulates the water resource quantity and development measures. The efficiency of this system is not known. However, it is argued that in India too water allocation mechanisms for irrigation would work better if management was handed over to farmers' associations. The study by Menon et al (2005), on the contrary, shows that property rights do not matter as much as the dependence of people on that resource, the timeliness or effectiveness of the delivery, and the existence of effective rules and mechanisms. In other words, granting of property rights is not the only way to achieve efficient allocation of water, effective rules and mechanisms can achieve it even within an existing system.

A BLUEPRINT FOR OPERATIONALIZING WATER RIGHTS IN RURAL AREAS

In this section, we try to propose a model for operationalizing the concept of according priority to drinking water over all other uses. Granting property rights over water can be a very sensitive issue.

As Bruns and Meinzen-Dick (2000) say, "Water rights are not just an analytical abstraction. People depend on water for their life and livelihood; people also get killed fighting over water. Around the world, competition for water is increasing. . . . Conflicting claims challenge the social institutions which mediate access to water."

It needs to be emphasized that individual women resort to a range of strategies for claiming and obtaining water. Government, religious and customary laws, development project rules and unwritten local norms may all address who should receive water, from which sources and for what purposes. Understanding water allocation should start from the local perspectives of those who use water, their daily experiences, the meanings through which they conceive of water and rights and the options they have available for acquiring water and defending their access to this vital resource. Research needs to be undertaken on such strategies in various regions of India. Only after being equipped with such knowledge, would we be able to determine how women's position or negotiating powers for getting access to drinking water can be strengthened.

The local rules get established via various types of negotiations. It needs to be recognized that decisions are not reached only through talks on a negotiating table. Negotiation could take the form of abstention, obstruction, resistance and sabotage. All of these forms have been used while negotiating rights over irrigation water. Sengupta (2000) describes a case where a village forcibly diverted the canal water, leaving the downstream canal people high and dry. After trying out various methods of persuasion, a village downstream finally decided to take law into its own hands. The villagers came in a mob and broke down the structure erected by the upstream village, releasing the water again for their village. Many people got killed in the process.

Such forceful means of negotiating accessibility to drinking water are not likely to be available to disempowered rural women. That means that whatever might be the strategies used for getting access to drinking water, many women will still have to undergo considerable hardship to fetch water. As discussed in the first section of this paper, there are numerous instances of women not being able to establish satisfactory access to water for domestic use. They are disempowered and are unlikely or unable to use means like obstruction or sabotage. Even at the negotiation table, they are not able to negotiate on an equal footing with others. Hence women, especially from water poor villages, need help in tackling the problem of accessibility to water.

Establishing accessibility to water also gets considerably affected by rules and laws of the state. Local laws prevail *within* the environment of state laws, however remote these may sometimes seem (Bruns and Meizendick, 2000). Local rules rarely exist in isolation from the state legal system. Once the laws are declared, the local system reworks these to lay down who may have what, how much the compliance will be with the law and to what extent and in what forms the violations will take place. Considering the importance of state laws in the negotiation process, we feel that their change in a positive direction can help in enhancing women's rights over water.

Thus, it might be worthwhile for the state to attempt to undertake the ownership of all water in the country, whether surface or underground. It might not be too far fetched an idea, as discussed in section 5, and there are other countries in the world that have tried it quite successfully. Under such a property rights regime, user rights can be given to all individuals for filling up 15 pots of water (or about 400-500 litres) a day from any well or canal in the village. With such rights, women can collect water for their domestic requirements from the nearest water body. Also, when a drought strikes and water remains in only one or two wells in the entire village (or only in a canal), women can rightfully collect water for domestic use from such water sources. Even if the river water is collected for supplying to urban areas, the villages close to the river should have the right to demand at least 500 litres of water per household. Then they would not have to walk for miles to get it.

Farmers can be allowed to use the water from their wells but *only after* the drinking water requirements of the village are satisfied. Each village will then need to quantify its drinking water requirements by discussing them in the gram sabha. Based on the requirements, the gram panchayat can decide the number of hours farmers can be allowed to use their wells per day (there would be no charge for using the well water by the well owners, the panchayat would only determine the number of hours they can be used), depending on the water table of the village. This would check excessive withdrawal of ground water and ensure sustainable drinking water supply over the long run. If there is water shortage in the village, all other uses of water, except that for domestic use, would be immediately stopped.

As discussed, in the case of Mexico, monitoring the actual extractions by concession holders and restricting the withdrawals to agreed levels could be an almost impossible task for the central authority. However, at the village level, where any passer-by can be watching when the field is irrigated, implementation of the laid down limits could be more feasible.

Alternatively, instead of specifying the number of hours the irrigation system is allowed to work, the gram panchayats can decide to impose charges on the user of ground water according the crops grown. The suitability of crops for a region depends on the natural resources available in the concerned region. If a crop requires too much of a resource (say water) that is short in supply in the region, the panchayat can decide to impose higher charges on those crops. Otherwise, a small fee can be imposed for protective irrigation. As seen in the case of Mexico (Shah et al, 2004), higher charges for water changed the cropping pattern: wheat area fell from 3,018 to 539 ha between 1993-2002 but sorghum area increased from 2,580 to 3,209 ha and barley area shot up from 57 to 1941 ha. Similar results might be seen with the scheme that we propose. It needs to be emphasized though, that the success of such a system would be dependent on the existence of effective rules and mechanisms for their enforcement, as pointed out by Menon et al (2005).

The proposed model may be considered impractical, given

the fact that the decentralized governance system has not worked well in many parts of India. At the same time, it could be argued that where decentralization has worked, it has made a notable difference. Thus the proposed model too might make a difference. Additionally, monitoring and control are relatively easy with a decentralized system; these are essential for the proposed model to work. Most importantly, it would be difficult for the centralized system to accurately estimate the water demand for each village and to prioritize water uses according to the water situation in each place. Hence the decentralized system of water allocation seems like a better system to propose.

Some Suggestions for Water Subsidies in a Public Allocation System

Under the public allocation system, drinking water does get priority over other uses. Here, as the privatization debate showed, the more relevant question is to determine how much to charge for the water. In section four, we had suggested that the state should try to provide the infrastructure for the water supply system, whereas the users should be asked to bear the operation and maintenance cost.

It was also mentioned that increasing water charges is a sensitive political issue. Therefore we suggest that water charges should be made progressive charges instead of flat rates. Delhi has progressive rates but they start at too low a level and do not go up high enough. To beat the political system, the lowest rates can be kept low but the progression of charges can and should be quicker. Water charges can be dependent not only on the water use but also on the type of house to which it is supplied. The charges can be low for a slum, but can be very high for bunglows with lawns , or for luxurious colonies.

We further propose that heavier levies be imposed on all users requiring water for luxury purposes (for example, residential colonies with swimming pool, sauna, etc.). Such measures would ensure better conservation of water and consequently, can lead to improved water supply to the water poor pockets of the city.

While such measures are taken for ensuring better allocation of water and giving first priority to drinking water, special programmes need to be designed to augment water supply as well as for conserving and reuse of water.

SUMMARY AND CONCLUSION

This essay argues that water for drinking purposes should be accorded priority over all other uses. Since it is women's responsibility to fetch water for the household, it implies that women should be given the first right over water.

Noting that accessibility to water is more hampered by water allocation rather than water availability per se, the essay concentrates on property rights: who is allowed to have how much water. None of the property rights regimes prevailing in the country at present assure first and foremost priority to drinking water for all. The legal requirements need to be revised to ensure such priority.

The accessibility to water is determined not only by the government, but by religious and customary laws, development project rules and unwritten local norms. The authority to allocate water, hence, should be delegated to the local level governments, where the gram sabha has the authority to decide whether to release water for other purposes or not. This would ensure local resource assessment based rules and effective monitoring of the implementation. Thus the solution to a macro problem of water allocation may lie in a micro—decentralized system of decision-making regarding water allocation.

While trying to allocate available water effectively, steps also need to be taken to augment water supply (through measures like rainwater harvesting and watershed management) as well as to reduce the wastage of water and encourage its reuse. If all this is done, women will not have to go through untold hardships just to acquire a few pots of water.

REFERENCES

Agarwal, Bina (1994) *A Field of One's Own: Gender and Land Rights in South Asia*, Cambridge: Cambridge University Press.

Bansil, P. C. (2004) *Water Management in India*, Delhi: Concept Publising Company.

Barlow, Maude and Clarke, Tony (2002) *Blue Gold: The Fight to Stop The Corporate Theft of the World's Water*, Delhi: Leftword Books.

Barlow, Maude, Clarke, Tony (2004) "The Struggle for Latin America's Water", *NACLA Report on the Americas*, 10714839, Jul/Aug 2004, Vol. 38, Issue 1.

Bhatia, Bela (1992) *Lush Fields and Parched Throats: The Political Economy of Ground water in Gujarat*, WIDER Working Paper 100.

Bosch, C., Hommann, K., Sadoff, C., and Travers, L. (2000) "Water, Sanitation and Poverty" in *Poverty Reduction Strategy Sourcebook: Water and Sanitation*, World Bank.

Bruns and Meinzen-Dick (ed) (2000) *Negotiating Water Rights*, Delhi: Vistaar Publications.

Cosgrove, W. J. and Rijsberman, F. R. (2000) *World Water Vision: Making Water Everyone's Business*, World Water Council, London: Earthscan Publications Ltd.

Datta, Bisakha (ed) (1998), *And who will make the chapattis?: A study of all women panchayats in Maharashtra*, Kolkata: Stree Publishers.

Faruqui, Naser (2003) "Balancing between the eternal yesterday and eternal tomorrow: economic globalization, water and equity" in *Rethinking Water Management: Innovative Approaches to Contemporary Issues*, edited by Figueres et al, London: Earthscan Publications Ltd.

Government of India (2001-02), Ministry of Water Resources, Annual Report

Iyer, Ramaswamy (2001) "Water: Charting a course for the future", *Economic and Political Weekly*, March 31, 2001.

Iyer, Ramaswamy (2003) *Water: Perspectives, Issues and Concerns*, Delhi: Sage Publications.

Jairath, Jasween (2003) "Drought of Sanity and Flood of the Absurd: Politics of water discourse", *Economic and Political Weekly*, February 15, 2003.

Jyotishi, Amalendu and Rout, Satyapriya (2005) "Water rights in Decaan region: Insights from Baliraja and other water institutions", *Economic and Political Weekly*, Vol XL No. 2, Jan 8, 2005.

Menon, Vineetha, Paul, Antonyto, and Nair, K. N. (2005) "Dynamics of Irrigation Institutions", *Economic and Political Weekly*, February 26, 2005

Ostrom, Elinor (1990) *Governing the Commons: The evolution of institutions for collective action*, Cambridge: Cambridge University Press.

Rajesh (2000) "Rajasthan: Drought, Debt and Poverty", *Economic and Political Weekly*, June 17, 2000.

Reddy, Ratna (2002) "Water security and Management: Lessons from South Africa", *Economic and Political Weekly*, July 13, 2002.

Rosegrant, Mark, Cai, Ximing and Cline, Sarah (2002) *World water and food by 2025: dealing with scarcity*, IFPRI, Washing DC (taken from www.ifpri.org/pubs).

Sengupta, Nirmal (2000) "Negotiations with an uniformed bureaucracy: Water rights on system tanks in Bihar", in *Negotiating Water Rights*, ed. Bruns and Meinzen-Dick, Delhi: Vistaar Publications.

Shah, Anil (2002)"Women, water, irrigation: Respecting Women's priorities", *Economic and Political Weekly*, October 26, 2002.

Shah, Tushaar, Scott, Christopher, and Buechler, Stephanie (2004) "Water Sector Reforms in Mexico: Lessons for India's New Water Policy", *Economic and Political Weekly*, January 24, 2004.

Shen, Dajun (2003) "Water rights and their management: A comparative country study and its implications for China", in *Rethinking Water Management: Innovative Approaches to Contemporary Issues*, edited by Figueres et al, London: Earthscan Publications Ltd.

Engendering Health Rights in the New Global Economy

RAVI DUGGAL

> Man is the only creature that consumes without producing. He does not give milk, he does not lay eggs, he is too weak to pull the plough, and he cannot run fast enough to catch rabbits. Yet he is lord of all the animals. He sets them to work; he gives back to them the bare minimum that will prevent them from starving and the rest he keeps for himself. (This quote is even more relevant for patriarchy and the New Global Economy).
>
> George Orwell: *Animal Farm*

INTRODUCTION

The last decade of the millennium and the first few years of the new millennium have witnessed unprecedented changes globally. The global transformation brought about by the new economic policies has certainly not shaped the world into a place where the misery suffered by masses has reduced in any significant way or violation of their fundamental human rights has lessened. In fact, the gulf between the developed and underdeveloped world has widened with a shift in control over the political economy from politics to economics.[1] (Eisenstein 1998, Appadurai 1996, Smith 1997) The new engines of change are not political ideologies but globalized economics which use the multilateral institutional route to shape international policies wherein the driving forces are not nations but a new breed of international bureaucrats who are increasingly coming from global business establishments or are economists and social scientists who are supporters of global business tenets. Hence it is not surprising that the new Prime Minister of the largest democracy in the world, India, is an international economist who is also supported by another international economist as head of the Planning Commission of the same nation and in tandem they are changing the direction of India's political economy to fit the curves of the new global political economy.

Thus World Trade Organisation (WTO), General Agreement on Trade and Tariffs (GATT) and General Agreement on Trade in Services (GATS), Intellectual Property Rights (IPR) and Trade Related Aspects of Intellectual Property Rights (TRIPS), International Monetary Fund (IMF) and World Bank (WB), Multilateral Investment Guarantee Agency (MIGA), Asian Development Bank (ADB) and other affiliate alphabetical combos have taken over global governance. All these multilateral bodies are controlled by business interests based in finance capitals of the developed world and foist their agenda of promoting capitalist globalization in an increasingly unipolar world. This process started towards the end of the last millennium continues into the new millennium.

So if this is the way the world is changing, then the human rights agenda, which is often in conflict with capitalist globalization because the latter often violates various human rights, including health rights, also needs to follow a similar trajectory of multilateral or multinational initiatives. Thus alternate alphabetical combos which seek to reclaim human rights have emerged to challenge the capitalist globalization—World Social Forum (WSF), Peoples Global Action (PGA), Peoples Health Movement (PHM), Earth Charter Initiative (EHI), NGO Coalition for the International Criminal Court (CICC), Jubilee 2000, the International Campaign to Ban Landmines (ICBL), International Gender and Trade Network (IGTN), Global Health Watch (GHW), Trans National Institute (TNI), Transparency International (TI), Women's Environment and Development Organisation (WEDO) etc. All these are civil society initiatives and believe that not only is Another World Possible but also that Another World is Necessary and these initiatives also actively use multilateral treaties and declarations such as the International Covenant for Civil and Political Rights (ICCPR), the International Covenant for Economic Social and Cultural Rights (ICESCR), the Convention for Elimination of Discrimination of all forms Against Women (CEDAW), the Child Rights Convention (CRC), Health For All (HFA), ICPD Program of Action, Beijing Platform, Agenda 21 etc. to demand respect, protection and fulfillment of various human rights from governments across the world.

Thus the new global economy is the new arena for conflict and negotiations for various human rights, including health rights. Experience over the world shows that if citizens of a country have to enjoy basic quality health care as a human right then:

- The State must be an active player
- The financing of health care has to be under some form of public monopoly or single-payer mechanism
- A lack of purchasing power is not an impediment to realize the highest attainable standard of health
- The private provision of health care is well regulated and
- A law mandating all the above has to be enacted

This is the experience of most of Western Europe (UK, Germany, Netherlands, Sweden etc.), Canada and a few countries from Latin America (Costa Rica, Brazil, Chile, Cuba) and Asia-Pacific (Japan, Australia, South Korea, Thailand, Sri Lanka) (WHO 2002). By contrast the USA, India and a number of underdeveloped countries which have weak state intervention and participation are unable to respect, protect and fulfil the right to the highest attainable standard of health as mandated by Article 12 of ICESCR and explained in General Comment 14 pertaining to this Article. (UNCHR 2000).

HEALTH AND HEALTHCARE

Health is increasingly becoming a tradable commodity and GATS is facilitating that process wherein liberalization of the service sector, including health services becomes negotiable. Globally the delivery of healthcare is increasingly in the private domain, though in many places, especially the welfare capitalist economies, financing of healthcare is through a public mechanism (OECD 2003). In India, for instance, provision of healthcare as well as its financing is a public private mix with overarching dominance of the private sector, especially in financing (largely out-of-pocket) (Duggal 2004). This makes India highly vulnerable under GATS because the political economy of healthcare in India is such that it cannot use the exemption clause in GATS negotiation for the health sector (Srivastav 2004). The promotion of medical tourism in India is a classical case which enhances the vulnerability of India in GATS negotiations. And what is worse in India's case is that it has not even used effectively the compulsory licensing clause of the Doha Declaration of Public Health under TRIPS in its new Patent Act. Since India is a major producer (8 per cent of global volume and 95 per cent of this in the private sector) and exporter (over 50 per cent of its production) (MoCF 2004) of pharmaceuticals it is not keen about compulsory licensing.

India has the largest private market for healthcare in the world with 82 per cent of health expenditure being accounted as out-of-pocket (NCMH 2005). In fact even in the US, which has the largest health economy in the world accounting for 15 per cent of its GDP, the State contributes to over 40 per cent of health spending through the Medicare and Medicaid programs. (OECD 2003) In recent years the introduction and raising of user-fees in public health institutions in India has added to the personal burden of health expenditure, especially for the poor. As though this were not enough, public investment in the health sector since the macroeconomic reforms of the nineties has declined and this is reflected in drastically reduced capital expenditures and no further expansion in the public health infrastructure. (Duggal 2005) Further revenue expenditures on health have declined both as a proportion to the GDP as well as percent of total government spending, and within this reduced expenditure allocative inefficiencies have increased especially after the 5th Pay Commission. (Ibid)

The above has further reduced the credibility and acceptability of the public health system and one sees declining utilisation rates of public health facilities. (NSSO 1998)[2] On the other hand the dominance of the private health sector is increasing but with absolutely no regulation and minimum standards being followed.

The medical profession pays no heed to self-regulation, ethics and has never looked at the possibility of an organized system of healthcare. In fact the profession is losing control to the corporate sector, which is now looking beyond the hospital sector at not only diagnostics but also consultant services and general practice. Such a scenario is bound to impact on costs and increases the burden of the patients. Such a situation is not good for 70 per cent of the country's population that lives in poverty or at subsistence level.

The health status indicators amply testify to the poor state of health and healthcare in India. Our trajectory has been worse than the low-income country average over the years and we reached that level only in the nineties and we are stagnating at that level. Infant and child mortality rates which had shown substantial improvements in the eighties with stepped up public health investment under the Minimum Needs Programme (MNP), especially in the rural areas, are presently not only stagnating but the rural-urban gap which was narrowing down is again getting wider. Apart from the rural-urban divide, there are issues in health and healthcare related to various vulnerable sections of the population and these are not only related to poverty and class concerns but also social concerns. Both access and health outcomes for women, dalits, adivasis, and other minority communities, show clear differentials in terms of adversities in health and healthcare. NFHS-2 and NSSO 52nd Round data provide strong evidence for this (NSSO 1998 and NFHS-2 2000).

While the existing situation is very dismal, the changing political economy does not show too much promise of change for the betterment of health and healthcare; unless of course there is a radical transformation in the political commitment. For this to take place the support of civil society pressures and demands for a transformation of the healthcare dispensation will be needed. The changing political economy demands reduced State participation in the economic sphere both in terms of policy and intervention. Its logic is that economic growth will impact poverty positively and increase purchasing power. The economic growth of the last decade and a half tells us that this does not happen because the impact of growth on poverty depends on how additional incomes get distributed. Global income distribution data shows that the share in income of the top 20 per cent countries increased from 70 per cent in 1960 to 89 per cent in 1998, that of the bottom 20 per cent declined from 2.3 per cent to 1.2 per cent and the middle 60 per cent declined from 28 per cent to 10 per cent, increasing the Gini coefficient from 0.54 to 0.70. (UNDP 1999) In fact Amartya Sen argues that economic growth may not necessarily be a driving force for better equity in health by citing the examples of Kerala, Sri Lanka and China who achieved good and equitable health outcomes independent of economic growth (Sen 2001).[3] Thus the new political economy has failed to strengthen the welfare role of the State. Under SAP and other related measures, economic growth increased and the State's intervention in the economy declined but so have Tax: GDP ratios and consequently investments, expenditures and interests in the social sectors. This trajectory of growth has worsened the situation for the poor and subsistent population of the country.

One very clear impact is declining state investments in the health sector. With rising debt burdens of the State, the social sectors are the first to receive the axe. There has been a declining trend since 1991 in social sector expenditures, especially by the Central government and this is best reflected in compression of grants to the states for social sector expenditures. (Duggal 2005) Health care expenditures too have been affected both in quantitative terms (declining real expenditures) and qualitative terms (increasing proportion of establishment costs and declining proportion on medicines, equipment, maintenance and new investments).

Another very striking impact is the rapidly rising cost of medicines. With a large dependence on the private health sector even by the poor this has meant extreme hardship. With the drug price control virtually on its way out and with India having signed the WTO treaty on IPR we are moving closer to international prices of drugs. The combined effect of the above facts makes a deadly mixture that results in reduced access of the poor to health care. Since the poor too have been active users of private health care their dependence on it makes the case for "right to health care" becoming a political agenda even a more distant dream.

At the global level the World Bank is propagating selective care for selected (targeted) populations under the public domain. (World Bank 1993) The WHO too has dropped its Health For All commitment and fallen in line with the World Bank thinking. This global pressure on the Indian State is evident through its policies of focusing on selective services (MoHFW 2003), for instance RCH and AIDS receive overriding support over primary health care or basic referral services.

Another trend that further reduces access is the increased corporate control of health care. New medical technologies have helped complete the commodification of health care and this has attracted increased interest of the corporate sector, which has jumped into the health care business in a very big way. The State has nurtured the private sector over the years and corporatisation is only a logical progression of the State's vision of health care provision. Some examples:

- Medical education is almost wholly State financed (though in the last decade private medical education has expanded rapidly) and its major beneficiary is the doctor who sets up private practice after his/her training.
- The government has provided concessions and subsidies to private medical professionals and hospitals to set up private practice and hospitals. It provided incentives, tax holidays, and subsidies to private pharmaceutical and medical equipment industry. It manufactured and supplied raw materials (bulk drugs) to private formulation units at subsidised rate/ low cost. It allowed exemptions in taxes and duties in importing medical equipment and drugs, especially the highly expensive new medical technologies. It has provided free land, capital as well as assured clientele for large private hospitals like Apollo and now it is even promoting medical tourism.
- The government has allowed the highly profitable private hospital sector to function as trusts which are exempt from taxes. Hence they don't contribute to the state exchequer even when they charge patients exorbitantly.
- Construction of public hospitals and health centres are gener-

ally contracted out to the private sector. The latter makes a lot of money but a large part of the infrastructure thus created, especially in rural areas is inadequately provided hence cannot meet the health care demands of the people.

- Medical and pharmaceutical research and development is largely carried out in public institutions but the major beneficiary is the private sector. Development of drugs, medical and surgical techniques etc. are pioneered in public institutions but commercialisation, marketing and profit appropriation is left with the private sector. Many private practitioners are also given honorary positions in public hospitals which they use openly to promote their personal interests.

GENDER DIMENSIONS

Inequities based on gender overall in India, when viewed in terms of access to healthcare or even health outcomes, may not appear to be very strong given the "larger issues" of livelihood, poverty, caste, rural-urban residence etc. But the evidence of patriarchal oppression is clearly there and best reflected in the declining sex-ratios, especially the child sex-ratios, due to the strong son-preference syndrome. Further, within various categories of inequities we do see gender differentials, which are more adverse for women. Thus gender inequities come out as quite complex and cross-cutting and hence cannot be viewed only in the context of a specific sector like health.

The Constitution of India through Fundamental Rights assures equality through Articles 14, 15, 16 and prohibits any discrimination based on sex. The Constitution has also made provisions for affirmative action, like reservations in access to education and employment, as well as in contesting elections, for groups which are recognized as having a disadvantage, and this includes quotas for women in various arenas where women are grossly under-represented with the objective of creating some level of gender equity. Apart from the provisions in the Constitution and various laws that support Constitutional mandate, support also comes from International Treaties and Declarations which India has signed and ratified. Thus the International Covenant for Civil and Political Rights (ICCPR), the International Covenant for Economic, Social and Cultural Rights (ICESCR), the Convention for Elimination of All Forms of Discrimination Against Women (CEDAW), the Child Rights Convention (CRC) etc., as well as various declarations which are based on provisions of these treaties like Health For All, ICPD Program of Action, the Beijing Declaration and Platform for Action, Declaration of Commitment on HIV/AIDS, the United Nations Millennium Declaration and Millennium Development Goals (MDGs) etc., provide further mandate for gender equity.

The above constitutional and legal provisions have no meaning if adequate resources to realize the mandates are not provided. Thus the right to equality before law may be a fundamental right but if vulnerable sections like the poor, adivasis or women do not get legal aid then the right has little meaning. For instance the 93rd Amendment of the Indian Constitution incorporated the right to education but the State has not been able to realize that right because it has been unable to commit the required quantum of resources and this gross violation of a fundamental right hence has no redressal. Further, the limited resources that are allocated and spent are often done in a very discriminatory manner leading to regional, class, social, and gender based inequities. With respect to health all these inequities operate and they are also synergistically linked.

What then are the consequences of gender inequities for health? Under a patriarchal social regime the consequences mostly target women. And hence one sees persistent gender disparities in health outcomes and in indicators of access to healthcare which favour men (Table 1). Critical indicators like infant and child mortality or maternal mortality for instance provide strong evidence of gender disparity. While male children at birth suffer higher mortality (neonatal mortality which is biologically determined), post-one month of being born girls begin to face discrimination as is clearly revealed in post-neonatal mortality and child mortality rates which are more adverse for girls. In the post neonatal period biology has a very little role to play and it is mostly social and economic factors that play a role.

Similarly discrimination in access to healthcare, especially maternal health services like antenatal care and safe deliveries, contributes to women's greater adverse health outcomes. Women suffer higher levels of morbidities but these are more likely to remain untreated as compared to men. Further women are larger users of public health facilities especially for hospital care and when the new macroeconomics impacts public health by reduced investments and expenditures or introduction of user fees under so called health sector reforms it is women who bear the larger brunt, not only in terms of their own health but also by increasingly becoming informal care takers in homes which because of low purchasing power may not be able to access private health services or the now user-fee charging public health services. In fact when resources are scarce as in the case of poor households, then in the distribution of resources for health care, when one has to purchase it, women and girls are more likely to be neglected. (Standing 2002)

Another impact of the New Global Economics in developing countries like India comes from the low-cost and deprofessionalised approach advocated by World Bank et.al. for the reason that these countries have limited resources. This advice from World Bank and other donors is in their own self-interest so as to assure that such countries are able to service their international debt repayments and hence discourage public agencies from investing further in medical care and get them to promote medical care in the private domain. The result of such a policy is clearly seen in India with a sophisticated, well developed and internationally competitive private health sector which now caters to global medical tourism. It is precisely these sets of policies that are destroying public health in India and further enhancing inequities in access to healthcare, and especially inequities based on gender.

CONCLUSION

It is clear from the above discussion that health and healthcare of the people of India, and especially the poor and various vulnerable groups, are being threatened. India was doing quite well on the health front until the late eighties and then it got SAP(ped) with macroeconomic reforms which spelt disaster for public health.

At the same time the private health sector found the space and opportunity to increase its presence—it is in this period when the Indian pharmaceutical sector went global, India became a destination for medical tourism, the corporatisation of healthcare happened and public health services in India begin to get privatized by charging user fees.

All this has contributed to increased vulnerabilities in access to healthcare and health outcomes, including gender injustice. To change this we have to debunk the policy route to health and healthcare and adopt a rights-based approach. The world over where health care is provided universally to its citizens it uses the rights framework and a single-payer mechanism to assure universal access to healthcare. It must not be forgotten that health is a public/social good and if marketised is subject to severe market failures and gross inequities. (Stiglitz 2002) Nowhere in the world have out-of-pocket payments led to equity and universal access in healthcare because health is a public/social good and this we need to reiterate strongly to reeducate the macroeconomists of this world, including our Prime Minister.

Table 1: Gender Disparities in Health Outcomes and Healthcare Access

Health/Care Indicator	*Unit*	*Male*	*Female*	*All*
	*Maternal and Child Health**			
Maternal Mortality Rate	Per 100,000 live births	-	540	-
IMR (SRS 2003)	Per 1000 live births	57	64	60
Infant Mortality Rate	Per 1000 live births	74.8	71.1	73
Child Mortality Rate	Per 1000 age 1- <5 yrs.	24.9	36.7	30.6
Under 5 mortality rate	Per 1000 age 0-5	97.9	105.2	101.4
Neonatal Mortality Rate	Per 1000 live births	50.7	44.6	47.7
Post Neonatal Mortality Rate	Per 1000 live births	24.2	26.6	25.3
BMI below 18.5 kg/m^2	Weight for height in kgs/m^2	-	35.8	-
Anemia of any grade	percent	-	51.8	-
Weight for age children	Percent below -3SD	16.9	19.1	18
under 3 yrs	Percent below -2SD	45.3	48.9	47
Height for age	Percent below -3SD	21.8	24.4	23
	Percent below -2SD	44.1	47.0	45.5
Weight for height	Percent below -3SD	2.9	2.7	2.8
	Percent below -2SD	15.7	15.2	15.5

continue

Table 1: *continue*

Health/Care Indicator	*Unit*	*Male*	*Female*	*All*
Fully Immunised	Percent children 12-23 months	43	41	42
All Antenatal checkup	Percent	-	20	-
No antenatal check up	% pregnant women in Rural	-	40	-
	% pregnant women in Urban	-	14	-
Number of antenatal Checks	Median for Rural	-	2.5	-
	Median for Urban	-	4.2	-
Institutional Deliveries	Percent in Rural	-	24.7	-
	Percent in Urban	-	65.1	-
RTI/STI symptoms	Percent	12.3	29.7	
Awareness of HIV/AIDS	Percent	60.3	41.9	
	*Access to Healthcare***			
Point prevalence on	Percent in Rural			
day prior to survey	Percent in Urban	2.8	3.0	2.9
		2.7	3.0	2.9
Acute morbidity in	Per 1000 in rural	41	44	42
last 15 days	Per 1000 in urban	39	43	41
Chronic morbidity	Per 1000 in rural	13	14	13
in last 15 days	Per 1000 in urban	13	15	14
Hospitalisation rate in	Per 1000 in rural	14	13	13
last one year	Per 1000 in urban	20	20	20
Untreated ailments	Percent in rural	15.8	18.3	
	Percent in urban	8.1	8.8	
OPD use of public facilities	Percent of treated ailments	19.5	20	19.7
Inpatient use of public facilities	Percent of hospitalisations	44	47	45.3
Expenditure on OPD cases	Rs. Per ailment Rural	151	137	144
	Rs. Per ailment urban	187	164	175
Expenditure on Hospitalisations	Rs. Per hospitalisation	3778	2510	3202
	Rs. Per hospitalisation	4185	3625	3921
Borrowing/sale of asset	Percent of cases rural	46	40	44
	Percent of cases urban	26	23	25

Sources: * All maternal and child data, unless otherwise specified is from NFHS-2 for year 1998

** All morbidity, treatment and expenditure data from NSSO 52nd round.

NOTES

[1] This is reflected in the fact that 25 per cent of global output in 1998 was by transnational corporations and more than half of the 100 largest economies in the World are corporate conglomerates and not nation states (Petchesky, 2003). Further in 1999 the combined wealth of the top 200 billionaires of the world is $1135 billion in contrast to the combined income of only $ 146 billion of 582 million population of the least developed economies (UNDP, 2000)

[2] The recent 60th NSS Round (2004) results give further evidence to this trajectory of declining use of public health facilities. (NSSO 2006)

[3] What is interesting to note is that economic growth in Kerala and China is today reducing equity in health outcomes. In both these countries neglect of the health sector and declining public investments by the State and increasing presence of private health care has adversely impacted health. Sri Lanka has survived these adversities because of the continued state support to the health sector.

REFERENCES

Appadurai A. 1996. "Disjuncture and Difference in the Global Cultural Economy", in A Appadurai (ed.). *Modernity at Large—Cultural Dimensions of Globalisation*, University of Minnesota Press, Minneapolis.

Duggal Ravi. 2004. "Financing Health Care in India—Prospects for Health Insurance", *Express Healthcare Management Journal*, March 1-15, 2004.

—— 2005. "Public Health Expenditures, Investment and Financing under the Shadow of a growing Private Sector", in Gangolli, Leena, Ravi Duggal and Abhay Shukla (eds) *Review of Healthcare in India*, CEHAT, Mumbai

Eisenstein Z. 1998. *Global Obscenities—Patriarchy, Capitalism and the lure of cyberfantasy*, NewYork, New York University Press.

MoCF. 2004. *Annual Report, Department of Chemicals and Petrochemicals*, Ministry of Chemicals and Fertilizers, GOI, New Delhi.

MoHFW 2003. *National Health Policy*, Ministry of Health and Family Welfare, New Delhi.

NCMH 2005. *Financing Healthcare, National Commission on Macroeconomics and Health*, GOI, New Delhi.

NFHS-2 2000. *National Family and Health Survey -1998*, IIPS, Mumbai.

NSSO 1998. Report No. 441, 52nd Round (1996), NSSO, GOI, New Delhi.

NSSO 2006. Report No. 507, 60th Round(2004), NSSO, GOI, New Delhi.

OECD 2003. *OECD Health Data 2003*, OECD, Paris.

Petchesky Rosalind 2003. *Gendering Health and Human Rights*, Zed Books, London.

Sen Amartya 2001. *Economic Progress and Health*, in Leon, D and G Walt (eds.) *Poverty, Inequality and Health*, New York, Oxford University Press.

Smith N 1997. "The Satanic Geographies of Globalisation—Uneven Development in the 1990's," *Public Culture* Vol. 10, No. 1.

Srivastava Ajay 2004. "GATS—The Indian Scenario", paper presented at "Business for Development": Challenges and Options for Government and Business After Adoption of WTO "July Package", Manila 21-22 Oct. 2004.

Standing Hillary 2002. "Towards Equitable Financing strategies for Reproductive Health", IDS Working Paper 153, Brighton.

Stiglitz Joseph 2002. *Globalisation and its Discontents*, New York, Norton.

UNCHR 2000. Committee on Economic, Social and Cultural Rights Twenty-second session 25 April-12 May 2000, Geneva.

UNDP 1999. Growing Disparity Globally www.poorcity.richcity.com/entundp.htm accessed 20th August 2005.

UNDP 2000. *Human Development Report 2000*, New Delhi, Oxford University Press.

World Bank 1993. *Investing in Health, World Development Report 1993*, New York, Oxford University Press.

WHO 2002. *World Health Report 2002*, Geneva, World Health Organisation.

Macroeconomic Methodologies, Approaches, and Policies

Why Gender Matters

PADMINI SWAMINATHAN

Assumptions that women's biology, moral reason, intelligence, contributions to human evolution, economic well-being, or to historical change are inferior to men's are not idiosyncratically held beliefs of individual 'subjects'; they are widespread assumptions of entire cultures institutionalized in global and local practices and discourses. These assumptions have constituted whole fields of study, selecting their preoccupying problems, favoured concepts, hypotheses and research designs; these fields have in turn lent support to male supremacist assumptions in other fields (Harding, 1995: 1).

Starting off our thought from the lives of those who are assigned body and emotional labour is an empirical and theoretical project. It does not automatically flow or erupt into the consciousness of those who perform it. Women have had to learn to characterize their activities in terms of a double-day of work, to recognize sexual harassment not as 'boys will be boys' but as a violation of our civil rights; to see rape not as a consequence of our 'asking for it' or of the inevitability of some deranged men acting out; to see their lower wages not as a reflection of their lower natural talents and abilities or their natural obligations to domestic work, but as a matter of economic exploitation. Feminist insights are empirical and theoretical achievements, requiring political and scientific struggles against the dominant institutions and their discourses (Harding, 1995: 24).

My aim is to show how gender analysis has challenged and enriched many of the standard assumptions and concepts utilised in analysis of the economy, be it peasant studies, paid and unpaid work, care labour etc., even if or even though precious little of this understanding has translated into women-friendly economic policies and/or shaken the disciplines of our educational institutions. This essay is informed by a two-fold purpose: one, to highlight in no particular order some of the crucial contributions of Women's Studies research to our understanding of the functioning of our economy in order also to foreground the critical importance of gender to macroeconomic concerns, methods and strategies. Two, a field-based study undertaken in a few villages in rural Tamil Nadu in the latter half of 2004 provides empirical support to several of the analytical observations made here while also providing a critique of the disjuncture that the women in the villages perceived between macroeconomic concerns and the reality of their lives. The essay is organized as follows: it begins with an overview of the crucial macro-economic concerns that have/ substantive and differential impacts on the lives and livelihoods of households. The subsequent sections build on these perspectives using insights gained from field studies; in the process they also highlight the specific contributions of women's studies to these perspectives and concerns.

We begin with a discussion of our research experience relating to employment, livelihoods and of the rural economy in particular.

MACROECONOMIC CONCERNS: EMPLOYMENT

A discussion of the employment scenario in India provides a broad platform to bring and link together issues relating to poverty and livelihoods, including from a gender perspective. It also presents an interesting contrast to the manner in which the theme of poverty has been dealt with in policy and praxis. While poverty eradication, poverty elimination, poverty alleviation, etc., were/are frequently and interchangeably touted as goals, full and 'decent' employment was never and still is not a goal, much less integrated into plans of development, either sectorally or as underpinning the overall growth objective. Discussions around the generation of employment generally get reduced to how many person-days of (invariably manual) employment that special employment schemes can generate; these (populist) schemes are part of the government's welfare programmes. Hence apart from the fact that they lie outside the 'main' development programme of the government, their periodicity, sustainability, spatial spread and such other logistics of their operationalization depend crucially on factors such as the fiscal situation of the state concerned, the political and other 'benefit' that the government of the day can derive from such a programme, etc. In other words, rather than welfare measures supplementing income derived from employment, for the large majority of the population, State provision of employment is itself a welfare measure.

In an interesting exercise, Dev and Mooij (2002) have analysed the budget speeches of Finance Ministers starting from 1988-89. Among other things they find that all the twelve budget speeches analysed by them were generally silent about employment creation in the regular economy. While they found separate sections devoted to agriculture and industry, there was hardly any mention of employment and labour market policies, except of specific anti-poverty employment programmes.

> It is ironical that the first time that the labour market is specifically discussed in a budget, it is to make the point that lay-offs, retrenchments and closures should be made easier... It would be no exaggeration to state that, as far as one can judge from these budget speeches, India in the 1990s had no employment policy... A new term brought into the budget speeches in 1999 is empowerment... This empowerment has nothing to do with changing power relations or a redistribution of productive assets" (ibid: 52).

Further, according to the authors, the post-1998 budgets reveal the implicit interpretation of poverty by the government. "It (poverty) is a residual interpretation—in contrast to a relational one. Poverty is seen as something that can disappear with a capital injection. A relational interpretation, on the other hand, would hold that poverty is the result of social and economic relations: the poor are poor as a result of their position within the social and economic structure" (ibid: 52).

What the above discussion reveals is that the disjunction between development and employment generation is in-built in the basic conceptualization of the annual budgets of the government. In a different way the same point is reinforced in the *Report of the Task Force on Employment Opportunities* (2001) and the *Report of the Special Group on Targeting 10 Million Employment Opportunities* (2002). Both Reports emphasize the fact that there has been a steady decline in the job creating capacity of the economy, which decline has accelerated since 1993-94. Further, both Reports also discuss the aspect of 'quality' of existing employment and of that being generated in the economy. In particular, the Reports' exercise of disaggregating unemployment data reveals that the rate of unemployment is higher among the educated than among those with lower levels of education.

> The high rate of unemployment among educated youth is in many ways the core of the problem because it creates a sense of despair across a wide section of the population including not only the educated youth but also their parents and families. It needs to be emphasized that the aspirations of this group cannot be met just by creating any employment opportunities . . . The problem of unemployment in this category can only be solved if *high quality* employment is created (emphasis added) (Government of India, Task Force Report, 2001: 28-29).

The Special Group Report (Government of India, 2002) emphasizes another dimension of the problem of unemployment in the country, namely, the inter-state differentials in unemployment rates. More significantly, it attempts to relate State Domestic Product and employment growth and comes up with interesting results. These include the following: of the 16 major states, there are three with very high and increasing unemployment rates. These are Kerala, Tamil Nadu and West Bengal. Of the three, Kerala has comparatively lower growth rate of GDP but higher employment elasticity, whereas Tamil Nadu and West Bengal have high growth (above 7 per cent) but with very low employment elasticity. The Report therefore records that, GDP growth rate *or* high labour intensity in production *exclusively* will not reduce unemployment. "For reducing unemployment, the challenge is to combine a high growth rate with high employment elasticity (that is, labour intensity in production) by proper sectoral and technology choice" (ibid: 31). Like the Task Force Report, the Special Report also highlights the growing incidence of unemployment among the educated youth, but goes beyond by disaggregating the data, state and gender-wise.

Ghose's (2004) study of the employment scenario in India, among other things, brings out the gender and class dimensions of the problem. According to Ghose, women's employment conditions are worse than men's in several respects. First, the average quality of women's employment is worse than that of men's. The share of regular employees in the total employed is much lower for women (9.2 per cent) than for men (18 per cent). At the other end, the share of casual wage-labourers in total employed is much higher for women (42.5 per cent) than for men (31.1 per cent). These facts also imply that women's employment is much more concentrated in agriculture compared to men's; nearly 74 per cent of employed women work in agriculture compared to 54 per cent of employed men. Second, underemployment is significantly higher for women in all sectors. This, of course, is not surprising, since women depend much more on self-employment and casual wage-employment than men. Third, while there is little unemployment among persons of both sexes with little or no education, educated women actually face a much higher rate of unemployment than educated men. In 2000, for persons with tertiary education, the rate of unemployment was less than 9 per cent for men but 27 per cent for women. Thus unemployed women, on average, have a significantly higher level of education (10.3 years) than unemployed men (8.7 years). Finally, as is widely known and documented, women generally earn significantly lower wages than men (ibid: 5111).

Based on an overall review of current employment and labour market conditions in India, Ghose concludes that:

> The core of the employment problem is that of the working poor, and overcoming it must be the priority objective of employment policy at this juncture . . . it is in the world of the working poor that child labour and widest gender inequality are to be found. . . Besides, it is arguable that addressing the problem of the working poor will create the conditions for improving the average quality of regular wage-paid jobs, *while improving the quality of regular paid jobs is most unlikely to address the problem of the working poor. . .* priority must be placed on generating and sustaining a process of labour transfer from self-employment and casual wage employment to regular wage employment. For, in the absence of such a process, special employment schemes—the main instrument available for reducing underemployment and for increasing the real wage rate for casual labour—will need to be implemented on an ever-expanding scale just to prevent the problem of the working poor from worsening (emphasis added) (Ghose, 2004: 5111).

But is the economy geared towards 'generating and sustaining a process of labour transfer from self-employment and casual wage employment to regular wage employment?' We engage with this and other related questions through an illustrative study of Tamil Nadu's economy.

FROM THE FIELD; GENDERED PERCEPTIONS AND OBSERVATIONS ON DEVELOPMENT, EMPLOYMENT, AND LIVELIHOODS

Tamil Nadu is generally perceived as one of the well-developed and fast growing states of the country, which perception has enabled the state to attract considerable amounts of foreign investment. Nevertheless, levels of poverty, as measured by the NSSO using the head-count ratio, indicate that 'the poor are over-represented in Tamilnadu' (Ghosh, 1998: 7). The conventional notion that growth powered by the secondary and tertiary sectors would generate sufficient employment so as to absorb surplus labour from the primary sector has not taken place; on the contrary, the primary sector continues to maintain its rank as the largest employer of the rural people even as income from the primary sector has declined over time. In an attempt to understand the nature of risks faced by the poorest among the poor and also their coping mechanisms, we undertook a 'livelihood assessment survey' in several villages across Tamil Nadu between July and October 2004.[1] The relevance of reproducing here the observations from the survey lie in the remarkable manner in which people on the ground, women in particular, in their own words linked their inability to make a transition to a better life because of the disjuncture that they perceived between the macro-economic issues of employment and growth on the one hand, and on the other, the low scale and poor quality of the otherwise 'functioning' welfare institutions in their villages. A quick glance at the employment scenario in Tamil Nadu based on secondary data is in order before we get into the field details:

1. Official sources, namely, The *Report of the Task Force on Employment Opportunities* (Government of India, 2001) and the *Report of the Special Group on Targeting 10 Million Employment Opportunities* (Government of India, 2002) clearly endorse the fact that employment growth in the economy, as a whole, particularly for the best part of the nineties, has been inadequate. Data further indicate that the growth rate of employment is less than the growth rate of the labour force indicating an increase in the unemployment rate and this is a matter of concern. The inter-state differentials in unemployment rates make these concerns even more serious. For instance, the unemployment rate (on the Current Daily Status basis)[2] has reached a figure as high as 20.97 per cent in Kerala; and West Bengal is next with 14.99 per cent, *followed by Tamil Nadu at 11.78* of their respective labour force.
2. We have already alluded above to the fact that data reveal no strong correlation between inter-state SDP growth and employment growth and that, of the 16 major states, there are three with very high and increasing unemployment rate—Kerala, Tamil Nadu and West Bengal. Understanding the incidence of unemployment in a more disaggregated form (*gender and age-wise*), we get the following disquieting scenario. Incidence of unemployment is very high among some groups, such as rural females and among youths (15-19 years) in

particular. Among the female youth in rural Kerala, the unemployment rate is as high as 45.8 per cent; in West Bengal it is 39.1 per cent and *nearly as high in Tamil Nadu.* Among urban females also the incidence of unemployment is high—50.4 per cent for Kerala, 27 per cent for West Bengal and 16 per cent for Tamil Nadu. This shows that apart from the genuine problem of generating employment for the rural sector in particular, positive policies are needed to generate employment keeping in mind the youth, educated and skilled (Government of India, 2002).

3. An analysis of the trends in the sectoral shares in income and employment in Tamil Nadu shows that though there has been a decline in the share of the primary sector in income, this has not been accompanied by a significant shift in the share of employment. Consequently a very sizeable section of the labour force (nearly 50 per cent) continues to depend on the primary sector. The average income of persons depending on the agricultural sector is considerably less than that of those working in the secondary and tertiary sectors. The prevalence of poverty in rural areas is widespread mainly due to the low productivity of workers in the agricultural sector and the seasonal nature of employment (Government of Tamil Nadu, 2003: p. 19).
4. The working population in Tamil Nadu was 27.8 million in 2001, an increase of approximately 3.6 million from the 24.2 million in 1991. Nonetheless, what is worrisome about the 2001 Census results, according to the TN HDR is that the number of marginal workers has gone up from 1.4 million in 1991 to 4.1 million in 2001. This suggests that the increase in WPR during this time period is largely accounted for by an increase in marginal workers as opposed to main workers. The number of main workers increased by less than a million (Government of Tamil Nadu, 2003: pp. 19-20).
5. Whichever data is used (Census or NSS) and whatever be the terms used to capture the status and quantum of work (principal/subsidiary, or main/marginal workers), what stands

out starkly is that women are overwhelmingly represented in the subsidiary/marginal categories.

6. There are two important aspects to women's 'work' that need to be noted: one, the 'growth' in employment has largely been in the marginal/subsidiary category and most women 'captured' as workers figure overwhelmingly in the marginal/subsidiary category (Ghosh: 1998). Two, it is now officially acknowledged that concepts and methods used by NSSO to net work and workers are not able to capture satisfactorily the range of activities of the poor and of women in particular (Hirway, 2002). In different ways, both aspects emphasize the deterioration that marks the livelihood options of sections of our population.

In several ways our field visits corroborated some of the observations based on secondary data analyses. These include, declining employment opportunities, reduction in number of days of employment, increase in unemployment among all sections, but particularly among females and among the youth, etc. The field visits provided crucial insights on the manner in which the vulnerability of the rural agricultural households has increased overtime.

At the outset, it needs to be recorded, that, across the villages, and among almost all sections of the agricultural labouring population, the risk and therefore vulnerability due to declining agricultural activities (the most important source of livelihood for those with land as well as for those without land) has increased considerably. The villagers in general, women included, traced the decline in agricultural activities to a combination of factors: continuous failure of monsoons, depletion of ground water, change in cropping patterns, changes in institutional patterns that govern agrarian relations, etc., all of which has combined to erode the livelihood base of much of the agriculture-dependent population. Public intervention programmes by their very design and nature have been singularly ineffective in addressing regressive agrarian structural factors, caste for example, and have more often than not contributed to problems rather than to solutions.

A direct economic consequence of this combination of factors is the decline in the number of days of employment, hitting hard the landless agricultural labouring population in particular. Most villages have no other major activity that can provide alternate employment (and therefore some source of income) to the erstwhile labour employed in agriculture. Because of this dip in their major source of income, the landless households among the agriculture-based employment groups are the most vulnerable since they have nothing to fall back upon. Consequently, these households are forced to cope by cutting down the number of meals they take in a day, discontinue schooling of their children, delay seeking medical attention for their ailments, default on repayment schedules on their loans, and/or become more indebted, thereby further increasing their vulnerability. The gender question that emerges here is the differential impact that this vulnerability holds for men and women: while to some extent men venture out in search of coolie work, at times even staying out for days together, such options are not available to women. They have neither the resources nor the support system to enable them to make these search trips. At the same time, we need to stress that a resolution to this gender problem does not lie only (or not even) in enabling women to go out in search of coolie work, but in addressing the larger question of the erosion in the main source of livelihood of these populations.

A fall in and/or lack of income has other adverse fallouts. For example, women in one village pointed out that *all* children were not in school and further that there was considerable dropout at the middle and higher levels for one or several of the following reasons: deteriorating income standards meant that they were forced to pull out their children from classes that did not serve noon-meals and also because they could not meet other school-related expenditure such as travel (since for classes beyond 8th standard the children have to travel outside the village), and notebooks. In some cases older children had to discontinue schooling in order to share household responsibilities while their parents went out in search of work. In quite a few villages, girls' education was constrained by the fact that the only school in the village had classes only upto the 8th standard. Thereafter the parents would have to invest resources in travel and other expenses to enable their daughters to pursue their studies further. A combination of limited income as well as poor transport meant that, while parents expressed their willingness and desire to educate their daughters further, they could not translate this desire into practice. Hence, beyond the 8th standard, the gender gap in educational level becomes stark.

Another dimension of the gendered nature of the problem relating to education is the following: in almost all villages women clearly expressed the point that, while they were happy that some among their village children, girls as well as boys, had managed to study up to the 12th standard, they were very aware of the futility of being 'educated' only up to the 12th. It was pointed out that, pursuing education beyond the 12th was expensive even in government higher educational institutions and also at times non-accessible (because of non-fulfillment of eligibility criteria by these children). Not all could afford to educate *all* their children; forced to make a choice, the parents opted to expend on higher education and hostel accommodation for their boys rather than for girls. *The parents had a reason for this gendered choice*[3]*:* opportunities for employment outside of the ones available in the village, namely, agriculture, were nil, unless the 'educated' chose to go to large metros and towns. While in fact a few boys from these villages have found some service jobs in metros like Chennai (like lorry booking, cleaner jobs with transport companies, etc), similarly 'educated' girls were handicapped by lack of social support and economic opportunities, and were therefore confined to their households. Villages close to metros such as Chennai were sourced for adolescent girl labour to work in garment units particularly in the export processing zone; the latter organized pick up and drop services for such labour but most villagers were reluctant to send their daughters to these units.

All sections of the population were extremely anxious about the uncertainty facing their children, educated or otherwise. Their hopes of a better future for their children were shattered because of their realization that the children had no future either in the 'traditional' occupation, that is agriculture (which was declining), or in 'modern' occupations; the latter required more and different kinds of qualifications that the village population could, as of now, ill afford. Women were frustrated that their work and levels of earnings were not sufficient to enable their children to rise above a certain level of education and/or acquire any form of professional skill. This in turn implied that they could not get into better paying jobs—a necessary condition for reducing the intensity of insecurity of their lives and very existence.

While the nature of problems encountered by adivasi villages in hill areas, like Semmanarai for example, are not very different, in such places the topography of the area further compounds the problem of access to services like education and health. Conventional solutions that generally mark all government intervention programmes are neither suitable nor viable for such locales. The government's Adivasi welfare programme includes the construction of schools with hostels (the Government Tribal Residential Schools). For the children of the hill areas that we visited, this facility was still being implemented. At the time of the visit only a huge hall had been built which also doubled as a hostel. This 'hostel-cum-school hall' is up to the 3rd standard only and has two teachers for about 60 children. Clearly the tribal people and children have a long way to go.

We encountered a range of observations on the theme of 'health'. In quite a few villages, the provision of safe drinking water by the government under one scheme or the other has dramatically reduced the incidence of water-borne diseases. Again, in almost all villages, except the remote tribal village of Semmanarai, institutional delivery is the norm; and therefore pregnant women were somehow transported to the nearest hospital at the time of delivery. In Semmanarai, on the other hand, generally traditional dais help out during pregnancy; otherwise women have to help themselves or in times of emergency women are carried to the nearest point till a bus or jeep arrives to transport such cases to the nearest hospital.

A government health worker visited most villages, including Semmanarai, on a particular day of the week. But the health worker confined herself generally to examining women and children and only occasionally men. Kalyanpoondi village, was the only one that had a functioning PHC (Primary Health Centre), in all other villages such centres were dysfunctional. In fact most women told us that they could not recall when the PHCs in their villages had been last open. In the case of Kalyanpoondi (where the institution of Panchayat is functioning in large part in the interests of the villagers and which in turn accounts for the functioning nature of most village public institutions), the PHC has a resident ANM (Auxiliary Nurse Midwife) and is visited regularly by a doctor. Here, the ANM accompanies cases that require hospitalization to the nearest town—a distance of nearly 8 kms. In all other villages, the distance to the bus stop and the regularity of transport dictates in most cases how soon or late pregnant and/or sick persons reach the nearest health facility. The non-functioning of institutions such as the PHC has serious implications for the health of the population, which factor worsens for the poorest among the population and for women in particular (the latter very often need to be accompanied to the health facility). The observations made by the women in Kizhkathipoor for example, sums up the nature of the problem. According to them, in the short run, the non-functioning of the PHC combined with the financial and physical inability of the poor (in particular) to seek medical care in the nearby town means that their recovery from illnesses, however minor they may be, gets delayed with adverse consequences for their ability to seek work. In the long run, prolonged periods of unemployment and therefore inability to eat sufficiently means that entire households are prone to all kinds of ailments because of poor nutrition. While Balwadi schemes are conceptualized to *supplement* nutrition for infants/children, and pregnant and lactating mothers, these cannot address the risks that households face because of the progressive erosion in their livelihood base.

A related point stressed by women was that lack of latrines affected women in particular, more so whenever it rained. The women were very vociferous in demanding that latrines needed to be provided to avoid long-term reproductive tract infections and other health problems connected with reduced intake of water because of having to relieve themselves in the open.

Women and young girls, in almost all the villages we visited, were very critical of the poor communication facilities in their villages, since more than for men and boys, a lack of crucial infrastructure facilities reduced their options in several ways. To reiterate some of the points already made in the context of accessing employment, education and health: women of villages (like Magaral) that were close to metros such as Chennai were very critical of the poor connectivity of their village. They have to walk almost three kilometres to catch a bus to Chennai. In addition, the poor frequency of buses to Chennai also means less opportunity to seek work and/or health facility outside the village. A similar complaint was made by the women of MK village, who, in addition stated that the 1½ km trudge to the bus stop and back had to be made in the dark since there was no lighting facility. Women in Kalancheri pointed out that the combination of a non-functioning PHC in the village and lack of transport meant that just transporting a pregnant woman to a hospital located in the nearest city (Thanjavur) for delivery would cost anything between Rs 300-400 one way.

While some problems such as decline in employment opportunities, limited access to higher levels of education, particularly for girls because of poor transport connectivity, etc. cut across classes and castes within the village, quite a few problems were specific to particular classes and castes depending on their endowments and location within the village. For example, in Kizhkathipoor, the SC women had been provided with 'houses' under the government's Group Housing scheme for SCs but the entire segment has no electricity. (Most parts of the rest of the village have electricity). Besides, in this and in most other villages we found these group houses to be of extremely poor quality—leaking and falling apart—particularly in all those cases where the inmates have not been able to pay adequate bribes. In places like Semmanarai, most group houses remain empty for the simple reason that the hill people find them totally unsuited for the weather. Given the inability of the government to change its stipulation of materials and design according to the topography and living patterns of people, it is not surprising that well intended schemes of government have failed to make the expected impacts.

The physical location of the Christian Dalit colony in Kalyanpoondi, for example, about 3 kms away from the main village, has contributed in no small measure to them being deprived or poorly serviced by otherwise functioning public institutions located within the main village. The colony people feel that not only their location but also the fact that they have converted to Christianity has worked against them since, because of this religious conversion, they are not able to access facilities otherwise due to Dalits. The ration shop is located in the main village; officially, supplies to the entire village, which includes the colony, are downloaded and accounted for in the main village. Despite repeated requests, the panchayat president has not been able to put in place a system whereby supplies meant for this colony can be delivered in the colony itself. Similarly, the balwadi for the village is located in the main village. Supplies meant for the children and pregnant/lactating mothers of this colony are deposited in the main village. However, it is physically not possible for the children and pregnant women of the colony to travel 3 kms on a day-to-day basis to the main village to access these supplies.

Another dimension of the different perspectives and emphasis expressed *within* a village has to do with the class status of the population. Thus for example, the women of the main landowning class of Kalyanpoondi village, namely, the Reddys, feel that the prime institution that needs to deliver quality service is the school in their village. According to them while their village had a functioning school where education was provided up to the 12th standard, where the Panchayat has ensured that teachers come to the school on a regular basis, where the school itself is well endowed in terms of classrooms and playground, where noon meals, text and note books are provided, etc., nevertheless, there were specific problems such as lack of teachers with specialized qualifications, such as mathematics and science. This deficiency was beginning to impact adversely on their children in that the latter were not able to cope in these subjects in competitive examinations, which in turn deprived their children of seats in institutions of higher learning.

The institution of SHG has a pervasive presence in almost all the villages that we visited except the Adivasi village of Semmanari. What came out quite clearly is that the nature of activities and the ability of SHGs to sustain these activities have a lot to do with the general level of economic activity in the village, the level of cohesiveness of the village population, plus the institutional support provided by the Panchayats in the villages. Thus for example, despite the downturn in agricultural activities in Kalyanpoondi, the dynamic thrust provided by the present village panchayat president has enabled most village women to form themselves into several SHGs and go into dairy business on a fairly large scale. While one set of SHGs has facilitated the purchase of milch animals, another set has taken up the task of planting grass in about 10 acres of land in order to be able to provide steady feed for the animals. The dairy activity is relatively young, just about five months old at the time of our fieldwork in August 2004 and hence it was too premature to say whether it was viable or not. The women in the SHG-sponsored dairy business were earlier wageworkers in agriculture. Even though they have ventured in to the dairy business to provide themselves an alternate source of income, the continuing failure of monsoons (that would impact adversely on the growth of grass) made them wary of sourcing further loans since they were not sure whether they would be able to repay without defaulting. Nevertheless, according to the men and women of the village, the formation of the SHGs and their foray into the dairy business has transformed to quite an extent the gender scenario in the village of Kalyanpoondi. The decline in agricultural activities in the village has catapulted the SHG-facilitated dairy business into a prime economic activity of the village. Being an activity of the SHGs means that women have come to play an important visible role. But women were quick to point out that the day-to-day operations of the business occupied all adult members of the household almost full time. In fact, it was openly admitted that, a large part of women's time was devoted to running the SHG office (maintaining accounts, collecting dues, taking decisions on sanctioning loans, depositing the money in the nationalized bank; the latter required the women to travel by two buses and almost the whole day). There is, as it were, a reversal of roles, with women 'administering' and men 'working'.

Similarly in Magaral, the SHGs are in the forefront of organizing and getting public institutions to function as well as becoming accountable to the village. At present Magaral has 18 SHGs, ranging from those that are just 6 months old to those that have completed 6 years. However, unlike Kalyanpoondi, only one SHG has ventured into income generating activity. (This lone SHG has just been sanctioned a loan for dairy business). A feature of SHG activity in Magaral is that, initially, only SCs (the numerically dominant caste in the village) had formed themselves into SHGs. But of late, and particularly when it became known that public money for a range of activities would flow only or mainly through SHGs, the women of the dominant land-owning caste of the village, namely Naidus, have also formed themselves into two SHGs. Interestingly, the Naidu women are forced to interact with the SC women in federation meetings, where the office bearers are almost all SC women.

Across the villages it came out quite clearly that the institution of the SHG has mitigated to a considerable extent the dependence on usurious moneylenders and in the process it has also contributed enormously to bringing women to the forefront of village level activities. But the inability of SHGs to plunge into new ventures is severely constrained by the general decline in agricultural-related employment, the main source of income for most of the households in the villages that we visited. In all these villages, the SHG loans are used largely for consumption purposes. For some segments of the population (the SC segment of Kalancheri village for example) the continuing drought-like conditions, the lack of alternate employment opportunities, is impacting adversely on their SHG loan repayment schedule. The not-so-poor SHG women also were very clear that if they were to start income-generating activities, they would need enormous inputs and training to make these activities viable and therefore worthwhile. They admitted that their own motivation and enthusiasm to plunge into any new venture was very low; their argument was that if at least one member of the household had a steady source of income then it would motivate them to take the risk involved in getting into a new venture.

At a more general level, and in particular, because of the institution of SHG, the levels of awareness on a range of issues among most sections of women in almost all villages that we visited were quite high. The women themselves admitted that the SHG experience had given them tremendous opportunities to engage in the problems of the village, attempt to come to some consensus on how to address them, maintain records, conduct surveys, and present their points of view at different fora within and outside their village. Both in Kalyanpoondi and in Magaral, for example, the women were also sharp in observing (while listening to the discussion that the men were having) that the men were reluctant to admit that an important source of loans for the household was the SHG in which their womenfolk were active members. According to the women, it is they who have convinced their menfolk to come together to form SHGs. Most important, the women in almost all villages were also aware of the limits of SHG-sponsored activities and realized that while their SHGs could tackle short term contingencies and/or support them in times of crises, the SHGs were no alternative to large scale employments, good infrastructure and functioning public institutions—in all of which the State has a major role to play.

The organizational characteristics of the SHG and the built-in checks in its functioning have led to a strengthening of essentializing characteristics, such that unlike men, recovery rates of loan from women are several times better and therefore it is better to 'target' women rather than men of households in the matter of loans under various programmes. At several discussion meetings, the SHG programme was contrasted with the erstwhile IRDP programme, where recovery rates from men (who were the recipients of loans under the IRDP) was extremely low. What the women failed to relate was the structural dissimilarity of the two programmes; the IRDP was administered through banks that dealt with men of the households as individuals; it was left to the officials of banks to chase these individuals and recover the loans—a scenario that led to heavy transactional costs but very few recoveries. In contrast, the SHG has extremely low transactional cost. For the bank, the SHG is the unit for loan application. Peer pressure from the group ensures that defaulters fall in line or quit the group, since otherwise the group as a whole would not be able to source further loans unless existing dues are cleared.

It needs to be recorded here that given the fact that the prime source of livelihood of every village that we visited had been eroded particularly in the last 3-5 years due to failure of monsoons, ground water depletion and lack of water for irrigation, and also given the emphasis that every segment of the population including women placed on securing their livelihood, it seemed almost out of place, nay, cruel to focus beyond a point on specific aspects of either caste or gender-based violence. The women in particular also emphasized that they did not want any further ad hoc 'schemes' from the government; they posed two hard questions: one, restoring their source of livelihood, and two, enabling their children to make a transition to a better source of livelihood through higher education. These questions, in fact, made us re-examine the rationale of our 'social sector' and its relationship to 'economic development'.

The theme of macroeconomic management and social policies is an area that has been critically studied by feminists. Despite exhortations to the effect that macroeconomics and social policies need to be integrated, operationally the tendency in the macroeconomic domain has been to emphasize price stabilization and on reducing the role of the state while at the same time *adding* social policies to address issues such as poverty and women's empowerment (Elson and Cagatay, 2000). The adding-on-social policy-approach by definition cannot transform macroeconomic policies; but a transformatory approach would, ipso facto, imply that we re-think our macroeconomic policies and our approach to macroeconomics itself. The theme of gender budgeting is a good example but needs to be critically studied. As of now, in our opinion, what is practised in India is a loose form of gender auditing that is touted as gender budgeting; this audit of programmes for their levels of financial support to women-friendly policies is expected and envisaged to 'transform' macroeconomic management. The making of the budget itself is not examined from a gender perspective.

WOMEN AND NON-FARM LABOUR: INSIGHTS FROM RESEARCH AND IMPLICATIONS FOR POLICY

A considerable body of research has brought out the ways in which women's gendered identity has been central to the national and international drive towards cheaper labour but higher productivity and profits over the last few decades. In the process this body of research has also highlighted the strategies through which governments, transnational corporations and even trade unions have managed to continually erode potential and existing entitlements for women workers (Pearson, 2004: 607). The case studies of the units in EPZs are a good example of this combined onslaught. These include: a bid to attract foreign investment, the conditions offered to foreign investors/buyers by developing countries ensured that these major employers were absolved of virtually all responsibility for the welfare of their workers; despite the fact that units in EPZs are formal units, which in turn implies that national regulations stipulating wage levels, non-wage benefits, hours of work, safety regulations, etc., do apply, all parties have routinely managed to negotiate exemptions from these measures. Apart from exemptions, these formal units have managed to protect themselves also legally by not designating their women workers as 'workers', through a simple device of employing their workers through contractors; the latter are on the pay rolls of the employers not the women workers.

Amartya Sen's writings, particularly his argument that increasing women's freedom to work outside the home is crucial for increasing their freedom in domains such as the home, healthcare, reproductive control, etc., has been critically studied and commented upon by several feminist researchers. Feminists have critiqued the facile connections that are made between promoting women's workforce participation and increasing their agency. Without decrying the need for increasing women's paid employment outside the home, feminists have however directed attention to a number of factors that disempower women despite wage work. As Koggel (2003) puts it succinctly, "The central question . . . thus becomes: is Sen's account sufficiently discerning of the ways in which global forces of power and local systems of oppression operate and interact in ways that limit women's freedom and agency even when they have paid work?" (167). An equally important contribution of feminist analysis of women's work is the futility of merely suggesting that better data be collected and that through better data collection techniques and tools, women's work as economic activity rather than leisure can be netted. The case of women not being counted as workers, of home-based work increasing women's wage employment but not contributing to their participation in the public sphere nor enhancing their freedom and/or agency in the private sphere—clearly illustrates why simply improving the definition of work and the collection of data on labour is not enough. Better economic analysis needs to go hand-in-hand with more gender-sensitive policies.

How and Why Gender Matters: A Recapitulation

The picture of gender gaps in achievement/outcomes that one routinely encounters while analysing secondary data (be it data relating to employment, education, health, etc.), has more often than not led to the institution of 'welfare' measures ostensibly aimed at eliminating such discrimination and in also 'empowering' the discriminated. The persistence of poverty and vulnerability despite the 'social sector' and despite any number of studies documenting the linkages and connections between macro-economic policies and changes on the ground, has contributed very little to the way discrimination is perceived at the policy level and/or in the manner data are gathered. There is in fact, at the policy or macro-economic level, very little use for nuanced analysis (of the type provided above) of the underlying causes contributing to gaps/discrimination, vulnerability and disempowerment.

The official sanction that was accorded to conduct a Time Use Survey (Government of India, 2000) to net the range of activities as well as the time spent on these activities by different members of selected households across seven states of the country remains an exception. For us, the data thrown up by the Survey considerably substantiated and enriched the concept of gender division of labour, a term centre-staged by feminists to highlight, among other things, the assignment to women in particular the tasks of daily and generational reproduction. The term has, to put it mildly, revolutionized the concept of 'work', forced researchers, policy makers and data collecting agencies to rethink the categories of 'productive' and 'unproductive' work, and take cognizance of the multiple and simultaneous nature of much of women's work particularly in rural areas. Gender analysis has not only enriched the definitions of activities but is also instrumental in foregrounding the issue of the relationship between women's participation in production and their status in the household. The significance of the recognition of the multiplicity and simultaneity of much of women's work lies in the fact that it provides to a large extent an explanation of how households persist in the face of their impoverishment and diminishing income. The empirical picture presented above, in our opinion, goes further. It also engages with the question of why and how households are forced to take gendered decisions in their attempt to cope with the progressive and secular decline in the sources of their livelihoods.

In the West, the discussion initiated by feminist economists in particular around what has come to be subsumed under 'care labour' has in fact contributed significantly to three policy issues: pay equity, the valuation of non-market work and greater support for parental work (Folbre, 1995: 74). The inconclusive but ongoing nature of debates on these issues notwithstanding, in different ways, through these debates, feminism has challenged the patriarchal family, and helped establish new rights for women and children. At the same time feminists are aware that policies to recognize, compensate and provide paid leave for 'care work' superimposed atop gendered labour market structures and gendered notions of care giving are likely simply to reproduce gender gaps in employment and the gender division of care work (Morgan and Zippel, 2003: 73). In developing societies and particularly in the rural areas of these societies, where the concentration of poor households is the highest, the notion of institutional assistance for 'care work' hardly exists. On the contrary, the decline in public investment in rural areas in general, the low investment in infrastructure relevant to alleviating household drudgery (such as fuel, water and sanitation), and the bias towards facilitating infrastructure for private investment (such as investment in roads but not in public transport)—all this on top of decline in sources of livelihood means that the burden of keeping body and soul together falls disproportionately on women, the prime care givers in society as the latter is presently constituted. Our field experience described above bears testimony to these observations.

In a nutshell, the signal contribution of feminists and gender studies to macroeconomics is a questioning of the assumptions on which economic policies are anchored, a questioning of the methodologies that limit our understanding and approaches to economic problems, and a questioning of the solutions that it uncritically offers. Nevertheless, the relegation of gender to the social at one level, and the anxiety of feminist researchers including feminist economists to be seen as 'practically relevant' all the time, at another level, is one small example of the continuing tensions that keep surfacing largely also because macroeconomic policies have failed in their basic objectives but have had no qualms in transferring these failures to the 'social sector'—a euphemism for considering all these problems as 'women's issues'. How feminists engage with such reductionism is a challenge waiting to be addressed.

Table 1: Villages Surveyed for Livelihood Analysis

Sl.No.	*Name of the Village*	*District*
1	Adhikaripatti	Theni
2	Kadambur	South Arcot
3	Kalancheri	Thanjavur
4	Kaliyampoondi	Kanchipuram
5	Keelkadhirpur	Thiruvallur
6	M. Kolakudi	Cuddalore
7	Magaral	Thiruvallur
8	Nadukombai	Namakkal
9	Keelpachar	Thiruvannamalai
10	Sambakuttapatti	Salem
11	Semmanarai	Nilgiris

Source: *Livelihood Assessment Report*, Institute of Development Alternatives, Chennai, December 2004, mimeo.

NOTES

[1] The 'Livelihood Assessment Survey' was undertaken as part of the preparation for the Tamilnadu Empowerment and Poverty Reduction Programme. The survey covered 3864 households and a population of 16325 individuals spread over eleven villages in ten districts of the state. Three of these eleven villages are tribal villages. Forty per cent of the surveyed population is from the scheduled caste community, seventeen percent from scheduled tribes' community and the rest from 'others'. The male-female break-up of the surveyed population is 50.5 and 49.5 percent respectively. Nearly 15 per cent of the surveyed households are female-headed households. See Table I for names of villages surveyed and the districts in which they are located. (Livelihood Assessment Report, Institute of Development Alternatives, Chennai, December 2004, mimeo) HERE.

[2] The National Sample Survey Organization (NSSO) of India collects detailed information on the employment status of the population through large-scale, nation-wide sample surveys in which individuals are categorized as employed or available for work but not employed, using different criteria. Rates are calculated as percentages of the total labor force. The NSSO provides four different measures of employment and unemployment, each of which captures different facets of the

employment-unemployment situation. One of these is the Current Daily Status (CDS). Based on the reported time disposition of the person on each day of the reference week, person-days in employment (unemployment) are aggregated to generate estimates of person-days in employment/unemployment. The person-day unemployment rate is derived as the ratio of person-days in unemployment to the person-days in the labor force. This measure captures the within-week unemployment of those classified as employed on the Weekly Status. The CDS-measure of unemployment is widely agreed to be the one that most fully captures open unemployment in the country (Planning Commission, 2001: 15-16).

[3] Nussbaum makes a similar observation: "[Thus], many individual parents who have no objection to educating girls and boys on a basis of equality may be able to afford to educate only one of their children. . . In many cultural circumstances, existing employment opportunities dictate that the one educated must be a boy because his overall employment opportunities are greater and education is a necessary passport to these. So the neglect of female education may be a matter of survival for parents in many parts of the world" (2003: 340-1).

REFERENCES

Dev, Mahendra, S. and J. Mooij, 2002. "Social Sector Expenditures and Budgeting: An Analysis of Patterns and the Budget-Making Process in India in the 1990s", *Working Paper 43*, Centre for Economic and Social Studies, Hyderabad.

Elson, D. and N. Cagatay. 2000. "The Social Content of Macroeconomic Policies", *World Development*, Vol. 28, Number 7, pp. 1347-1364.

Folbre, Nancy. 1995. "Holding Hands at Midnight: The Paradox of Caring Labour", *Feminist Economics*, Vol. 1, Number 1, pp. 75-92.

Ghose, A. 2004. "The Employment Challenge in India", *Economic and Political Weekly*, Vol. 39, No. 9, March 2-9, pp. 853-866.

Ghosh, Jayati. 1998. "Assessing Poverty Alleviation Strategies for Their Impact on Poor Women: A Study with special Reference to India", *Discussion Paper 97*, United Nations Research Institute for Social Development, October.

Harding, Sandra. 1995. "Can Feminist Thought Make Economics More Objective?" *Feminist Economics*, Vol. 1, No. 1, pp. 7-32.

Hirway, I. 2002. "Employment and Unemployment Situation in the 1990s: How Good are NSS data?" *Economic and Political Weekly*, Vol. 37, No. 21, May 25-31, pp. 2027-2036.

India, Government of. 2000. *Report of the Time Use Survey*, Central Statistical Organization, Ministry of Statistics and Programme Implementation, New Delhi, April.

———2001. *Report of the Task Force on Employment Opportunities,* Planning Commission, New Delhi, July.

———2002. *Special Group on Targeting Ten Million Employment Opportunities Per Year,* Planning Commission, New Delhi, May.

Koggel, C.M. 2003. "Globalization and Women's Paid Work: Expanding Freedom?" *Feminist Economics*, Vol. 9, Number 2-3, pp. 163-183.

Morgan, K. J. and K. Zippel. 2003. "Paid to Care: The Origins and Effects of Care leave Policies in Western Europe", *Social Politics*, Spring, pp. 49-85.

Nussbaum, Martha. C. 2003. "Women's Education: A Global Challenge", *Signs: Journal of Women in Culture and Society*, Vol. 29, No. 2, Winter, pp. 325-355.

Pearson, R. 2004. "The Social is Political", *International Feminist Journal of Politics*, Vol. 6, Number 4, pp. 603-622.

Tamil Nadu, Government of. 2003. *Tamil Nadu Human Development Report*, in association with Social Science Press, New Delhi.

Notes on Contributors

RITU DEWAN is Professor, Department of Economics at the University of Mumbai, she heads the Centre for Women's Studies (Gender Economics), and is also the Coordinator of the Centre for Human Development. She has published widely and has over 20 books and 60 articles on aspects of development economics, gender economics, informal sector, rural economy, urban issues, labour markets, small-scale industries, environment, displacement, health, conflict, human rights, etc. She is also a consultant to the Planning Commission of the Government of India. United Nations. ILO, etc., as well as Honorary Advisor to the Kashmir Foundation for Peace and Democracy. Her research focus is generally the result of the demands of several on-going movements.

K. SEETA PRABHU works with the United Nations Development Programme (UNDP), India. She has guided and supported the preparation of a large number of sub-national Human Development Reports (HDRs) in India. Previously, she was Professor of Development Economics at the University of Mumbai and has also been Visiting Professor at Jawaharlal Nehru University, Delhi as well as at the universities of Oxford and Erasmus, Rotterdam. She has served as Advisor to the Planning Commission. India, as well as the Reserve Bank, state governments and others. Key among her publications to her credit are: Economic Reform and Social Sector Development: A Study of Two Indian States and Reforming India's Social Sector: Poverty, Nutrition, Health and Education.

WANDANA SONALKAR teaches Economics at Dr Babasaheb Marathwada University, Aurangabad where she also heads the Centre for Women's Studies. She is a founder member of Aalochana, Centre for Documentation and Research on Women. She has translated a definitive history of the Dalit women's movement in Maharashtra—*We Also Made History: Women in the Atnbedkarite Movement*—from Marathi to English.

AZANIA MOYA THOMAS completed her Bachelors and Masters degrees in Economics from the University of Mumbai. She worked as a Research Associate for the conference on Gender Economics organized by the UNDP where she also presented a paper on engendering market structures. Her current interest is in exploring Latin American Economies and micro-credit markets.

ANUSHREE SINHA is Senior Fellow at the National Council of Applied Economic Research (NCAER). She completed her PhD from Jadavpur University, Kolkata in macro modeling and subsequently carried out postdoctoral research at the Universities of Pennsylvania and Oxford. She has been a Senior Consultant to the United Nations Economic Commission (UNECA) in their initiative in mainstreaming gender to study the impact of trade liberalization in African countries. Currently a Visiting Scholar at the United Nations University, World Institute for Development Economics Research at Helsinki, Dr Sinha is involved in various international assessments and forums to study the impact or macro policies on the informal sector and women workers.

ROMAR CORRCA is the Reserve Bank of India Professor of Monetary Economics in the University of Mumbai. He was the Director of the Department of Economics till recently. He works on the tension between micro and macro in non-neoclassical frameworks.

ANJALI GOYAL is Executive Director, Finance (Budget) in Ministry of Railways and is responsible for preparing and controlling the budget of the Ministry of Railways. She has worked in the Railways in various capacities in ibe Finance and Accounts Departments lor the last more than 20 years. While on deputation to the Government of India from 2001–2006, she worked as Director Finance in the Minister) of Women & Child Development and was also responsible for general budgeting initiatives undertaken in Government of India, She worked closely with agencies like UNDP, UNIFEM and UNICEF.

ALKA PARIKH is aPH.D. from Cornell University, USA and at present is working as an Associate Professor with Dhirubhai Ambam Institute of Information and Communication Technology, Gandhinagar, Gujarat. Previously she was a Reader at Department of Economics, University of Mumbai, where she wrote this chapter. Her research has focussed on a variety of development issues including agriculture, education, unemployment and poverty, environment and development debates as well as disaster management.

RAVI DUGGAL, a Sociologist by training and a health researcher and activist by practice, presently works as an independent researcher/ consultant across South and Southeast Asia on governance and budget issues, especially in the health sector. He is also associated with the Peoples Health Movement and the Medico Friend Circle, both health activist groups.

PADMINI SWAMINATHAN is Professor at the Madras Institute of Development Studies. She holds the Reserve Bank of India Chair in Regional Economics. Her research interests include studies relating to industrial organization, labour and employment, occupational health issues—all from a gender perspective.